ABRAHAM'S CURSE

Also by Bruce Chilton

Rabbi Jesus
Rabbi Paul
Mary Magdalene

ABRAHAM'S CURSE

Child Sacrifice in the

Legacies of the West

BRUCE CHILTON

DOUBLEDAY

New York   London   Toronto

Sydney   Auckland

PUBLISHED BY DOUBLEDAY

Published in the United States by Doubleday, an imprint of The Doubleday Broadway Publishing Group, a division of Random House, Inc., New York.
www.doubleday.com

Book design by Michael Collica

Library of Congress Cataloging-in-Publication Data
Chilton, Bruce.
Abraham's curse : child sacrifice in the legacies of the West / Bruce Chilton. — 1st ed.
p.   cm.
Includes bibliographical references and index.
1. Isaac (Biblical patriarch)—Sacrifice. 2. Abraham (Biblical patriarch) 3. Child sacrifice. I. Title.
BS1238.S24C45 2008
222'.11064—dc22
2007030288

ISBN 978-0-385-52027-0

PRINTED IN THE UNITED STATES OF AMERICA

1 3 5 7 9 10 8 6 4 2

First Edition

Contents

ABRAHAM'S CURSE

Foreword

Only five years old, my younger son, Henry, answered the telephone and passed the cordless on to my wife. She called me down from my study, and the caller, a good friend who lives near the church I serve as priest, told me the news. She described what her son had seen: an area cordoned off by yellow tape, a person lying on the ground between the two main buildings, the church proper and the old rectory.

The two-mile stretch between my house on a college campus and the church—farmland, woods, and gracious homes—was lit by the autumn twilight in the Hudson River Valley, filling the air with colors and a still vibrancy unlike any other time of year. The tangible beauty of light seeming to hang in the air put me in a mood to wish away my gathering sense of dread. I had few defenses at my disposal for how cruel that evening would prove, how far its pain would reach.

A young woman lay fallen between the buildings. Her throat had been cut; the officer on the scene believed she was dead. To give the woman last rites, I went into the church to collect my stole and my vessel of oil. Then, outside again and kneeling next to the woman, I recognized her—a student whom I had met to counsel from time to time, named Anna.

Anna's eyes, still open and clear with apparent life, picked up the last rays of the sun. I anointed her forehead and prayed for her. The wound across her throat was dreadful. An autopsy later found that the knife-blow that killed her had chipped her spine. When my prayers had ended, I asked a newly arrived officer, apparently senior to the first, to cover Anna's body and face. He agreed without hesitation.

Recollection of an ancient text, not part of the last rites, stirred just out of reach of conscious recognition as I stood up. The memory had been awakened by the rays of the setting sun in Anna's eyes, yet resisted identifying itself. I was not surprised, or even frustrated, by the elusive memory; my mental processes had slowed to the speed of a waking dream. Tenants who rented rooms in the old rectory emerged from the house. Earlier that evening they had heard screams, one of them ran downstairs to find Anna wounded, and another had telephoned the police. Now they all stood outside, paralyzed by a scene none of us could understand. We prayed for Anna together until the gathering chill of the evening sent the tenants back into their homes.

I agreed to meet with them later in the old rectory. Most of that night saw me either talking with that small group, or in the church with students from the college, who were drawn in clusters to the site by news of Anna's murder. But before I attempted to counsel others, I excused myself to return my stole and vessel of oil to the sacristy of the church, to call my wife to let her know what had happened, and to take a moment's solitude. Walking west toward the side door of the church, I saw the last of the sun's colors disappear over the mountains across the Hudson River. Then the text that had stirred in my memory crystallized in my mind.

The memory related to the classic passage from Genesis where God tells Abraham to sacrifice his son Isaac. Abraham dutifully climbs Mount Moriah, binds his son with rope as he would a sacrificial lamb, and is about to slit Isaac's throat when an angel intervenes. This is the story of how a human being was "bound" ('aqedah) in order to be sacrificed.

Different versions of Genesis 22 circulated in an immensely varied tradition called the Aqedah or "Binding" of Isaac in Rabbinic sources, and—with key changes—in both Christian and Islamic texts. Several ancient interpreters stated, or implied, that Abraham *did* cut his son's throat, and that Isaac had bled out and was offered in the sacrificial fire.

In texts I had studied in England twenty years before Anna's murder, as Abraham positioned the knife at his son's neck, Isaac looked up to heaven and saw angels there. Abraham's nearest approach to heaven was indirect, through what was reflected in Isaac's eyes; the offered son saw God's presence and God's will in a way the sacrificing father could not. The angel that stayed Abraham's knife was Isaac's vision, which his father saw only by reflection. Anna's throat and Anna's eyes had brought to life an image whose visceral power came home to me in that moment's silence in the sacristy as never before.

The events involved in Anna's murder in 1998 and its aftermath were complex, but the dreadful simplicity of the act, the slaughter of a young woman with a hunting knife, matches the simplicity of her killer's testimony during his successful insanity defense. A voice, he said, had ordered the murder, and his use of drugs had made him compliant. A festival a week before the crime had celebrated the Afro-Caribbean god Ogun, whose knife is believed to liberate vital forces from the victims he sacrifices. The cult of Ogun represents the same impulse with which the Aqedah struggles. A primordial compulsion had visited the doorstep of our church, as it has visited countless doorsteps before and since, taking the life of an innocent victim.

The laws of New York State provide for the psychiatric treatment of a murderer rather than his imprisonment, if the killer is not responsible for the killing. A quasi-religious motivation for the crime plays into the argument for treating a killer as a patient. In the judgment of the court, an impulse like Abraham's had motivated Anna's killer to do his crime.

Three years after Anna's death, I was in my church on another tragic day, but with a larger congregation. The attacks of September 11, 2001, took lives, broke up families and businesses, and robbed millions of people of the sense of security they had once enjoyed. Those who gathered that evening in the church, some of them remaining in meditative prayer long after the service ended, had either suffered losses directly or were drawn in sympathy to those who had suffered. They struggled to understand the motives of the hijackers, and of suicide bombers in the Middle East and elsewhere, who were proclaiming themselves martyrs.

In the weeks that followed we learned of the letter of guidance found in Mohamed Atta's bags, left behind in Boston on the day of the attacks. The letter gave instructions for ritually purifying one's body, reciting the Qur'an before boarding the plane, and remembering, "You must make your knife sharp and must not discomfort your animal during the slaughter." Following a pattern discernible within the Qur'an, in a story directly comparable to the Aqedah of Genesis 22, the Atta letter makes the sacrifice of Ibrahim (the Arabic equivalent of Abraham) and the willingness of his son to be offered into a model of true martyrdom.

Islam is by no means unique in using the Aqedah as a model for martyrs and as a justification for violence. As Judaism has praised the sacrifice of Abraham, and Islam the offering of Ibrahim, Christianity since the first century has contended that Jesus accomplished in actions the offering that Isaac only symbolized. The key Christian belief in Jesus as the sacrificial Lamb of God reinterprets and recasts the image of Isaac in Genesis.

Fundamentalist Christians have been particularly invested in this theology, and one of their number unleashed domestic terrorism in the United States well before Mohamed Atta's attack. Timothy McVeigh, a former soldier in the American army who belonged to the militant Christian Identity movement, bombed the Alfred P. Murrah Federal Building in Oklahoma City on April 19, 1995. One hundred sixty-eight Americans died and more than five hundred were wounded by McVeigh's truck bomb. When asked about the children in a day care facility whose lives he had ended that day, McVeigh allowed that there had been "collateral damage." He welcomed his own execution on June 11, 2001, at the federal penitentiary in Terre Haute, Indiana, by a lethal injection.

At the time of his death, Timothy McVeigh kept his stoical façade up until the end and said nothing. Yet prior to his execution, he released a portion of the poem "Invictus," by the Victorian poet William Ernest Henley, as his last words:

> It matters not how strait the gate,
>   How charged with punishments the scroll,
> I am master of my fate:
>   I am the captain of my soul.

In McVeigh's mind, his self-sacrificial attack on a corrupt and sprawling government ennobled him, and gave even the innocent victims of his improvised bomb—the children and adults he referred to as "collateral damage," who lost their lives in his cause—the only nobility they could ever achieve.

In the same year that saw the bombing in Oklahoma, Yigal Amir shot and killed Israeli prime minister Yitzhak Rabin in Tel Aviv, on November 4, 1995. Amir justified his murder on the basis of the Torah, the sacred Law of Moses and the Rabbis. He explained that Yitzhak Rabin wanted to cede too much land to the Palestinians and contended that "when you kill in war, it is an act that is allowed" according to the Torah of Moses. The land given to Israel by divine covenant is worth killing for as well as dying for, as in the time of Moses and his successor Joshua. Asked whether he had acted alone, Amir named God as his accomplice.

Amir was not the only member of his sect to embrace sacrificial violence. Meir Kahane, to whose ultra-orthodox cult Amir belonged, wrote to his young son Binyamin Zevson on God's behalf: "Sacrifice yourself, and sanctify my Name. . . . It is an obligation upon every Jew to do the same if the need arises." A deep conviction running through Christianity and Islam as well as Judaism makes the offering of the son a requirement for the patriarch to be proven truly worthy. The fact that Prime Minister Rabin was named Yitzhak, the name rendered as "Isaac" in English, only underscores that his killing and those like his are not merely ironies or coincidences, but part of a deep affliction within modern culture whose roots are biblical, and even (as we shall see) prebiblical.

Abraham's story has never been ours more than it is now, because his motivation has never been more evident in our actions. Naming that compulsion to take innocent life in the belief that sacrifice is noble goes beyond the incidents of any single crime, and takes us into the foundations of human culture and of how people understand the divine. My only real resource for dealing with the murder of Anna and its aftermath was that I had some previous familiarity with the forces behind the slaughter of innocents. Now I see that the forces involved in that singular death on the doorstep of my church have been unleashed on a much wider scale.

The Christian soldier, the Israeli conscript, the Muslim jihadist are all poised for conflict and prepared for death, armed by their training and motivated by an ethos that is thousands of years old. The impulse to praise martyrdom, and therefore to encourage susceptible adolescents to become martyrs, is embedded in the cultural DNA of the West. By examining the Aqedah and how it has been developed and deployed within the Abrahamic religions, and the enormous impact it has had on the way we think and feel, I hope to lay bare the sacrificial roots of violence and the driving force behind martyrdom.

Once self-sacrifice is at issue, the individual stands only for the collective, and morality in the usual sense of that word dissolves, whether for the American soldier in Iraq or the Palestinian suicide bomber in Jerusalem. We live on the edge of a prolonged sacrificial commitment, in a "War on Terror" whose end is as obscure as its purposes and methods are ill defined. Understanding what it is we're talking about when we speak of human death as a "sacrifice," as parties in armed conflict frequently do, has become crucial for us. We are not merely living through a political crisis, although it is also that. Powerful cultures rooted in the memory of Abraham are on the cusp of giving in entirely to their sacrificial drive with instruments of sacrifice more terrible than ever before.

The violence that seems to engulf us is neither random nor unpredictable, but derives from forces whose ways have been traced for millennia in texts that can leave us informed about our own motivations instead of bewildered by our fate. But to confront those forces demands that we engage a story that is often passed over in confused silence or explained away, and that we search our way through the disturbing questions the Aqedah raises.

For all its horror, the Aqedah is as familiar as the archetypal stories of the Fall, the Flood, and the Exodus. In Genesis 22, God "tested" Abraham, commanding him to sacrifice his son Isaac. Father and son journey for three days and then climb Mount Moriah. After making the necessary preparations, when he has bound his son, Abraham raises his knife, ready to carry out God's command. Abraham's haunting willingness to slay his own child, implicitly young and innocent although his age is not specified, makes the Aqedah the darkest of the Bible's classic scenes, a strange counterpoint to the stories of promise, deliverance, and justice that readers expect from Scriptures concerning a just God and his righteous people.

According to Genesis and Exodus, God was hard on Adam and Eve, ruthless in dispensing with Noah's generation by means of the Flood, and exacting in destroying the firstborn of Egypt. Yet those stories convey a sense of purpose and a standard of justice along with God's harsh, sometimes violent punishments. Unlike the primordial couple in Eden, Noah's unrighteous contemporaries, and the oppressors whom Pharaoh epitomized, Isaac was innocent. The boy was too young to have done real harm to anyone, and his obedient willingness charges the events with pathos.

Isaac's youthful innocence comes with his identity as the child of God's covenant with Abraham. God had promised Abraham that his descendants *through Isaac,* Sarah's first child and Abraham's true heir, would inherit the blessings of the land. The laconic description of Abraham's steady preparation to sacrifice this child of promise, the miraculous offspring of aged parents, deepens the horror of the story. Is this unspoken reversal of the promise of God's covenant with Abraham a throwback to when Yahweh, like other gods, liked the taste of human blood, innocent blood, and children's blood best of all? Does the Aqedah contradict all claims—Christian, Jewish, and Muslim—that God is merciful in his justice; does this story unmask him as a cruel tyrant whose bloodlust trumps any promises he might make?

The Aqedah takes anyone who hears the story up to Mount Moriah, to that place where we will give all that we have and all that we are, where we will hand over what is more precious to us than our lives, because we think we should or we must. God tests, and we are convinced we must pass the test. In that moment on the mountain, Abraham acts as deliberately as McVeigh, Amir, or Atta.

For no other reason than God's command, issued without argument or explanation, Abraham brought his child to the brink of death. Both in their interpretations of this story and in wars they have sanctioned on divine authority, the Abrahamic religions have persistently pushed believers and their children beyond that brink.

Understanding why they have done so, and how Abraham's curse has been handed on to secular cultures, involves understanding the Aqedah.

How could God have asked Abraham to sacrifice his son, and how could Abraham have been willing to obey? Once the demand is made and Abraham proceeds to offer sacrifice, does the angelic intervention represent God's point of view, or a desperate expedient by the storyteller to end the scene with Isaac still alive?

The issue in this book is not whether Genesis or any other text is right about God, but how its authors understood God, and—even more important—how they used Abraham and his son to understand human beings. The logic of the Fall or the Flood or the Exodus is ruthless, but it remains logic aimed at righteousness; there is a measure of justice and integrity in the divine-human interaction. But why would God invent a test that he then canceled, and how can Abraham wind up being the most callous parent imaginable at exactly the moment when God confirms the covenant with him? What vision of human nature does the Aqedah convey, and why has it proven powerful in the Abrahamic religions and in the cultures of their inheritors?

Jewish and Christian interpreters in the ancient period joined in a dialogue over the centuries, often trumping one another in claims to a superior understanding of the events of Genesis 22. They borrowed from one another, argued, insisted that they alone were right, and struggled for basic insight into God's nature and ours. They found a visceral, emotional force in the Aqedah, which pushed them, both

Christians and Jews, to imitate the actions of Abraham and Isaac, to offer themselves in martyrdom, and to instruct the young people of their time to become martyrs.

In the history of discussion of Genesis 22, as in countless other cases, scholarship tends to ask a narrow range of questions when confronting deep-seeking texts. Technical issues of dating sources are basic to scholarship, and I once spent considerable time and energy in the task, when I first researched the Aqedah in detail. I regret none of my investment in those questions, but I have realized over time that the debate concerning exegetical issues has distracted attention from the stunning development during the second century C.E. that both Judaism and Christianity argued vehemently that God *desired and accepted* human sacrifice. They did so for their own reasons, largely independently, and with differing motivations, but also within a prolonged argument over the true meaning of Genesis 22 that has never really ended. Did this text foreshadow Christ's gruesome death on the cross, as Christian interpreters maintained, or did Abraham really hack his son apart on Mount Moriah, as some Rabbis taught, in order to obey God's command? Either way, the divine approval of human sacrifice remains, and many texts on both sides of the Jewish-Christian divide called attention to that approval rather than attempting to soften it in any way.

The Judeo-Christian embrace of sacrifice, even to the point of spending human life, goes beyond acknowledging that death might be an occasional necessity. An entire literature of martyrdom, keyed in to the themes of Genesis 22 and often referring explicitly to that text, glorified those who gave their lives for their faith as ritual offerings that pleased God. The literary artistry of the texts belies the terrible heroism they endorse and the grisly suffering they describe.

What were the forces in Judaism and Christianity that caused ancient writers to portray the son, Isaac in one case and Jesus in the other, as a bloody and yet pleasing sacrifice? Since the time when both religions endorsed human sacrifice by divine mandate, how has that endorsement affected the behavior and the faith of Jews and Christians?

Those questions occupied me as the Cold War came to an end, and Americans began anticipating what, at the time, they called "the peace dividend." My expectations were less optimistic, because by then I had deepened my work on the question of why people engage in sacrifice, including human sacrifice and its modern surrogates. Once that question might have seemed abstract, of no more than passing interest to what passes for being the "real world." Although the whole idea of a "real" business world—separate from and superior to the worlds of values, ideas, science, and aesthetics—has long seemed to me artificial and pretentious, I saw no reason to take my discussion outside of an academic context. That is no longer the case; events have changed my mind.

Sacrificial violence, both as endured by believers and inflicted by them on others, has woven itself deeply into the pattern of Western history, and the rise of modernity has by no means broken that violent strand of motivation. During the twentieth century, confrontations between totalitarian and democratic states, pursued in two world wars and then between the Soviet and American empires made religious conflict *appear* to be on the wane, but the capacity of religions to produce brutal behavior remained powerful beneath the surface of events and has never been more obvious than it is today. There was, practically speaking, no "peace dividend," apart from public access to the Internet.

The West has instead moved almost seamlessly from an apocalyptic confrontation with Communism to an apocalyptic confrontation with Islam. To understand the forces that moved us and push us still into reactions that we can barely control, if at all, we need to turn to the story that has most persistently been associated with religious violence, the Aqedah. The three Abrahamic faiths—Islam included, only focusing on Isma'il rather than Isaac—have all provoked their people to martyrdom by speaking in terms of Abraham's sacrifice of his son, and making the Aqedah into the model of pure devotion to God.

To confront the Aqedah involves confronting a source of violence within our societies, and ourselves, which remains a powerful anthropological force in the West. Since the eighteenth century, however, fashions of thought have avoided that confrontation. The Enlightenment encouraged educated people to believe that they had transcended the sacrificial practices of their premodern ancestors. Religions, especially Christian and Jewish denominations during the nineteenth century, competed with one another to become rational rather than dogmatic. The Aqedah was left to art historians and biblical scholars, an apparent artifact of a bygone human era.

But what if the sacrificial era has not gone by? Suppose the impulse to sacrifice, even to yield up the lives of children to gain supernatural favor, is still with us. If you consider, not what we say about ourselves, but what we do in relation to one another, you would observe that the twentieth century saw more children sacrificed to one cause or another than any previous century saw offered to its gods. The shift from religious belief to secular cause has not changed the fact that the increase of violence against innocents appears unrelenting.

With brutal precision, Wilfred Owen, writing during World War I in "The Parable of the Old Man and the Young," encapsulated the experience of the twentieth century. In his poem, even divine intervention cannot control Abraham's impulse to kill his child:

So Abram rose, and clave the wood, and went,
And took the fire with him, and a knife.
And as they sojourned both of them together,
Isaac the first-born spake and said, My Father,
Behold the preparations, fire and iron,
But where the lamb, for this burnt-offering?
Then Abram bound the youth with belts and straps,
and builded parapets and trenches there,
And stretched forth the knife to slay his son.
When lo! an Angel called him out of heaven,
Saying, Lay not thy hand upon the lad,
Neither do anything to him, thy son.
Behold! Caught in a thicket by its horns,
A Ram. Offer the Ram of Pride instead.
But the old man would not so, but slew his son,
And half the seed of Europe, one by one.

Owen appreciated the motivating power behind the Aqedah, and realized that its mythic insight could key us in to realize why we behave as we do. The Aqedah has typically been read since the Enlightenment as marking the end of human sacrifice, but the reverse seems more accurate: sacrificial violence may be more uncontainable than ever.

Like Owen's poem, the influential variations of the Aqedah that we will examine state, with dreadful certainty, that no angel interrupted Abraham. Rather, he obeyed God's initial command and shed the blood of his son. These interpretations of the Aqedah have inspired cults of death in all three Abrahamic faiths, and the rhetoric of sacrifice has been passed on from its religious sources to the lexicon of politically inspired violence. Violence has been secularized during the great military campaigns of the past two hundred years, but by no means reduced in its extent or mortality. Moreover, since the end of the nineteenth century, powerful movements of fundamentalist interpretation—Christian and Jewish as well as Muslim—have arisen that demand literal sacrifice from their adherents. Whether from a secular or a religious perspective, we live in an age of sacrifice.

Looking into Abraham's mind, into the heart of sacrifice and its consequences, provokes dread, even "fear and trembling," the title of Søren Kierkegaard's meditation on Genesis 22. By virtue of this unsurpassed and unsurpassable book, Kierkegaard—the nineteenth-century Danish philosopher who designed his thought to serve faith—became a hero of existentialism during the twentieth century, after Walter Lowrie's translation of his work. *Fear and Trembling* made Abraham into a "knight of faith," the hero who places his trust in the paradox that God requires our all in order to give all in return. As in Jewish and Christian sources since the second century, Abraham's ennobling sacrifice was worthy of existential imitation. Kierkegaard compared himself to the patriarch when he decided not to marry his fiancée. Even that, we will see, repeats a claim deep in the Christian tradition, that celibacy is involved with Abraham's sacrifice.

Kierkegaard's contribution endures, both brilliant and unique, yet in its fundamental meaning it is also repetitious of Christian theology. He repeated the assumption that sacrifice is noble and that the story turns on Abraham's individual heroism. But the Aqedah is not only about that one man: his child, his wife, and whole cultures, yearning for survival and willing to sacrifice, weave themselves into the action. All together they represent realities of human motivation and response that ripple through societies, not only individuals. Abraham's curse remains our inheritance, because we live during a period of renewed sacrificial intensity, often without any awareness that violence since the First World War is unparalleled in its scale and in its choice of young victims. By untangling our actions from the atavistic impulse that kills children in the name of virtue, we can at last free Isaac from the cords that, had they remained tied, would have denied Abraham his progeny. Unless we do, unless Abraham's impulse and the means to transform that impulse are discovered, then Wilfred Owen will prove to be a prophet of this century as well as a principal poet of the last.

Part One

THE TEST

I

Sacrificial Species,
Human Offerings

Before Judaism, Christianity, or Islam existed, before people
could write, and before they founded cities, they sacrificed. The
species *Homo neanderthalensis* (flourishing between 110,000
and 35,000 years ago) interred both animal and human skeletons near
hearths evidently constructed for sacrificial gatherings. Remains of
young children found in Crete from the ancient Minoan civilization
at Knossos, dated during the middle of the second millennium B.C.E.,
were found charred, their bones nicked in a way that accords with
how Minoans prepared sheep and goats for ritual slaughter. Horrible
to conceive of, human sacrifice has nonetheless remained rooted in
human behavior from the time it emerged, deeply enough that the
impulse persists, encoded even in evolved societies.

Many investigators cherish Minoan civilization as a gentle oasis
in the midst of warring Mediterranean tribes. Human sacrifice, and
child sacrifice at that, contradicts what has been called "the Minoan
Myth." Evidence for the practice outraged one archaeologist, who
tried to explain away the skeletons as those of apes rather than human beings.

Sacrifice featured as centrally in primordial societies as it has been
marginalized and denied in modern cultures, repressed like a bad
dream of violence running rampant in the precivilized past. Yet sacrifice need not be any more destructive than a meal; ancient liturgies

often called for offerings of grain or wine rather than slaughtered animals of any kind. Wherever sacrifice is practiced, however, the *possibility* of a human offering emerges. Although tantamount to homicide, the desire to please the gods can break through, and often has broken through, a basic human taboo: not to kill one's own child. Two distinct but related impulses, the impulse to sacrifice and the impulse to offer children, wove themselves together during the ancient period and have emerged together persistently ever since in appeals to atavistic violence, articulated to this day in calls for young people to sacrifice their lives for the good of their faith, their society, their nation, or their family.

To see these forces at work requires getting beyond the reflexive denial, fashionable since the Enlightenment, that the desire to sacrifice sometimes drives human behavior. That fashion persists today, despite centuries of war in recent history, with its comforting assumption that human beings have no natural proclivity toward sacrifice *or* violence, but are guided by instinctive and rational self-interest. Leaving optimistic views of humanity behind to study sacrifice in any period is emotionally as well as intellectually demanding. To consider the incontrovertible and transcultural facts of sacrificial behavior, although they are endemically human, requires an act of will as well as of intellect. I have never met anyone who has not been shocked on first confronting unmistakable evidence that human beings killed their fellow humans—including their children—because they wanted to please their gods.

The inescapable reality of people's tendency to sacrifice, and their consent to offer their own children, has disturbed modern thinkers in the West, like the archaeologist who preferred to think of human bones as ape skeletons rather than concede that the highly developed, generally gentle Minoans had sacrificed children. The idea of child sacrifice awakens deep revulsion. Part of that reaction involves outrage, a moral rejection of the act. The willingness to offer a child in sacrifice, especially one's own child, seems utterly inhuman to many observers, specialists and nonspecialists alike, and they reflexively want to deny that child sacrifice ever really happened. If it did happen, they naturally think, then it should never have occurred. To reject sacrifice as a human activity has long been part of our Enlightenment makeup.

But to help account for the fateful pull of human behavior toward collective violence, we need to understand sacrifice, not deny it, and see how it develops into human sacrifice. Then, to fathom the persistence of Western violence in particular (both before and after the Enlightenment), we need also to examine how the Abrahamic religions have sometimes endorsed child sacrifice as a virtue by using the example of the patriarch's sacrifice to justify the martyrdom of the young. Following chapters will show in detail that Christians have marched to war, Jews have died to resist their persecutors, and Muslims have declared jihad, all with appeals and allusions to the example of Abraham offering his son. To understand the sacrificial motive for violence requires dealing with the evidence that people sacrifice, and that they believe in God, gods, or some other form of ultimate reality, which they are convinced they please with their devoted offerings, including their own children. Whether we like those facts or not does not augment or weaken their reality: they need to be explained for human behavior to be understood, and for it ultimately to be changed.

Despite the Enlightenment's view of human nature, human behavior since the eighteenth century has shown little sign of constitutional change. Even without official rituals of sacrifice, sacrificial acts abound, concentrated in times of war, but also ambient now, during the strange, vicious twilight of war and peace that has opened the twenty-first century. Adolescents, and preadolescents, join up with the Lord's Resistance Army in Uganda, the Shining Path in Peru, Al Qaeda in Afghanistan, the Aryan Nation in North America, various National Fronts in Europe and Australia, and Maoist cadres in Asia. However willing these children and youths may or may not be, the groups they belong to freely expend their young lives in war, calling their deaths a sacrifice. That reflex is as basic to these groups as it is for nations to organize armies of youthful men and women and to commemorate their patriotic and sacrificial deaths on national holidays. However twisted Abraham's offering may seem, generations of people—with every kind of faith and with no particular faith—have repeated his actions millions of times since he lifted his knife over his son, only unlike Abraham in Genesis, they have brought the knives of war down on their children, convinced that such slaughter is necessary and right.

Sacrifice is a powerful, primordial act. Living things are offered and consumed in sacred meals, concentrating the collective forces and hopes of the societies that host them, and as a result participants feel their own lives revive. People participate with their gods in collective enjoyment across cultures and throughout history, by eating what their gods eat, savoring what their gods savor, and dedicating themselves to create as their gods create. Sacrifice infuses powerless people with power as palpably as it feeds the hungry with delicacies, particularly meat, which their diets typically lack. Enjoyment and purpose, combined with participation in divine destiny, suffuse sacrifice as no other human activity. The continuing power of sacrificial thinking is rooted in that pattern of dedicated and energizing renewal, accomplished by sharing the products of human work in the presence of the divine. Human beings ritually join the divine world in the act of enjoying the good things of life, as they consume the benefits of their work together and anticipate further benefits to come.

In the past, sacrifice has been portrayed as an attempt to bribe the gods with monetary gifts, or to tap into the magical life force of an animal as it dies. Both these portrayals have their merits. Without question, commercial transactions were ordinarily involved in sacrifice, and the action of the priest or prophet who offered a victim often made him or her a magician in the eyes of worshipers, with special powers of insight and healing. But sacrifice is not a mere by-product of advancing commerce or of specialized magical powers. The reverse is more likely the case: civilizations emerged by transferring skills they had learned in a basic social activity—the communal, sacrificial meal with the gods—into daily life with increasing degrees of specialization.

Yet sacrifice is not an exotic, remote, or "primitive" activity. Whenever human beings share the products of their own labor with an awareness that this sharing occurs with divine approval, that is a sacrificial act. The Catholic Mass, the offering of a goat at the end of Ramadan, the Seder at Passover, formal meals to gather support for a common cause or to mourn a loved one's passing, are all linked to the primordial human impulse to offer and share our goods in anticipation of the good that is to come. The character of this activity is determined by a community's discernment of what should be shared, with whom, where, and when, and by its view of the divine or transcendent truth—be it God or gods or a principle or ideal—that measures the worth of their offerings. Both ancient and modern societies frame basic ethical concerns and establish shared values when and how they decide to sacrifice, on religious or other grounds.

Neither personal nor mass psychology fully explains ritual impulses. Both sacrifice and the practice of offering children on altars—sometimes ritual altars, sometimes metaphorical altars of convenience or warfare—are powerful inheritances from at least as long ago as the Stone Age. But the two impulses are *not* one and the same. Sacrificing a butchered goat or a bushel of milled grain or a vat of wine is obviously not identical to offering a human being. The two acts are distinct and different, however related they may be, and ancient religious literatures as well as interpretations of those Scriptures from Antiquity until the present day reflect deep insights that have freed people from confusing sacrifice generally with homicide. Genesis 22 is the principal ancient text, Antiquity's gift to a modern consciousness bereft of means to understand its own behavior, which permits us to parse the difference between deeply ingrained impulses whose confusion has produced disaster and poses an acute danger today.

Part of the power of Genesis 22, and its capacity to explore the connection between sacrifice and killing children, is the silent horror the text awakens in the reader. Laconic and rhythmic, the Hebrew narrative avoids mentioning emotions, and the terse description builds all the more in affective tension for that reason. Actions transpire without deliberation or choice, objection, or delay, as if the sacrifice of the child Isaac were a foregone conclusion.

Rendering Hebrew prose and poetry into English in a way that conveys the unique and varying styles of the Israelite Scriptures is a challenge, and can't be met unless the translator puts aside the practice of trying to make all biblical text sound alike. Versions authorized by various churches and Bible societies have perpetuated the convention of homogeneity, because it permits translations to be inserted seamlessly into services of worship in a recognizable, "biblical" English. Even efforts of literary translation carry on this habit in a new guise by attempting to find a single, consistent voice for the Bible.

But what strikes any reader of the Hebrew Bible in its original language is the variety produced when idiosyncratic voices meet and combine in the harmonics—and occasional dissonances—of texts produced over the course of centuries. The narrator of Genesis 22, coming from the source known to scholars as the Elohist (because it prefers to call God *'Elohim,* "God" in a majestic plural, prior to the revelation of Yahweh's personal name to Moses), is one of those unique voices. The Elohist source tells the story of Israel's beginnings, and is part of the whole narrative now included in the Torah or the Pentateuch, the first five books of the Bible.

The Elohist's particular contributions—the cycle of stories about Joseph, for example, and the depiction of Moses' visions—reveal a burning interest in prophecy. In Genesis 22 as well, the action pivots on Abraham's willingness to take correction from God's revelation, in the way the prophets did: only Abraham's obedience to the angel who intervenes saves Isaac's life and sustains God's covenantal promise to the children of Abraham, Isaac, and Jacob.

By the time the Elohist source was first crafted, during the ninth century B.C.E., the united kingdom of David and Solomon had been torn apart by civil war. Judea remained under the control of David's successors, but the bulk of the country—which appropriated the name of Israel—went a separate way, with its own king, altars, rituals of sacrifice, and ideas of what God truly desired. This Israel (called the Northern Kingdom in modern scholarship, to distinguish it from Judea) was more prosperous than its southern counterpart, more able and willing to trade and make alliances with surrounding countries and empires, and therefore more open to influences from cultures whose worship differed radically from the standards set out by the prophets of Yahweh. In this syncretistic environment, Israelites in the north embraced gods alongside Yahweh. Child sacrifice, one of the practices known from before, during, and after this period, became a pressing issue for the Elohist. The Aqedah represents the Elohist's response to the possibility that offering a son could seal a father's devotion to God.

Linguistic choices that went into telling the story give it its unique voice, alive with the exceptional nature of the events recounted:

> Then after these things God tried Abraham. He said to him, Abraham. And he said, Look—me. He said, Take now your son, your cherished one, whom you love, Isaac, and go your way to the land of Moriah, and offer him up there, an offering by fire on one of the hills that I say to you.
>
> Abraham awoke early in the morning, saddled his ass and took two of his young men with him, as well as Isaac his son, split the wood of the offering by fire, and arose and went to the place that God said to him. On the third day Abraham lifted up his eyes and saw the place from afar. Abraham said to his young men, Stay back here with the ass. I and the young man, we will go there. We will worship. We will come back to you.
>
> Abraham took the wood of the offering by fire and put it on Isaac his son, and took in his hand the flint and the knife, and the two of them went, together. Isaac spoke to Abraham his father. He said, My father. And he said, Look—me, my son. He said, Look—the flint and the wood, but where is the lamb of the offering by fire? Abraham said, God will himself see the lamb of the offering by fire, my son. And the two of them went, together.
>
> They came to the place that God said to him, and Abraham built there the slaughter pit, and arranged the wood, bound up Isaac his son, and put him on the slaughter pit above the wood. Abraham sent back his hand, took the knife to kill his son.

The routine of sacrifice permeates this narrative, determining the content of every action, punctuating each gesture, and grounding the whole plot in a relentless rhythm. That is why Abraham needs no more than the initial command by God—what to sacrifice, how, and where—to proceed along his way. Abraham knows what to do; inexorable ritual seems to drive him to a foregone conclusion.

Knowledge of the sacrificial sequence underlies the horror that the story evokes, as well as its action. Once Isaac is identified as the victim God wants, each move—ordinarily an anodyne increment in shedding animal blood for divine festivity—ratchets toward infanticide. Isaac focuses the narrative and its horror when he asks, "Where is the lamb of the offering by fire?" He knows what needs to happen, yet doesn't know Abraham's intent; his knowledge and his ignorance together make him the most acute observer of the events, as well as their innocent victim.

When Isaac, who is about to be sacrificed, asks innocently about the lamb, his question encapsulates the full power of Genesis 22. Its emotional impact derives, not merely from a masterful style of narration, but also from a fearless investigation of the connection between sacrifice and infanticide. Anthropologists and historians as well as theologians have seen different logical links implicit in this combination. Are these drives inevitably entwined, as some suggest? Does sacrifice in all its diverse forms mask a desire for human victims? Or does God test Abraham in order to disentangle genuine worship from bloodlust? In its original setting, the Aqedah addressed these issues as existential questions rather than as theoretical possibilities.

By the time of the Elohist, human sacrifice had been practiced for millennia. The end of the Stone Age saw the first urban communities and, in some cases, the institutional killing of children. Cities were the basic unit of human civilization, generating large markets, the production of surpluses that could be used to trade with other cities, specialized activities, armies, wars and casualties, the practice of victors taking multiple wives from the women of fallen enemies and comrades alike, central government, royal courts, and a central altar of sacrifice.

The urban temple, the foundation of the whole city, had to be seen as holier and more powerful, more attractive to the gods, than any other altar. Human sacrifice emerged as the price required to assure divine favor in building a city, the means of making the urban temple the ultimate altar. Several ancient myths depict the founder king of a city sacrificing his own child, his firstborn son, by slaughtering him on the foundation stone of the city in order to secure prosperity, and especially victory over enemies.

Before the Exodus of the people Israel from Egypt, human sacrifice had been practiced on the land that Israel eventually occupied, and was practiced after Israelite settlement. When God "tried Abraham," that trial was in no way hypothetical. Abraham climbed Moriah to worship his deity with his most cherished possession, following time-honored practices of peoples far more ancient than Israel, the Elohist source, and Abraham himself. But this narrative equally illustrates that sacrificing a person clashes with the usual practice and purpose of sacrifice in general. That's what makes the story a trial. Isaac's question about the lamb for the offering speaks from the heart of the Aqedah, posing the crucial issue: What is the fundamental difference, if any, between sacrificing a person and sacrificing an animal?

The answer of Israelite tradition to this question became clear in the celebration of Passover. The lambs slaughtered for this sacrificial feast symbolized not only escape from Egypt, but also deliverance from death. The word Passover, *Pesach* in Hebrew, means "limping" (or "skipping," as some scholars more delicately express the same kind of movement) and referred originally to the limping of the spring lamb, hobbled prior to being ritually slaughtered, sacrificed, and eaten. But the memory of deliverance from Egypt gave this nomadic ritual a totally new meaning (see the Book of Exodus 12:5–13). The lamb at Passover in the Bible is a true sacrifice, offered to honor God and to join with him in celebration, precisely because he did *not* kill the firstborn of the Israelites as he did of the Egyptians at the time of the Exodus (12:29). As in the case of *most* offerings, those who worshiped at *Pesach* enjoyed the sacrifice together with God.

Distant as modern sensibility is from the actual practice of these rituals, the common understanding of sacrifice is that the worshiper has to forgo any enjoyment in the occasion, assigning his own property to the deity without benefit to himself other than the deity's favor.

Pesach proves the contrary, as an instance of a "sacrifice of sharings" (*zebach shelamin* in Hebrew), when participants feasted during a meal enhanced by God's presence. Collective feasting together with sacrifice features commonly in ethnographic studies to this day, as it does in narratives of the patriarchs and Moses. A sacred meal formalizes Jacob's treaty with Laban (Genesis 31:51–54), for example, and Moses initiated his covenant, the solemn compact between God and his people, by means of sacrifice. At that time Moses brought his brother Aaron, his nephews Nadab and Abihu, and seventy elders up the mountain with him. All of them, the Book of Exodus explicitly says, "saw the God of Israel" (24:10) while they were eating and drinking: that festive communion is also an example of a sacrifice of sharings.

Sacrificial meals combined human and divine enjoyment; music, dance, and sacred drama as well as eating and drinking typified these occasions. In the ancient Israelite conception, sacrifice involved God's emotions, because Yahweh actively desired to consume a part of what is pure with his people, while they also enjoyed the benefit of the slaughter and joined one another in celebration. The joy of ritual offering, which suffuses sacrificial texts of every period and culture, challenges the understanding of most modern observers, who reflexively conceive of sacrifice as a dour, grisly ordeal—all payment and blood, superstition without benefit. Yet the fact is that Israelites did benefit, and not only in the favor of God: sacrifice involved consumption of more meat and wine than usual, as well as foods of better quality, entertainment, a break from work and routine, pilgrimage to Jerusalem (or other sites, depending upon the period), and social interactions with many more other Israelites than they ordinarily encountered during the week of feasting that major festivals involved.

When we understand sacrifice as a sacred meal, in which people and deity join, we begin to see a deep, common pattern within all known religions. Sacrificial activity involves taking foods that are of the highest standards, and bringing them to the deity for divine and human enjoyment. Standards of purity varied widely: the pig beloved by Zeus was anathema to Jews, the offering of Moses—as he said himself (Exodus 8:25–28)—was abominable to the Egyptians, and the camel sacrifice of the Arabs aroused the fascinated horror of British ethnographers during the nineteenth century. But the underlying principle, that effective offering occurs when a people shares its best with its deity, endures. That is sacrifice, pure and simple.

If sacrifice is first and foremost a sacred, celebratory meal, what is the connection between worshiping a deity and the ritualistic slaughter of a child? It seems a long way from the celebration of deliverance or plenty to the slaughter of a firstborn son, yet just that journey is plotted by Abraham's ascent of Moriah. Genesis's concise poetry puts into words and narrative a connection few texts explain.

What Abraham is called to do in Genesis 22 is, from a biblical point of view, monstrous. He trudges up Moriah to prepare human flesh for God's consumption, although the laws of ancient Judaism explicitly prohibit treating people as food, committing murder, approaching human blood, or engaging in infanticide. If sacrifice perpetuates the community's life, how is it compatible with murdering that community's future? The riddle of child sacrifice is that it is incompatible with the basic aim of ritual, to offer a pure and joyful meal, and yet it occurs. Sacrifice binds a community together, while offering a person, making a child a sacrificial victim, threatens that community's existence. Yet healing and destruction seem to have become inextricably entwined. How and why was that possible?

Genesis 22 investigates the origins of human violence by setting out the most graphic case imaginable. Horrific and unanticipated, violent acts change any setting in which they occur; a knife thrusting or slashing, punches thrown, a firearm discharged, or an explosion detonated—all put the people concerned into new relations with one another, even if tension had been mounting prior to the moment of violence. Relations after violence, of course, are likely to involve a cycle of revenge, such as has consumed the West and Islam in a long struggle of mutual retribution that seems to know no bounds. The Aqedah constitutes the model of sacrificial violence that cultures in the Abrahamic tradition have referred back to, have taken on themselves as a pattern of virtuous behavior, have imposed on their children, and have foisted onto one another in conflicts that pit one imitator of Abraham against another.

———

God's abrupt command to Abraham contradicts basic instincts of human affection. A sensitive reader might decide to reject the whole story of the Aqedah, to see it, not as in any way noble, but as a charter of abuse that *promotes* literal child sacrifice. But Israel no more invented the possibility of human sacrifice than it invented the idea of God or the practice of sacrifice generally; the Hebrew Bible explicitly deals with cases of human sacrifice apart from Abraham's abortive offering of Isaac. These instances, together with Genesis 22, indicate that child sacrifice marks critical passages, moments of danger that seem to require a disruption of sacrifice as ordinarily practiced, in a way that resonates with other ancient literatures.

War, famine, and plague could kill so great a proportion of the community that people who engaged in sacrifice came to believe that their god or gods enjoyed human victims. In the interests of warding off the divine thirst for blood, why not offer up a person, despite the loss involved, especially in times of danger? That thought may well have arisen spontaneously in the course of ordinary Israelite worship, but examples of human sacrificial victims surrounded Israel in any case, so that child sacrifice became an option that had to be confronted. There were Israelites who embraced the possibility. The Minoan case—of children butchered and cooked as choice meat—was not isolated. Such sacrifices may well have involved cannibalism on occasion, as in the case of the Aztecs millennia later. Although human sacrifice does not necessarily include cannibalism, once the barrier between animal and human victims is breached, the taboo against consuming human flesh also becomes vulnerable.

The transition from sacrifice to child sacrifice left enough traces in ancient sources to permit us to see how it occurred. In Israelite and ancient Near Eastern practice as well as in the rituals of Greece, Rome, India, and South America, specified parts of any sacrificial animal were offered to the flames, for the deity alone, while the participants enjoyed the rest. At times the whole victim belonged to the god, typically when a community felt that its collective behavior had brought about divine disfavor: then those who sacrificed would offer a feast for the deity alone, and not take part themselves. The food might all be consigned to flame, or a part distributed among the priesthood, but the point was that when the usual, festal communion between divine and human participants had been interrupted, the deity alone would benefit from a sacrifice in order to reestablish a broken relationship.

Once the offering of sacrifice went to the god alone as a valuable gift of restitution, and the connection with human consumption was broken, then the preciousness of human flesh could make it seem an ideal medium of worship in crisis. That is exactly how the offering of children is presented in the Hebrew Bible. In a narrative even sparer than the prose of the Aqedah, Mesha, the king of Moab, in the thick of battle against the kings of both Judah and Israel, "took his firstborn son who was to reign in his stead, and offered him for a burnt offering upon the wall." Instead of condemning this action, the passage goes on to narrate, "A great wrath came on Israel; they pulled back from him and returned to their own land" (2 Kings 3:27). In other words, the human sacrifice worked. Mesha, a contemporary of the Elohist source (during the ninth century B.C.E.), actually did what Abraham did not, and benefited as a result.

Mesha himself went on to have a monument inscribed to celebrate his victories over Israel and Judah, and to prove his devotion to Kemosh, the Moabite god. Speaking of his destruction of an Israelite city, Mesha bragged, "I killed all the people of the city as a sacrifice for Kemosh and for Moab." This inscription sets out the sacrificial perspective in which Kemosh was pleased by the human offering of Mesha's son and returned the favor with victory, for himself and for Moab, and to the evident benefit of Mesha, who celebrated triumph with yet more sacrifice.

Mesha's sacrifice of his son, near the same time that the Elohist source crafted the Aqedah, shows how deeply, without any connection to Abraham, the appeal of child sacrifice had worked into the consciousness of the ancient Near East. From the point of view of the god Kemosh, all the destruction of battle came as a sacrifice that he rewarded with victory for his people of Moab. From the point of view of the story in the Second Book of Kings, the sacrifice of Mesha's son in particular was so effective that divine "wrath" came upon Israel: apparently Yahweh either took pleasure in the human offering himself, or did not stand in the way of the pleasure Kemosh took in Mesha's sacrifice. The success of the desperate ritual, however it was explained, posed a disturbing question. If other peoples cherished their gods so much that they were willing to offer their children, could Israelites show themselves less devoted to their deity?

From an even earlier period, at the very origins of the biblical tradition, around 1200 B.C.E., comes the story of Jephthah and his daughter. In this story (from the Book of Judges 11:29–40), Jephthah vows to Yahweh that if Yahweh will help him destroy the mighty Ammonites in battle, he will offer as a burnt sacrifice the first person who comes out of his settlement to meet him afterward. Jephthah overcame his enemy against the odds, but to his horror his daughter came out to meet him, singing and dancing in celebration at the victory. But she urges her father to fulfill his vow. He agrees, giving her time to mourn her fate—and especially, the text says, "her virginity," her prospective death as a childless woman—before the flames consumed her. And every year, those in the tradition of Jephthah mourned the loss of his daughter, joining in springtime religious commemoration that combined the seasonal themes of death and fertility. "It became statute in Israel of long standing that the daughters of Israel went to recollect the daughter of Jephthah for four days a year" (Judges 11:39–40). That feast involved an ambivalent commemoration, of folly and heroism at one and the same time. Anyone who keeps a feast of death implicitly asks: Is such death actually necessary, and even desirable?

The Israelites' Greek counterparts asked the same question centuries later and wound up endorsing human sacrifice with an ambivalence all their own. Agamemnon—becalmed, and fearful that his mission to Troy would end with failure and death at sea—killed his daughter Iphigenia in obedience to a prophetic oracle. His offering pleased the goddess Artemis, and Agamemnon gained winds favorable to his journey. According to Aeschylus's version of this tale, Agamemnon's wife and Iphigenia's mother Clytemnestra killed *him* as a sacrifice to avenge this crime. Somewhat later, Euripides, in his *Electra,* has Clytemnestra let her jealousy show through, saying that if Agamemnon had slaughtered their daughter "to prevent the ruin of the city, to secure his home, to rescue his children, killing one on behalf of the others, it would have been explicable—but for the sake of Helen. . . ." Her reaction in no way denied that human sacrifice could be justified; what she rejected was that her husband sought to harness the power of human sacrifice on behalf of another woman.

Clytemnestra's consent to the principle of child sacrifice is eerily similar to the portrayal of Sarah in some later interpretations of the Aqedah we shall encounter in the course of this book, where she permits and even encourages Abraham to act. Aeschylus wrote around 458 B.C.E. and Euripides around 417 B.C.E., some four centuries after the Elohist first committed Genesis 22 to writing. But Iphigenia's fate had been a traditional story for centuries by the time Aeschylus wrote; the Greek story and the Hebrew story are independent, representing two cultures coming to grips with their bloody legacies of child sacrifice in differing but comparable ways.

Isaac and Iphigenia share key traits in common. Each child lies at a founding cultural moment of the society concerned: Isaac sanctifies the mountain that will bear the Temple in the Promised Land (2 Chronicles 3:1; *Jubilees* 18:13), while Iphigenia introduces Greek city-states to their power in the sea. Both Isaac and Iphigenia, in rich literatures of interpretation, are sometimes said to have died, sometimes to have been replaced by an animal at the moment of sacrifice, sometimes to have been transported to a divine realm—all depending on the version of the story one consults. The multiplicity of those versions, their mythic permutations and combinations, supports the finding of several researchers from a range of disciplines that stories of child sacrifice reflect how cities understood their own origins, and reveal why human beings across civilizations resort to self-inflicted violence in times of trial. Recourse to human sacrificial victims is a desperate measure, but once embedded in the mythology of any culture it becomes a reflex that reemerges to guide societies, not only in crisis, but also in the anticipation of crisis.

The cultural reflex of self-sacrifice and child sacrifice is pervasive and often comes to the surface when a society confronts a threat to its existence or its moral order. When President George W. Bush remem-

bered the passengers and crew of United Airlines Flight 93 storming
the cockpit of their airplane so that it could not be used to attack
Washington, he described them as reciting the Twenty-third Psalm
and giving up their lives on behalf of others. He did so in a speech he
gave five years after the event, in which he also characterized suicide
terrorists as "the face of evil." With rhetorical precision, he fastened
on an underlying sacrificial pattern that Americans could use to make
sense of what they had witnessed on September 11, 2001, and experienced as a threat to their existence. The passengers on the flight in
President Bush's vision were true martyrs, while the suicide terrorists
were not, neither dying heroically nor aiming to do good. The passengers of United Airlines Flight 93 (old and young) willingly gave their
lives to defend the nation's capital from a very real danger and offered
themselves in sacrifice for a noble cause.

The appeal of sacrificial rhetoric is powerful enough to move people to act, and even go to war. The depth of the cultural reflex runs below conscious control and transcends individual psychology and the
usual logic of ethical action. The Aqedah in all its variations reveals a
common human impulse, which it brings to mythic expression. True
myths are not just individual stories or novels or poems, however
great the compositions of artists in words may be; myths arise from
the symbolic interconnections that enable a community to act together, experience emotions together, and explain themselves to one
another with a shared vocabulary of values. Myth is the place where
religions first come to consciousness, which opens the prospect that
we can understand these deeply interior but also powerfully communal engines of social life if we attend to their mythic disclosures of
their deepest concerns.

Religions outside the Abrahamic faiths express the call to self-
sacrificial violence by means of similar myths: for example, in the
epic called the *Bhagavad Gita* in Hinduism, where the god Krishna
explains to Arjuna his duty to go to war; in the Dalai Lama's aphoris-
tic summary of Buddhism in his *Book of Wisdom,* that "you sacrifice
yourself in order to attain salvation for the sake of others"; and in the
orders of Adm. Takijiro Onishi that sent Japanese pilots to their deaths
by using their planes as flying bombs against American warships in
World War II. Admiral Onishi's subsequent self-inflicted death by rit-

ual *seppuku* demonstrates his deep connection with the reflexes that Genesis 22 lays bare, without his having a personal or cultural awareness of that text. Self-sacrifice and child sacrifice lie deeper and wider than the story of Abraham on Mount Moriah. Even assuming that the myth of Abraham's sacrifice could somehow be expunged or replaced, there are other Isaacs and Iphigenias in world mythology, ancient and modern, who justify the urge to sacrifice one's children and to defend the nobility of martyrdom by proxy.

At the time the first extant religious texts were composed, human society went through a pivotal shift that altered the practice of sacrifice and social relations as a whole. Ten thousand years ago the first cities emerged. With their central temples, their kings portrayed as sons of deities, their monopoly of power—economic, military, and religious—cities concentrated and mandated the social relations of their people, often by use of force. The existence of the urban complex required land, which implied aggressive and defensive wars, armies, and casualties of war. What some social anthropologists refer to as a "masculine" or "patriarchal" attitude is more accurately described as the mentality of war, which cities since their origins and the nation-states that followed them have institutionalized. They have promoted polygyny among victorious male warriors (to distribute widows and female orphans after battle), sacrifice by men alone (since males were valued over women in warfare), and the provision of large, expensive victims in sacrifice in order to seal the power of the urban state. The hierarchy of animal victims in sacrifice, including in regard to their sex, also reflects the greater value generally attached to males, although notable exceptions (such as the red cow in Numbers 19) may well reflect rites from a time prior to the dominance of cities.

Once the city emerged as the dominant reality in human relations, each claimed its land to the exclusion of all competitors. Along with physical territory, cities—through their temples and priesthoods as well as in the rule of kings deemed to be "sons" of divine patrons—also laid claim to mutually exclusive myths that framed what people did, how they felt, and why they served their gods in their particular ways. Warfare became increasingly destructive as opposing myths clashed and city went to war with city, or with opposing pre-urban societies—such as the seminomadic Israelites—that had also learned to use the methods of urban conquest.

Wars were no longer fought for practical gain or defense alone, but easily veered into what is described in the Hebrew Bible, where Israel, prior to becoming an urban culture centered in Jerusalem, nonetheless goes to war with cities using the tactics of their urban opponents. The Book of Joshua 6, for example, relates how the Gentile city of Jericho was subjected to *cherem*: the complete destruction of the people, domestic animals, and property of an opposing city, so that nothing remained but the metal that could be passed through fire and reforged for the purposes of the victors and their deity. This destruction was not a sacrifice in itself, but devotion to the victorious god of everything that had belonged to the former city, so that sacrifice could take place on purified ground.

Urban warfare had developed by the time that writing emerged (during the fourth millennium B.C.E.), so that its impact upon subsequent cultures, for example in epic poems of war from the *Iliad* to the *Bhagavad Gita,* was and remains inevitable. The Stone Age ethos of warfare and sacrifice has shaped human culture to the point that some anthropologists have argued that human beings are naturally disposed, even compelled by their nature, to offer human sacrifice. On this view, all societies are fated to follow the primordial impulse to offer up their young, just as they are fated to accept the necessity of war.

James George Frazer crafted the most influential version of this fatalistic vision of human nature and sacrifice at the beginning of the twentieth century. He portrayed "primitive" people as transfixed by the false, magical idea that by killing a person, sacrifice releases his vital spirit for the benefit of others. More recently, René Girard, a French literary critic turned social anthropologist, has argued a powerful variant of this theory. Girard maintains that the central problem of all primordial societies was how to diffuse envy. The desire for what the other has, to the point of wanting to eliminate one's rival altogether, was endemic—and prior to the development of law codes, violence lay just beneath the surface of common life. The drive to eliminate the envied other and take what he has, left unchecked, brings every human community to the brink of destruction, according to Girard, and past that brink unless a cure for competitive greed can be found.

By grounding his analysis of human sacrifice in the greed of human nature rather than in the supposedly magical quality of "primitive" thinking, Girard has developed a more plausible variant of Frazer's theory. He has also crafted an elegant scenario of how primordial societies deal with their essential violence that seems to account for a wider range of historical and ethnographic evidence than Frazer's sweeping generalizations do. But as we consider Girard's scenario, beautifully articulated though it is, we need also to keep in mind that he asserts it was played out in *each and every* society that has ever existed, when there is no direct evidence to that effect. Although he claims all cultures have followed his scenario, he is in fact the first person to have written the script.

To compensate for the destructive envy in the heart of every person, human groups, according to Girard, find a scapegoat. They focus their envy and their desire to resort to violence by fixing on a single victim, preferably a victim with traits that set him apart from the community at large. In that way, the community can be strengthened, or at least feel it has been strengthened, by impulses that would otherwise be at cross-purposes with common life. When the generalized violence is projected onto a specific victim, the scapegoat is made to bear the blame for the ills that afflict society, including shortages that people complain about, famines, plagues, and other disasters. If victims can be portrayed as strange to the point that they might exert the malefic capacities of a sorcerer or witch, so much the better: that makes the community's resolve to remove the agent of pestilence all the stronger.

The logic of scapegoating drives the community, acting as a mob, in concentrating its violence on the single victim, to eliminate the supposed cause of their ills, and finally they murder the scapegoat. As time goes on in the normal course of social life, according to Girard's theory, the problems blamed on the scapegoat in fact resolve themselves, and the community credits the scapegoat's death with that benefit. At that point, memory turns completely mythological, and the community "remembers" the victim as dying *voluntarily* for the common good. That is a crucial moment, because for Girard that is when the scapegoat becomes a god. What we call sacrifice is in his view nothing other than the ritual reenactment of the victim's allegedly willing death, which confers supernatural benefit.

In Girard's analysis, every single cult of sacrifice in all societies stems from a specific moment of aggression against a scapegoat, and from the conversion of the scapegoat into a god after his death. Behind each ritual, there is a lynching. His claims have provoked considerable controversy, and have also drawn wide popular support, since he first made them. Part of their appeal is the fascinating detail of Girard's proposed mechanism for how the mass psychology of violence culminates in human sacrifice, but it has often gone unnoticed that his theory, drawn from many different examples, does not correspond to any documented historical or ethnographic example of ritual. Unless his theory can be shown to account for the whole range of evidence concerning sacrifice, rather than a few elements cherry-picked from very different times and cultures, it will have to be set aside with the equally inventive but unsupported scenarios of Frazer and Freud.

Girard's reduction of all sacrifice to instances of projected aggression does no justice to the dimensions of communal festivity, enjoyment, and release that sacrifices usually involve. Temples in antiquity, whenever we encounter evidence of them, were typically places of enjoyment and feasting rather than of austerity and violence. Girard has fallen into the trap set by modern usage of the term "sacrifice," which typically refers, not to festivity in the presence of the divine, but to self-inflicted harm and punishment. Whether that kind of a sacrifice is in baseball or on a battlefield, we admire the act, not because it brings pleasure to the person who suffers harm on behalf of others, but because he or she has been willing to serve the greater good at personal cost. This modern development reflects a tendency to assume that all sacrifice requires human suffering.

But that tendency only sharpens the need to address the basic issue: why sacrifice, a generally joyful activity, becomes conflated with violence against human beings. The question emerges in ancient societies, where human sacrifice was ritualized, and in modern societies, which sees sacrifice in terms of human death for a cause, or in some other way as related to suffering and hardship, and uses sacrificial language to motivate people to make war. Girard begs that question by assuming that violence was there all along, at the base of *all* ritual activity. He has, in effect, written his conclusion into his assumptions.

Girard provides many examples, from cultures on every continent, of practices involving human sacrifice, and derides anthropologists who have ignored or played down humanity's violent origins. At times he launches into eloquent, lusciously intemperate attacks on how academic fashion refuses to consider that Christianity might contribute to our understanding of how violence can be dealt with: "We are classicists first of all, then romantics, primitives when necessary, eager modernists, neo-primitives when we are fed up with being modern, Gnostics constantly—but biblical? Never." This defense of Christianity is more than an onslaught on political correctness (although it is that, among other things): rather, Girard combines his reductionistic analysis of sacrifice with a full-fledged defense of Christianity as the *sole* religion that can get humanity past its violent origins. Having posited that all sacrifice originates in violence and perpetuates violence, Girard then announces that Christianity is the only cure for violence.

Girard takes this drastic second step in his theory—which is, if anything, even more controversial than the first step—by analyzing the outcome of the mechanism of the sacrificial scapegoat. He locates a fatal flaw in ritual's capacity to displace communal violence. Because temples are places that commemorate violence, however dimly practitioners might be aware of that fact, their rituals ultimately provoke just the brutality they are designed to reduce. That is why primitive and ancient societies (Girard's favorite example being the Aztecs) fall into war, cannibalism, ritual killing, and other examples of human sacrifice.

According to Girard, Christianity is the one religion that offers humanity a way of extricating societies from their endemic and seemingly constitutional violence. The Christian insight—the equivalent of revelation, as Girard specifically asserts, and fundamental within the New Testament—is that Jesus was executed without cause. He was an innocent victim, and by asserting his innocence the New Testament reveals that human violence against scapegoats is unjustified. By stripping away the violent origins of humanity and all its religious institutions, Girard claims that Christianity did what no other religion or philosophy did or could do.

René Girard's passionate, carefully calibrated logic bristles with asides, gory illustrations of human sacrifice, and wry comments on the culture of academia. No one in the discipline of studying religions, apart from true believers in postmodern orthodoxy, can fail to enjoy his position as a timely corrective to deeply ingrained fashions within universities and colleges, where both Judaism and Christianity are routinely denigrated, where cultures designated as "other," "alternative," or "different" are uncritically praised, and where taking up causes has replaced philosophical reflection on the ethical implications of inquiry. For those reasons alone, Girard has made a contribution worthy of the philosophes of the eighteenth century, and in my opinion his work as an intellectual is even more considerable than his influential literary criticism.

Yet at each increment in his logic, I have to disagree. Just as a violently murdered scapegoat simply does not appear in the ancient or ethnographic sources as the origin of sacrifice in every culture, so I cannot agree that Christianity discovered innocent suffering: it is present in the Hebrew Bible (Isaiah and Job), in the mythology of Egypt (Osiris) and Babylonia (the *Epic of Gilgamesh*) as well as Greece (Iphigenia), in the philosophy of China (Taoism's praise of the long-suffering Lao-tzu), and in stories of how sacrifice began from Africa and South America that speak of innocent animals who give their lives. Girard is well aware of most of these materials, but he claims that only the clarity of the New Testament permits us to see these traces of "revelation" in pre-Christian texts.

This exceptionalism becomes egregious, in my view, when Girard goes on to claim that societies based on sacrifice will inevitably prove violent, while Christian societies, provided they persist in the service of their unique revelation, alone hold out the prospect of a peaceable world. Although I deplore the facile assertion (still popular among the postmodernists, whom Girard rightly condemns) that Christianity has brought more violence to the world than any other religion or philosophy, I cannot see my way to agreeing that it has brought noticeably less.

Moreover, the very texts Girard cites to prove that Christianity is a religion of peace, because it asserts Christ died without justification, appear in the New Testament in contexts that in fact justify animosity toward Jews. The most obvious example is Matthew 27:25, where "all the people" of the Jews plead for Jesus' death, and say to Pilate, "His blood is upon us and upon our children," a scene that became a charter for violent Christian pogroms against Jews during the Middle Ages. Christianity in every age has been plagued by violence, as are other religious cultures and modern secular societies; gruesome examples of deliberate torture, execution, and suicide in the name of God or of civic virtue crop up regularly in histories of many periods and in recent periodicals. It simply will not do to make ancient sacrifice the scapegoat for modern brutality. Any serious body count tells against the proposition that America has broken the curse of the Aztecs, much less its biblical variant, Abraham's curse.

But while the logic of Girard's position seems to me unreliable, a basic aspect of his technique of reading has proven invaluable. Time and again when dealing with sacrificial and ritual texts and then comparing them to archaeological evidence, he has been able to show that ancient sources downplay or deny the violence involved in killing, although slaughter of some kind is an indispensable act within most rites.

The evidence of Carthaginian child sacrifice provides a case in point. During the first century B.C.E., Diodorus Siculus reported on the ancient practice at Carthage, revived during time of war, to offer children to the local god (*History* 20.14.6): "A bronze statue of Cronos among them extended its hands, palms up and inclining toward the earth, so that the children set on it rolled down and fell into a chasm filled with fire." According to Diodorus's account, two hundred children were selected for this treatment, and another hundred were volunteered for the rite. Here there can be no doubt but that child sacrifice was practiced ritually, and Diodorus refers to human sacrifice among Egyptians (1.88.5), Celts (5.31.3–4; 5.32.6; 31.13.1), and

Messenian Greeks (8.8.2) as well. But archaeological investigation at Carthage in particular both confirms Diodorus's account with skeletal remains and inscriptions and uncovers another, related feature of child sacrifice. The inscriptions so far discovered refer to gifts offered to the various gods of Carthage rather than to who was offered in the flames or the method of killing the children, most of whom were less than two years old. These inscriptions illustrate what Girard has also shown time and again: myths associated with sacrifice frequently conceal the violence involved, both in extent and in kind.

Myth, Girard has shown us, is the vehicle by which sacrifices may become engines of brutality, by glossing over or occluding the suffering of victims while stressing the benefits of their death and their readiness to die. My principal difference with Girard is that I think the evidence shows that mythic distortion can happen at *any* time, rather than only at the moment of sacrificial origin, and that modern myths—from films about war to tales of heroism among police and firefighters—are no less apt than their ancient counterparts to cover the bloody facts of innocent suffering with the alleged glory of country, religion, ideology, or tribe.

René Girard's claim that the Christian Bible alone releases people from the compulsion of human sacrifice illustrates a trait common among theories that insist the impulse derives from our nature. If the pathological behavior is truly organic, a part of being human, then it follows that the only possible cure must lie in some higher power. For Frazer, that higher power was science as an answer to superstition; for his contemporary Sigmund Freud, it was psychoanalysis as an alternative to religious illusion; for Girard, it is the New Testament as a replacement for the relativistic postmodern canon. In each case, the power of the ideas and of the minds behind them is palpable, but the shaping of evidence to fit the theory concerned is no less obvious.

The fatalistic argument that human beings are endemically inclined to kill their own as sacrifices does not take account of the range of evidence, and easily serves as the prelude to claiming curative powers for the analyst's preferred ideology. Violence is clearly implicit in sacrifice, because life needs to be taken for the divine feast to take place. When the actual purpose of the sacrifice is to take life so that it is expunged rather than enjoyed, however, that requires a fresh and powerful myth to justify the new aim, especially in the case of offering human beings.

Sacrifice and human sacrifice can only be confused by means of convoluted ancient myths or equally complicated modern theories. Killing a person blots out the joy that feasting usually brings. For that reason, Israelite offerings directed solely to God, to honor him or to restore the people's relationship with God when sin had vitiated it, consisted of plants and animals that in principle were edible. A child could never be consumed by an Israelite according to the Torah, or by people in most societies in which human sacrifice is known. The pivot of the ritual of human sacrifice is no longer communion with the god, but giving the god a priceless, irreplaceable life that only the god can consume. It is an exceptional action in the midst of crisis, rather than routine.

Iphigenia presents a fine model of this new form of offering, beneficial to her father only because his act pleases Artemis. The sacrifice costs Agamemnon dearly, and its only purpose is to pay a price beyond all wealth in order to please the goddess and advance the war against Troy. The more sacrifice advances along the lines of intentional destruction in honor of the divine, a deliberate consumption of what is best and dearest without human beings taking part in what is offered, the more the best offering will appear to be human.

Just as the figure of Iphigenia can inform us of the deep, contradictory forces at work in the connections among sacrifice, war, and infanticide, so the Aqedah offers insight into the depths of these impulses in the Abrahamic traditions. The Bible neither introduced the world to human sacrifice nor completely replaced it with Jesus' teaching of loving one's neighbor. The expectation that biblical texts have that sort of power definitively to shape and change human behavior fetishizes the Bible. The Bible is not coherent enough or ancient enough to be the sole source of human sacrifice, and the New Testament does not in fact prohibit all sacrifice or all violence. Biblical texts are valuable, but not in any monolithic way, as if they served a single ideology.

In the last analysis, the Bible is a collection of disparate myths that were generated from early in the Iron Age (in stories dating from approximately 1200 B.C.E.) until 100 C.E. All they include—history and poetry and proverb and fable and an astonishing range of other literary genres—are irreplaceable indications of how humanity has thought about itself and God and the world in their mutual relationships over uninterrupted chains of tradition spanning a millennium. Deciding that the Bible is the source of human sacrifice is implausible and encourages a refusal to investigate the ambivalence and variety of the Scriptures of Judaism and Christianity, as they wrestled with the possibility, implicit in their cultural settings, that children might or should be offered on the altar of God. Pursuing Girard's course also flattens out the diversity of the Bible, reducing its message to a uniform counsel of nonviolence that has characterized neither Judaism nor Christianity as a whole in any period, ancient or modern.

The Bible reflects the culture of the ancient Near Eastern city, which was the formative influence on ancient Israelites. Israelites absorbed that culture in their own distinctive ways, but also in obvious dependence upon the more powerful empires that surrounded them. The Assyrian cult, an elaborate ritual centered on a temple where worship guaranteed the prosperity of the empire, featured a rite of making children "pass through fire," in the words of the Hebrew Bible. Some Israelites attributed Assyrian dominance to this practice, especially after 722 B.C.E., when the whole Northern Kingdom of Israel fell to the Assyrians after the destruction of Samaria, the Israelite capital. No wonder many in the south, in the remaining kingdom of Judah, decided that the best policy was alliance with the Assyrians.

That policy of accommodation extended to an extensive program of remodeling the Temple in Jerusalem to make it look like the Assyrian temple in Damascus (2 Kings 16:10–20). King Manasseh of Judah during the seventh century B.C.E. pursued the logical climax of this liturgical reform, and "made his son pass through fire," an offering to the deity called Moloch (2 Kings 21:6). Obviously, then, the story of Isaac in Genesis did not prove strong enough to close the question of child sacrifice. Jeremiah prophesied against others in Judea, not of the royal family, who continued this practice, and he promised divine retribution, saying in Yahweh's name that they did "something I did not command, and it did not enter my heart" (Jeremiah 7:31). It was as if the people Jeremiah spoke to were unaware of Genesis 22 as we know it.

In fact, in the shadow of interpretation, as we will see, an alternative plot was explored: in this narrative, Abraham *did* slay his son, so that Israel's foundation was laid in innocent blood. Abraham was cast in the mold of the judge Jephthah. The Scriptures of Israel as actually interpreted left the issue of child sacrifice unresolved, with consequences that directly shaped Judaic and Christian theology and have left us with impulses that we wrestle with to this day.

II

Martyrdom, the Jewish Invention

Panicked by threats to their survival, societies sometimes sacrifice their children in order to avert extinction. That tendency has been well documented by historians and anthropologists. But Abraham's curse goes behind the *possible* reversion to this pattern within the Abrahamic faiths. Uniquely among the religions of the world, the three that center on Abraham have made the willingness to offer the lives of children—an action they all symbolize with versions of the Aqedah—a central virtue for the faithful as a whole. Child sacrifice is not merely a possibility: it is incorporated within the pattern of faith, not as a requirement of literal ritual, but as an ethical virtue that every believer should be prepared to emulate.

A Mesha or an Agamemnon or a Jephthah offered his child's life under duress. In each case the desperate circumstances of the act are evident, and emphasized by the ancient literatures concerned. How did that kind of story, of heroic desperation, transform itself into a wider imperative, directed to believers as a whole—Christian, Jewish, and Muslim? That change, like most religious changes, came unbidden, and with a degree of violence that today can scarcely be imagined. Judaism, a religion that few people now associate with martyrdom, produced a charter for martyrs, making the willingness to follow the example of what happened on Moriah into an imperative for all, the ethic of Abraham's curse.

Judaism went through a revolution during the second century B.C.E., when the Maccabees successfully pushed back an attempt by the Seleucid Empire to extinguish Judaism. The Maccabean movement produced a rich literature of resistance and retaliation that galvanized partisans into conventional and guerrilla warfare. The Aqedah proved key to the Maccabees' success, because they made Abraham's offering a model for all Israelites, presenting a form of child sacrifice as the ideal of faithful devotion. The Maccabean demand for true Israelites to offer the lives of their young did not involve a physical altar, but it was no less lethal for that, because it *did* expect literal martyrdom from those who were true to the Torah.

This expectation came with two related and core principles of faith, both associated with the interpretation of Isaac's offering on Moriah and with his miraculous release from death there. Everyone committed to the covenant, following Isaac's example, was to be prepared to suffer and die, and every righteous Israelite, especially those who suffered as martyrs, could expect to be raised physically from the dead, delivered from the abyss as Isaac had been.

Each of these principles, self-sacrifice as well as resurrection, had a history prior to the Maccabees, but Maccabean interpreters brought the concepts together under the pressure of historical events and made them central to Judaism, modeling behavior for Jews as a whole. Today both these Maccabean principles are associated more with Christianity and Islam than with Judaism, but in fact they are Judaic in origin, and none of the Abrahamic religions can be understood unless the phenomenon of Jewish martyrdom and the accompanying expectation of afterlife are assessed in their original setting.

Before the ravages of suicide bombings in recent years, the word "martyr" had a nostalgic ring about it in the West, eliciting memories of medieval artwork that glorified saints who suffered agony and death rather than deny their faith. Countless renderings of Saint Sebastian pierced by multiple arrows now excite aesthetic admiration, but when they were created, these works were designed to enlist heroic efforts for suffering in the name of Christ, perhaps in military campaigns against heretics or Muslims, or by means of lifelong devotion to ascetical practice.

The medieval quest for martyrdom appears distant from modern motivations, yet the call for young people (usually adolescent males) to offer their lives for God and country, for the virtues of the West and the security of those at home, remains a staple of political rhetoric down to our own time. The appeal of becoming a martyr endures, although use of the word has been largely banished from public discourse in the West since the Enlightenment (and has been just about zeroed out since September 11, 2001, except in its pejorative sense, to discredit Islam). Early in the eighteenth century, the Earl of Shaftesbury made religious zeal of the type that produces martyrdom synonymous with fanaticism. After Shaftesbury, various denominations of Christianity competed with one another to show how tolerant and moderate they truly were.

Many Jews during the nineteenth and twentieth centuries bought into a similar conception of their religion, as enlightened, tolerant, and moderate rather than as zealous and inclined to produce martyrs. Backing away from the glorification of martyrdom during the Middle Ages, Reform and Conservative Judaism stress the rational quality of faith, while those who call themselves "secular" Jews claim that Judaism is really not a religion at all, but a matter of regard for the traditions and values of a people. You would not be likely to guess, listening to these voices, that a deep commitment to martyrdom and the belief that went hand in hand with martyrdom—the resurrection of the physical body—originated in Judaism, not Christianity. Worship in synagogues over the centuries and to this day, shaped by the fierce dedication of the Maccabees to their martyrs' creed, praises the God "who revives the dead," and includes the blowing of a *shofar* (ram's horn) on the solemn day of the New Year, following the command in the Talmud: "Blow with a ram's horn before me that I may remember for you the Aqedah of Isaac, the son of Abraham, and I account it to you as if you yourselves were bound before me."

The Maccabees mainstreamed resurrection and martyrdom as integral to Jewish faith. For that reason, the Mishnah—the most basic digest of the oral Torah of Judaism, published around 200 c.e.—promised a part in the world to come to "all Israel," but specifically excluded those who denied the resurrection as a teaching of the Torah (tractate Sanhedrin 10:1). As an article in the *Encyclopedia Judaica* points out, "Belief in resurrection is firmly attested from Maccabean times, enjoined as an article of faith in the Mishnah," and specifically endorsed in prayers, as well as in the teaching of Maimonides. The facts of history sometimes prove awkward to fashionable views. But those facts cannot be ignored: a Judaism that tries to deny its roots in belief in the resurrection and the praise of martyrs only hides from itself, and makes it more difficult to see why ancient Christians prized martyrdom and Muslims later followed suit.

Not merely during the Maccabean and Rabbinic periods, but also in the modern Middle East, some Jews have heard the call to martyrdom; a few have shaped crucial events with violent acts. In 1994 an American-Israeli follower of Rabbi Meir Kahane named Baruch Goldstein came armed to the Tomb of Patriarchs in Hebron and entered the Ibrahimi Mosque, as it is named in Arabic to honor Abraham. Goldstein opened fire, killing 29 people and wounding 150. A memorial to him near Hebron, later removed by the government, praised him as a "saint" and "martyr," and his grave still draws pilgrims who admire his example. Kahane and those like him have made Judaism, once characterized as a religion of rationality, seem quite different, a sometimes mysterious, mystically violent faith. Religions as a whole no longer appear as innocuous as was once claimed on their behalf, and the underlying motivations of faithful Jews and other believers arouse public concern. Belief can no more be written off as a matter of purely private opinion than the actions of believers can be assumed to be benign. The tide of Enlightenment piety, with its appeal for self-interest and moderation, has ebbed; new forces, sometimes expressed with destructive zeal, have displaced the old consensus about how faith should be understood.

Ancient Jewish interpreters shaped the classic paradigm of the heroic martyr who is a model for all the faithful that is basic to Abrahamic religions and still influences behavior and national policy in the West, even in countries that maintain a legal separation between Church and State. The lure of martyrdom is never naturally outgrown, but persists and adapts to changing circumstances so that the death of the young in righteous battle, or as innocent victims who adhere to the truth despite the threats of evildoers, is cast in a heroic light, and often explicitly as a sacrifice. The hope of understanding how to deal with the impulse toward martyrdom lies in our capacity to understand how and why it emerged. A historical perspective on theology, that permits us to see when and under what circumstances the martyr's crown seems the greatest accomplishment conceivable, will give us insight into what otherwise must remain a terrifying mystery.

Judaism was shaped by the Maccabees. Their scribes copied or wrote the last books in the Hebrew Bible as it has been handed on for centuries, and their thought was fundamental to the Rabbis who came after them. The Maccabees take their name from Judah, son of Mattathias, whose victories in battle won him the sobriquet "the hammer" (*maqaba'* in Aramaic). Usually known by this name in its Greek and Latin forms, Judas Maccabeus and his brothers took the land of Israel back from its occupiers, and then extended its boundaries to cover more territory than ever before, even under David and Solomon. While Judas and his brothers Simon and Jonathan reshaped the map of Israel, scribes and interpreters in their entourage and others who celebrated their accomplishments reshaped the understanding of the Torah.

Ancient propaganda for the Maccabees portrays their enemies as inveterate anti-Semites and the Jews as a peaceable and united people, firm in their faith, who turned to war only as a last resort. Some strains of modern scholarship, influenced by a desire to defend Judaism, still adhere to this portrayal. But historical assessment yields a different, richer, more interesting and complex story, and reveals how Abraham's sacrifice of Isaac became a model for how believers as a whole, not just heroes such as the patriarchs, should put their faith into action, even at the cost of their lives.

Maccabean interpreters of Genesis 22 made the Aqedah into a call to martyrdom. The imperative to become a martyr and join the armies of the suffering righteous is neither an artifact of medieval Christianity nor the unique excess of Muslim militancy today, but an intrinsic dimension within the Abrahamic tradition that derives from a specific, formative moment in the history of Judaism. Many Jews responded to what they saw as the direct threat to the existence of their religion with the offer of their own lives during the second century B.C.E.; the Maccabees motivated themselves—and their children in particular—with the example of Abraham's offering of Isaac, and they succeeded in a program of conquest never equaled by Jews before or since.

The Maccabees and their allies constructed their ideal of martyrdom in direct response to the politics of their period. A martyr was to be a "witness," the basic meaning of the words *martus* in Greek and *'eyd* in Hebrew, a person whose faith was so deep that, in testimony to Jewish belief, he or she resisted the surrounding culture to the death. According to this Maccabean theology, there was no middle ground between true belief and the powers of this world; the choice was not between remaining faithful and compromise, but between martyrdom and collaboration with the enemies of Israel. This remorseless standard—applied specifically to children and women as well as men—makes a willingness to die the litmus test of true faith.

Changes in the Seleucid Empire, which arose after the death of Alexander the Great in 323 B.C.E. in lands he had conquered in the eastern regions of his campaigns, provoked the emergence of the ideal of the zealous martyr. An unprecedented form of persecution eventually emerged in cruel contrast to earlier Seleucid practice. Many people in Judea had welcomed the Seleucid conqueror, Antiochus III, a strong leader who displaced the Egyptian Ptolemies definitively in 198 B.C.E. He offered key concessions to Jerusalem and extended protections to Judaism in the manner of Cyrus the Persian and Alexander the Greek before him. Jews had long been accustomed to life as a subject people, and proved to be loyal subjects for as long as their religious autonomy was respected.

Problems came the way of Jews in Judea when Seleucid power weakened after Antiochus III died. As often happens, weakness translated into draconian efforts by the new monarch—Antiochus IV—to compensate for his shortcomings with propaganda to idolize his status. He had acceded to the throne in 175 B.C.E. by displacing his nephew and having him killed, and needed to use every means available to enhance his prestige. Antiochus IV took to calling himself "Epiphanes" (manifest divinity), pretending to divine status in the manner of Near Eastern monarchs. He also consolidated his position by means of an extensive cultural program of Hellenization; Greek language and ways became imperatives under his rule, not just tendencies or fashions.

Antiochus IV's combination of the Near Eastern conception of the divine status of the monarch with a proselytizing fervor for Greek religion and culture mounted a threat to Judaism such as had never quite been experienced before. Antiochus Epiphanes wanted more than the simple conquest of land; his ambition was to alter the practice, character, and beliefs of Judaism, including worship in the Temple. This threat was all the more acute, because Antiochus was powerful enough to co-opt Jews within his program, including prominent members of the priesthood headed by Menelaus, the high priest. Menelaus symbolized Jewish collaboration with Antiochus IV. In 172 B.C.E., he promised Antiochus a 50 percent increase in annual tribute if the king would appoint him high priest in place of Jason, who had also bribed his way into office (2 Maccabees 4), and Antiochus promptly agreed.

Antiochus IV pursued ruthless methods to achieve his ends; events would prove that he was willing to resort to violence and torture. Yet when he first had his forces occupy Jerusalem, he was responding to a genuine threat to his hegemony, and the responses of the Jewish population varied enormously. In 169–168 B.C.E., striking out hard to confirm his control over his own lands and contiguous territories, Antiochus IV attacked and conquered most of Egypt, thwarted from taking Alexandria and making himself a new pharaoh only by the intervention of the Romans, who demanded his withdrawal from the territory. During this confused time a false rumor spread that Antiochus had died, and the high priest whom Menelaus had supplanted, Jason, attacked Jerusalem and stormed the city, besieging Menelaus and his supporters. Antiochus considered Jason's incursion an act of rebellion; on his return from Egypt, he went to Jerusalem, drove Jason out, and reestablished Menelaus's authority; according to 2 Maccabees 5:11–14, Antiochus massacred forty thousand Jews and sold an equal number of men, women, and children into slavery.

To compensate himself for his trouble, Antiochus also pillaged the Temple of huge sums of money, sacred vessels, and furnishings (2 Maccabees 5:15–23; 1 Maccabees 1:20–24). He even "dared to enter the holiest sanctuary in all the world, having as guide Menelaus—who became a traitor both to the laws and to his country" (2 Maccabees 5:15). Worse was yet to come. Antiochus arranged for a foreign cult in the sanctuary (1 Maccabees 1:41–64; Josephus, *Antiquities* 12.248–256), including the sacrifice of swine on the altar. A high-stakes player, Antiochus IV had gambled and lost a great deal in Alexandria; in response, he resorted to a tried-and-true policy of Hellenization to confront local rebellion in Jerusalem. In the extreme execution of his policy, however, Antiochus courted fresh disaster.

After Antiochus's grotesque intervention in the Temple, one high priestly group moved to Egypt, where the priest Onias IV built a temple at Leontopolis, complete with sacrificial altar, an alternative to the Temple in Jerusalem (*The Jewish War* 1.31–33; 7.420–432). This temple appears to have been of limited influence, but its very existence is proof of deep divisions within ranks of priests, and within Judaism as a whole. Not everyone resisted Antiochus, even in his most repugnant policies (as Josephus openly says in *Antiquities* 12.255), and even those who objected did not always agree to stay and fight in Jerusalem. Enough did remain, however, to alter the course of history and the definition of Judaism.

In 167 B.C.E., Antiochus IV prohibited the practice of numerous Jewish laws, including observance of the Sabbath and circumcision, and he systematically destroyed copies of the Torah. He intended to remove from circulation the book that stood in the way of his reforms; instead, he made the Torah into a symbol of revolt. Within the Jerusalem Temple itself, the government erected an "abomination of desolation upon the altar of burnt offerings" (1 Maccabees 1:54–64), offering their impure sacrifices to foreign gods. Those who refused to eat of these sacrifices were killed, while those responsible for performing circumcisions were executed. Children who had been circumcised were also murdered, their lifeless bodies hung around their mothers'

necks. According to 2 Maccabees 6:10, these women were then pa-
raded through the city and thrown to their deaths from its walls.

During the period when Onias's group established a temple of pro-
test in Egypt, within territorial Israel another group emerged, defined
by their desire to remain faithful to sacrifice in Jerusalem according to
the Torah and by their resistance to the demands of Antiochus. This
group was known as "the faithful" (the famous *chasidim,* a Hebrew
term that conveys the capacity of faith to access divine compassion,
chesed). Among them was Mattathias, a country priest from Modin.
His son was Judas Maccabeus, who gave Israel and Judaism the most
powerful priestly rule Jews have ever known. He turned piety into
disciplined revolt, including an alliance with Rome (1 Maccabees
8) and a willingness to break the Sabbath for military campaigns (1
Maccabees 2:41), which resulted in the restoration of worship in the
Temple according to the covenant in 164 B.C.E. (1 Maccabees 4:36–61).
The key to the Maccabees' surprising victory, however, was that their
movement was not merely priestly or military. Rather, it united Jews
of different castes, classes, and roles who were willing to show their
devotion to the Torah by committed action and, if necessary, physical
pain and death.

This movement necessitated a vigorous rejection of Hellenism,
which by this stage had become so extreme that it was easy for Jews
to reject. In deference to Hellenistic sensibilities, some young Jewish men who had been circumcised, including priests, were willing
even prior to the time of Antiochus's excesses to endure the medical
procedure called *epispasm,* a stretching of the skin along the penis, in
order to restore the appearance of a foreskin so that they could compete naked and without embarrassment in gymnastic competitions
(1 Maccabees 1:14, 15; *Antiquities* 12.241). The vehemence of the Maccabean response to the Seleucid challenge involved their recognition
that the disaster of Antiochus's abomination had been welcomed by
compromise, so that dedication to the Torah became the only true
virtue. Zeal for the Torah came to be identified with a global rejection
of the hegemonic culture as well as with a willingness to perish rather
than accommodate to its idolatrous values.

The brutal suppression of Judaic practices by the Seleucids ratcheted up the vehemence of Mattathias and his sons. The highly par-

tisan accounts in the First and Second Books of Maccabees do not make clear how many people complied with the imperial decrees to forsake Jewish practices and how many resisted. The emphasis in 2 Maccabees on the extraordinary courage of those martyred, as well as the reference in 1 Maccabees to some resisters fleeing into the wilderness, intimates that only a minority of Jews accepted physical martyrdom rather than acquiesce with, accommodate to, or evade Antiochus's demands.

Both Antiochus Epiphanes and Menelaus profited financially and in status from their control over operations in the Temple. The crucial importance of Judean revenues became apparent when Menelaus, unable to pay the taxes he had promised to the king, was summoned to the city of Antioch, the Seleucid capital. To pay his debt and thereby preserve his position, Menelaus took gold vessels from the Temple, selling some to Tyre and other cities for cash, bribed Andronicus, the king's viceroy (2 Maccabees 4:30–50), and bought his way back into Antiochus's favor.

But all these skilled political operators miscalculated the intensity of the resistance of the zealous few who pioneered the virtues of guerrilla martyrdom. One warrior, 1 Maccabees reports (6:44), "gave himself to save his people and to acquire an eternal name" by attacking a Seleucid elephant, one of their weapons of war. He slashed through the enemy to get under the beast, disemboweled it, and died in gore, crushed by the elephant's weight. The drive toward martyrdom in war made an unlikely victory possible by means of extreme heroism, incited by the praise of the martyrs' sacrifice in Maccabean literature.

The rebels countered Menelaus's acquiescence to Antiochus's demands by insisting upon absolute loyalty to the Torah in order to return the community at large to the covenantal blessings. The Torah itself, of course, especially the Book of Deuteronomy (see chapters 27–30 above all), had long insisted upon obedience to its demands as the condition sine qua non of Israelite prosperity, and had threatened grievous punishment for disloyalty to God. But the Seleucid attempt to retool Judaism as a Hellenistic religion had added a sinister dimension to the lure of idolatry. Because Antiochus acted with the connivance of Menelaus, the authority of the Temple and its sacrificial power seemed to endorse the Seleucid reform; only the personal commitment of rebels, in the view of the Maccabees, stood between Israel and catastrophic apostasy. This heroic individualism, portrayed as a more stable foundation than even the Temple, made every faithful Jew into a replica of the patriarch Abraham, whose choice to leave the gods of Mesopotamia behind him made the existence of Israel possible.

Devoted loyalists were living sacrifices on behalf of the community, propitiating God for the sins of the past and the present; Genesis 22 became a principal point of reference to describe how the offering of oneself might save Israel as a whole. In the First Book of Maccabees, Mattathias—the father of Judah and his brothers—is quoted as laying out his program of complete loyalty to the covenant in the face of seemingly impossible odds. In a speech at his death (1 Maccabees 2:52), Mattathias gives Abraham as the prime example of the kind of obedience that conditions demanded. "Was not Abraham found faithful by a test?" he asks, alluding to the Aqedah.

What he goes on to say evokes how vital Abraham's obedience on Moriah was to the Maccabees. Mattathias concludes, "and it was reckoned to him for righteousness." The Book of Genesis uses that same phrase, but in the original passage Abraham is not called righteous because he was willing to offer his son, but simply because he "believed in God" (Genesis 15:6). At that point, the Aqedah is still seven chapters away, and decades in the future by the chronological reckoning of Genesis. Genesis 15 concerns, not Abraham's willingness to kill his child, but his faith that one day he would have children to inherit the land of Israel. For 1 Maccabees, Abraham's unconditional faith is not enough: Abraham's real virtue, the virtue demanded of every Israelite, includes the willingness to sacrifice one's child. That is the true proof of righteousness.

The portrayal of Abraham as proving his righteousness is further detailed in the noncanonical *Book of Jubilees,* which derives from a group that had been allied with the Maccabees, separating from them later in the second century B.C.E. According to *Jubilees'* version of the story, the Aqedah was the seventh, climactic test of faith that Abraham faced, so that his heroism is marked (17:17–18). Yet *Jubilees* also makes the example of Abraham pertinent to Israelites as a whole, individually and collectively, by comparing his test at the time of the Aqedah to what Job, the Judaic equivalent of Everyman, had to endure. In *Jubilees,* Satan (called by an alternative Hebrew name, Mastemah) challenges God to test Abraham, claiming that the patriarch loves his son more than he does God (17:16), a precise echo of the opening of Job. By introducing Satan into the Aqedah, *Jubilees* protects God from the charge that he commanded human sacrifice, and at the same time equates the Seleucid persecutor with the Prince of Darkness that all the faithful are to resist.

Although deepening political divisions set those who opposed the Seleucids into differing camps over time, they agreed on the Aqedah as the symbol of the faithfulness demanded of all Jews. The author of 2 Maccabees praises Judas Maccabeus only with restraint (compared to 1 Maccabees), ignores his brothers, and attributes the defeat of Antiochus IV and the salvation of Israel to the fortitude of the Jewish martyrs and to divine intervention rather than to military prowess. Differing further from 1 Maccabees, 2 Maccabees places the responsibility for the sufferings of the Jewish people and the desecration of the Temple on *both* the Jewish people and the Seleucid ruler. Because many of the people (especially the leaders) sinned by deserting Jewish law in favor of Greek ways, God brought punishment to Jerusalem. But the fidelity of the martyrs anticipates and brings about the community's reconciliation with God according to 2 Maccabees, whose theology is less activist and yet more radical than that of 1 Maccabees.

Second Maccabees values martyrdom over military resistance. Recounting the stories of the martyrs Eleazar, an aged scribe (2 Maccabees 6:18–31), and a woman with her seven sons (2 Maccabees 7), the narrative praises their sacrifice and encourages all who hear their stories to be equally faithful. The martyrs give speeches expressing their fidelity to God's law, their desire to set a good example for those who come after them, and their confidence that in the resurrection from the dead their mutilated bodies will be replaced and restored.

Eleazar, age ninety, refused to eat pork forced into his mouth, and even to eat kosher meat disguised as if it were pork (the suggestion of a sympathetic executioner). He summarizes both his personal sense of responsibility and the book's perspective when he says, "By manfully giving up my life now, I will show myself worthy of my old age and bequeath to the young a noble example of how to die a good death willingly and nobly for the revered and holy laws" (2 Maccabees 6:27–28). Viewed from the angle of the community's commitment to the Torah, death was preferable, not only to apostasy, but even to giving the *appearance* of apostasy.

The mother of seven sons shows herself even more radical than Eleazar in her commitment; her ordeal is set in a surreal encounter with Antiochus Epiphanes himself. After seeing six of her sons being tortured to death for their refusal to eat pork—by whips, cords, cutting of flesh, amputation, and fire—the mother refuses Antiochus's advice that she encourage her last remaining child to transgress his ancestral traditions. "In derision of the cruel tyrant, she leaned over close to her son and said in Aramaic, their native language, 'Son, have mercy on me, who carried you in my belly for nine months, nursed you for three years, nurtured and brought you up to your present age . . . Do not be afraid of this executioner, but become worthy of your brothers and accept death, so that in mercy I may receive you again with them'" (2 Maccabees 7:27, 29). After the death of her youngest child by the cruelest tortures of all, the mother also suffers execution. By then she has already endured worse than death, strengthened by having—as the text says (2 Maccabees 7:21)—"aroused female thought with male resolution." In the conception of this Maccabean theology, women achieved a greater motherhood even than giving birth by providing their children as martyrs in the resolute manner of Abraham.

The Second Book of Maccabees pioneered a style of presentation later repeated and intensified in Jewish, Christian, and Muslim stories of martyrdom, portraying physical suffering in exquisite detail. Flayed skin, amputated limbs and tongues, bodies mangled in unspeakable ways, and death by slow burning—repeated in literatures of martyrdom ever since that time—all find their precedents in two chapters (6 and 7) of 2 Maccabees. This violence, however, was by no means gratuitous, although the martyr's fate is the precursor of guileless victims' in the modern genre of horror, both literary and cinematic. Rather, blood and pain sealed the accomplishment of sacrifice, and encouraged further sacrifice by arousing admiration, awe, and the desire to follow noble examples of the triumph of devotion over fear. In this way, 2 Maccabees put into action the praise of Abraham that links his pivotal role specifically to his willingness to offer his son. The deep horror of pork within Judaism to this day derives from this Maccabean moment of resistance to the Seleucids, not only from the Torah, which has no more of a problem with swine than it does with rabbit or camel. With that repugnance comes a dedication to resist those who pervert Judaism, by a martyr's death if necessary. The second century B.C.E., the Maccabean century, made Abraham's willingness to sacrifice his son, together with the willingness of Israelites to give their children to the cause of the Torah, into the model of what Jews should do as Jews.

The Seleucid threat to Judaism came and went, only to be replaced by Roman hegemony, which was established over Jerusalem in 63 B.C.E. Centuries of sporadic violence followed, between the successors of Judas Maccabeus and Rome, the empire that devised the most efficient machine of state terror known in Antiquity. During this long struggle with the Romans, a shift occurred in the depiction of Abraham's offering of Isaac, even among Jewish interpreters who supported the Romans. Because previous studies of the Aqedah have been literary in their orientation, scholars have not observed the direct correspondence between the portrayal of events on Moriah and historical conditions in Judea and the Diaspora. Just as Maccabean literature remains inexplicable unless its emergence is seen within the context of Seleucid policy, so Roman hegemony proves key to understanding the later development of the Aqedah, much as Roman politics has influenced nationalistic mentalities and public policies in the West.

Interaction with Roman culture later, during the second century C.E., included having to take account of Christianity. But before that time there is very little indication that Christian theology, at best a marginal influence, contributed directly to Jewish teaching in regard to the Aqedah. Until Christianity became a public voice, at which point cross-fertilization and combat with increasingly prevalent claims about Jesus clearly *did* become a factor within Judaic interpretation, the underlying Maccabean logic played out in the confrontation, not so much with the Church's teaching, as with Roman military and political power.

During the Roman period, Abraham's obedience as proof of his virtue remained, but Isaac's willing complicity with his father—reflecting a determination necessary for a martyr—emerged as a principal theme. Philo of Alexandria, Hellenistic Judaism's preeminent intellectual during the first half of the first century C.E., pictures Abraham as a priest with his son as a victim (*On Abraham* 197–98), and also makes exactly the connection that we explored in the last chapter, between sacrifice and allegedly noble warfare. Philo even refers to Isaac as being God's "son," because divine intervention had made his birth possible, and because Isaac was perfectly obedient (*On Dreams* 173). In a radical departure from the biblical text that is characteristic of ancient Judaic interpretation (midrash), Abraham did not even have to bind Isaac in Philo's description (*On Abraham* 176), but—articulating an image frequently portrayed by Western artists during the centuries after Philo—simply placed Isaac on the altar, a willing victim of sacrificial slaughter.

Another first-century Jewish intellectual, Josephus, had been a Jewish general in the disastrous revolt that resulted in Rome's destruction of the Temple by fire in 70 C.E. He defected to the Romans when his campaign in Galilee failed; in addition to his changing his allegiance, his name eventually changed from Yosef bar Matthiyah to Josephus. In libraries in the West, he is called Flavius Josephus, because the Flavian dynasty of Rome protected him. When he came to write his *Antiquities of the Jews* in Greek (c. 93 C.E.) from the comfort of his property in Italy, a gift from his Roman protectors, Josephus nonetheless let slip some of the Maccabean theology that had briefly motivated him as a young man—and spurred many Jews to embrace death rather than capitulate to the Romans.

Josephus makes Isaac into a warrior-martyr. Perfectly obedient to his father, Isaac knew exactly what he was doing, because he was *twenty-five years old* (*Antiquities* 1.227), no longer the youth of the Hebrew Bible, but the same age as the kind of soldier Josephus commanded in the field. Josephus takes pride in relating how, in the midst of an array of adventures, he organized the young men under his command at Jotapata in Galilee to commit mass suicide rather than surrender to the Romans. Drawing lots, each offered his naked throat to a brother-in-arms turned executioner. Once the executioner had struck, he in turn offered his own neck to another colleague.

Josephus escaped his own order as general, convinced by a revelation, he said, that power was passing from Jerusalem to Rome by divine will (*Jewish War* 3.141–408). Instead, the defeated general who had seen his own troops embrace an honorable death in the manner of Isaac gave himself up to Vespasian. Becoming a propagandist for Vespasian and his son Titus, Josephus accepted Flavian protection for the rest of his life. In depicting the scene on Moriah, Josephus may allude to Agamemnon and Iphigenia in Euripides, signaling his desire to bring together Judaic and Hellenistic culture. Although allusions are notoriously difficult to pin down, this is one of the sacrificial resonances we explored in the last chapter among various cultures in Antiquity that have long been appreciated. The links that bind together Isaac's offering, sacrifice, and martyrdom by military means are not merely theoretical possibilities emerging out of modern approaches, but have been openly acknowledged for the better part of two thousand years.

In any case, there is no doubt whatever but that Josephus makes Isaac into a willing martyr (*Antiquities* 1.232), who rushes to his sacrifice and his fate. Defeat at the hands of the Romans made Jewish interpreters emphasize the noble sacrifice of Isaac to the point that new elements—his adult maturity and rush to be offered, for example—supplemented or supplanted what was written in Genesis 22. The later, famous case at Masada in 73 C.E. was not an isolated incident, but represents a pattern of suicide-martyrdom that had been promoted by generals such as Josephus, who conducted the failed revolt against Rome after 66 C.E. The Maccabean martyrs had been glorified both by divine approval and by eventual victory for their nation: under Rome, the Jewish martyr's only reward was divine approval, and he embraced his fate to the point of joining in mass suicide.

God's approval for the martyr's death would be signaled supernaturally, by physical resurrection, another key element in the theology of the Maccabean period that survived, and in fact was enhanced, during the Roman period. Belief in a life after death did influence prophets before the time of the Maccabees, but Daniel 12:1–3, written as the Maccabees came to power, marks the first time that Judaic sages clearly embraced the conviction that a resurrection for judgment before God awaits people as a whole, so that the righteous will be rewarded and the wicked punished. But the Book of Daniel does *not* portray resurrection as literal or physical: the righteous who are raised are instead compared to celestial bodies that shine like the stars. *The Book of Enoch* (58–62) similarly portrays the afterlife of the just as taking place among the angels in heaven. In contrast, 2 Maccabees powerfully and explicitly insists upon the resurrection of *physical* bodies. One of the seven sons of the supremely righteous mother offers his tongue and his hands to his executioners, speaking of God in periphrasis as "heaven" (2 Maccabees 7:11): "From heaven I obtained these; and for his laws I despise them; and from him I hope to acquire them again." Maccabean theology saw the willingness to become a martyr and physical resurrection as related and essential components of faith.

In the way that they developed the characteristic Jewish belief in resurrection, the Maccabees and their allies revealed a fascinating ambivalence toward the surrounding Hellenistic culture. Although they resisted Antiochus IV to the death, and their successors pursued a policy of revolt against Rome long after it had become a hopeless cause, they all were also willing to write in Greek, and to incorporate key concepts of Hellenistic thought, including immortality, within their teaching. The cultural ambivalence of the martyr, whether considered as a historical person or as a character in literature, has been characteristic of martyrdom in many different societies.

The two principal works of Maccabean literature, First and Second Maccabees, are preserved only in Greek. For that reason they belong to the books of the Bible called the Apocrypha: even if originally written in Hebrew (which was probably the case in the instance of 1 Maccabees), those originals are lost, "hidden" (*apocryphon* in Greek) as Saint Jerome piously maintained during the fifth century C.E., or just plain nonexistent. Maccabean zealotry appealed throughout the Diaspora, because Jews in several parts of the Roman Empire faced not only constant pressure to assimilate, but also violent persecution, as vicious as it was sporadic. Philo in first-century Alexandria wrote an account of his own embassy to the emperor Gaius (or Caligula) in order to reverse the local outbreak of pogroms against Jews. Key Jewish works from this period, including the Wisdom of Solomon, reflect the oppression of Jews living in the Diaspora even as they adopted Hellenistic modes of thought and life in order to support and promote Jewish values, history, and practices.

The literature of martyrdom typically emerges, like Maccabean texts, not from within the stable traditions of a religion, but at the margins, where conflict with other cultures takes place and therefore the issue of cultural survival is fraught. The Maccabees came to power after a period of unprecedented accommodation to Hellenism, and they then expressed their zeal for the Torah, and wielded their power, with the tools of Hellenism: the Greek language, military discipline inherited from Alexander the Great, and a Hellenistic conception of sacred rule, according to which the Maccabees claimed both the monarchy, although they were not of the house of David, and the high priesthood, although they were not of the family of Zadok.

Martyrs typically live within or quite near the very cultures that they reject, and use whatever social advantage they can gain in order to combat those cultures. As a result, the martyr might appear well assimilated to an occupying society in terms of language, status within the community, and accommodation to the prevailing power. Judas Maccabeus was about as much a surprise to the Seleucids as were British suicide bombers who attacked London's transport systems on July 7, 2005, all of whom were brought up and educated in England. Marginalization is part and parcel of the martyr's persona across cultures and throughout history; the greatest zeal often comes with a sense of familiarity with and alienation from the hegemonic culture, together with suspicion of the hierarchy of one's own religion as being too prone to compromise.

The volatile mix of Israelite and Hellenistic values in Maccabean theology grew more blatant during the Roman period. Highly detailed, rhetorically flamboyant descriptions of torture inflicted on the martyrs, set within exhortations and apologetic speeches exchanged among the characters, created an intensely emotional atmosphere, even as they promoted disciplined resistance. The devotion of these martyrs in works such as Fourth Maccabees, written at the turn of the first and second centuries C.E. to praise the heroism of Jewish resistance, might as well be that of Sebastian and Catherine as depicted in medieval Christian sermons, because the Maccabean inheritance lies at the heart of the cult of martyrdom in all the Abrahamic religions.

Even the final reward of the martyrs, immortality, is described during the Roman period in terms drawn from Hellenistic thought. When Fourth Maccabees comes to describe the young men who embraced death rather than desert the Torah, the description is a mix of the image of the eager Isaac that Josephus had presented, along with the Hellenistic term "immortality" (*athanasia*) and a metaphor drawn from Hellenistic games: "all of them, as though running a race for immortality, hastened to death by torture" (4 Maccabees 14:5). The author even believes that the martyrs atone for Israel's sins, like animal sacrifices, by their blood. The aged Eleazar prays for his people: "Make my blood their purification, and take my life in exchange for theirs" (4 Maccabees 6:29). The death of martyrs is portrayed as redemptive for the sins of Israel (4 Maccabees 17:20–22) so that sacrifice, the imagery of Isaac, and the promise of afterlife all combine to move the martyr to his ultimate offering. In a single, striking image, the author portrays Isaac as unafraid, even when he sees his father's hand coming upon him with a *sword* (4 Maccabees 16:20), rather than the knife of the Hebrew text of Genesis, depicting the sacrificial scene in Genesis 22 in terms of execution under Roman arms.

In a work from early in the second century, called in its Latin version the *Liber Antiquitatum Biblicarum* (or *The Book of Biblical Antiquities*, a rewriting of the primordial stories of Israel), a fully mature Isaac calmly informs his father that he had been born into the world to be offered as a sacrifice to God (*Liber Antiquitatum Biblicarum* 32:2–3). He is the perfect reflection of the ideal of martyrdom, the prototypical witness to the value of the Torah in the face of danger, pain, and death.

The Book of Biblical Antiquities also represents a transitional moment, fueled by the reality and the remembrance of martyrs who really did die, *when Isaac was seen as an actual sacrifice,* provided by God to reveal the meaning of ritual offering. This is the moment, very early in the second century C.E., when the term "Aqedah" came into its own, because it was a reference to the way a sheep or a ram was tied up for slaughter, foreleg to hind leg. Isaac became a ritual offering and his death appeased God for the sins of Israel.

This human sacrifice emerged as the paradigm of all sacrifice at a crucial moment in Israelite history. The Romans had burned the Temple down when they occupied Jerusalem in 70 C.E., preventing the public practice of the sacrificial ritual that had until that time been the principal seal of the covenant. How could God allow this place, the intersection of heaven and earth, to be defiled by Gentiles? The fundamental challenge of the Romans to Israelite identity made a second great revolt, during 132–135 C.E., as inevitable as it was inevitably disastrous. *The Book of Biblical Antiquities,* written either between these two wars or after them both, has Isaac say that his willingness to die at Abraham's hand proves that God has made human life a worthy sacrifice (32:3): only this prototype of offering remained after the Temple's destruction, and it became imperative within Judaism that Isaac's offering should be seen as complete and perfect, at least as far as Isaac's intention was concerned. That interpretive move permitted Jews to conceive of the covenant continuing even after the most visible sign of the covenant, sacrifice in the Temple, had been wiped off the face of the earth.

When Abraham placed Isaac on the altar as a burnt offering, both father and son were rejoicing as well as ready to act (*Liber Antiquitatum Biblicarum* 40:2–3). Here the older theology of the Maccabees finds its capstone. Although *The Book of Biblical Antiquities* stops short of saying that Isaac died on Moriah, it stands as the earliest reference to Isaac's "blood" (*Liber Antiquitatum Biblicarum* 18:5): "on account of his blood I chose them." The intention of father and son was so perfect, their offering was accepted as if it had been completed, and that "blood" seals the election of their progeny. In the case of the interpretation of Genesis 22, we can clearly see that the turn toward the primordial reflex of child sacrifice is the consequence of violent external forces (the Roman demolition of the Temple) combined with a theology designed to enable the community to survive in desperate circumstances (Maccabean martyrdom). Yet the offering of the son is *not* completed, as René Girard's theory would require, in the original story presented in Genesis 22, but rather in later interpretations of Genesis 22, the Aqedah proper.

Isaac's "blood" in the Aqedah stood for sacrifice, and—because the Romans had burned the Temple down in 70 C.E. and then razed the remaining masonry in 135 C.E.—Isaac came to embody the only sacrifice that God would or could accept. During the second century (see the Mishnah, Ta'anith 2:5), some Rabbis taught that the sound of the ram's horn with prayer and fasting would cause God to answer the community as he had once answered Abraham's need on Moriah with the provision of a ram. The Aqedah eventually took the place of offering the daily sacrifice required in the Temple, the Tamid lamb, when blood was poured into the altar's flames. Centuries later, around 450 C.E., the Rabbinic midrash, or interpretation, of the Book of Leviticus explained that, when any Israelite reads about the Tamid, God remembers the Aqedah (Leviticus Rabbah 2:11). Because the Aqedah is presented as the true ideal that the offering of the daily lamb recollects, Isaac and the martyrs took the place of the discontinued ritual in the Temple.

The Aqedah, produced with the resources of Judaism in its confrontation with Hellenistic culture (and quite apart from Christianity until this time), demonstrates that the offering of children is not a primordial instinct that "civilized" culture controls. To the contrary, the capacity of literate civilizations, the inheritors of Stone Age cities, to conflate children and sacrifice and war and religious duty into a single myth or metaphor such as the Aqedah assured that no developed society in the Abrahamic tradition has ever perished for a want of willingness to shed innocent blood.

Once the connection between Isaac's Aqedah and ritual sacrifice had been made, it was possible for it to be articulated in various sacrificial contexts. A second-century midrash, for example, called the *Mekilta*, has God explain in Exodus 12:13 why he will pass over houses where he sees lambs' blood at the threshold of Israel's doorways during the first Passover: "when I see the blood, I see the blood of Isaac's Aqedah."

In this creative reading, typical of the ancient genre of midrash and quite unlike a strict commentary in the modern sense, the association of the Aqedah extends into a new paschal connection without breaking the earlier connections with the Tamid sacrifice.

The precise reasons for this innovative association with Passover only become plain when Christian claims during the second century (discussed in the next chapters), which presented Jesus' death at Passover as the true sacrifice foreshadowed by Isaac, are taken into account. But Isaac's status as the prototype of martyrdom and sacrifice made that Christian theology possible, and enabled Rabbinic Judaism to reply to the association between Christ and Isaac on the part of those whom the Rabbis considered heretics.

In his role as the prototypical martyr offering his life, Isaac crossed the line from readiness for sacrifice into sacrifice itself. When sacrificial blood is at issue, what God sees might be considered metaphorical or literal, and there is good evidence that Rabbinic interpretation took the image both ways. Perhaps, some interpreters said, Abraham went so far as to nick Isaac's carotid artery, so that he lost a quarter of his blood before his father was stopped in the course of his sacrificial routine.

As this trajectory of interpretation developed, Isaac's awareness about all the events around him also sharpened. Now he was no longer twenty-five years old, but thirty-seven, and he approached the sacrifice, not as a zealous martyr, but in mournful humility, tears falling from his eyes as—contradicting Philo's picture—he asks his father to bind him fast, so that he will not struggle and blemish his body, which had to be perfect to be acceptable as a sacrifice. When the classic midrash Genesis Rabbah came to completion during the fifth century, Isaac's determination became quieter and deeper than in earlier interpretations, and for good reason. By then Constantine's recognition of Christianity a century before had put Judaism as a religion in a more perilous position than ever before within the Roman Empire.

The sacrifice that Abraham made of his son by this stage meant to some interpreters, not only that Isaac's blood was shed, but also—in the presentation of the Babylonian Talmud (Ta'anit 16a)—that he had been *reduced to ashes.* No more extreme statement of the completion of the ritual could be imagined. By the same token, means had to be imagined by which Isaac could appear again in the biblical narrative: God must have raised Abraham's son, the child of promise, not merely from death, but from the ashes of a sacrifice by fire. Isaac symbolized a human offering that pleased God, but at the same time the will of God for Israel's survival by any means necessary, including physical resurrection from the dead. Isaac was redeemed from Moriah, no matter how far the sacrifice had gone, just as the people Israel had returned from what seemed certain extinction in Babylon, and centuries later—in the theology of modern Zionism—had denied the Third Reich its carefully planned genocide.

Genesis Rabbah (chapters 55–56) in its present form took several centuries to evolve, and it interleaves many different traditions. Once these changes were incorporated within the Aqedah, Isaac was furnished with a temperament, character, and spiritual experience commensurate with his resurrection. By that stage, *Isaac's* Aqedah had taken on a literary fullness such that Isaac nearly eclipsed Abraham within the narrative of events on Mount Moriah.

No longer, for example, did God simply test Abraham, as in the Hebrew text, nor did Mastema push God to act in the way he does in the *Book of Jubilees* out of jealousy of Abraham alone. Instead, Isaac and Ishmael have a dispute (Genesis Rabbah 55.4), in which Ishmael brags that, since he was circumcised at the age of thirteen, his devotion was greater than Isaac's, who—circumcised as an eight-day-old infant—had neither choice nor consciousness in the matter. Isaac replied that, were God to ask all his members in sacrifice, he would not deny them. The Aqedah then transpired.

The pure, mature intention of the thirty-seven-year-old Isaac has him rewarded with a vision of heaven at the precise moment when Abraham lifted the knife to slaughter him, seeing the angels that his father could only perceive by their reflection in his son's eyes. It is impossible to know the number of deaths, the degree of pain, or the longing for transcendence that went into this image, which came into mind as I gave my student Anna her last rites, but it is evident that in this midrash as in others, actual experience is as important as the biblical text in revealing God's will for his people. In the world of midrash there is no such thing as an extraneous detail, but countless opportunities to see human experience from the point of view of the Scriptures.

During the time he was dead, having died at his father's hand, it is said that Isaac studied in a heavenly academy, run by a supernatural figure named Shem (Noah's son), who is identified with Melchizedek, the mysterious figure who once gave Abraham a priestly blessing (Genesis 14:18–20). Isaac then returned to normal life when God raised him from the dead. Now the point of his age comes into clear focus, because he is of sufficient maturity to teach the wisdom that he learned in the heavenly academy.

Just by looking at two key elements in Genesis Rabbah—the dispute between Ishmael and Isaac, and Isaac's return to life from the academy of Shem—the allusive quality of the interpretations is obvious, and all the more so when read in the context of the many other interpretations also presented in Genesis Rabbah. Are we to believe that the brothers really fought prior to the Aqedah, and that Isaac came back from the dead, when so many other readings are possible? Today scholars still debate those points, yet it seems wise not to insist on literal readings when Genesis Rabbah so carefully constructs a series of possibilities for virtually every turning point in the story.

Side by side with these creative and often surreal developments in the story of the Aqedah, the laconic power of the original text of Genesis remained. Many Jews saw their experience of persecution by Romans, whether under a pagan or a Christian aegis, as impossibly cruel compared to Abraham's trial. In a midrash on the Maccabean story of the woman who saw her seven sons die, the mother embraces her last child before his death and says, "My son, go tell Abraham, our father, 'My mother says to you, Do not take pride, claiming, I built an altar and offered up my son, Isaac. Now see, my mother built seven altars and offered up seven sons in one day. And yours was only a test, but I really had to do it.'" Even as she gives her audacious message to her son, the woman articulates the Maccabean belief that her child will live again to speak with Abraham, and she takes up the Maccabean imperative to sacrifice life, limb, and children for the sake of faith.

The Judaic Aqedah put these convictions in narrative form, in Isaac's resurrection and in his competition with Ishmael, and gave Christianity and Islam opportunities to develop interpretations that suited their characteristic teachings on sacrifice and martyrdom. From the Maccabean period on, martyrdom was no longer merely an extreme response to social crisis by means of human sacrifice, such as occurs sporadically in most religious cultures; instead, Mount Moriah occupied a permanent place at the center of ethics, and self-sacrifice had become a standard virtue. Not only in the specialist literature represented by the Talmud, but also in the Aramaic versions of Scripture that were recited in synagogues for all who attended, Isaac offered his neck willingly for sacrifice, was praised by the angels, and gave his blood so that it would be remembered at the time of the Passover. The historical conditions that brought about this new theology were unique, but the persistence of the confrontation between loyal Jews and imperial oppression—whether by Seleucids or Romans—at a time of relatively high literacy within Judaism ensured that the image of the glorious martyr would be embedded within Jewish literature. Judaism has made Isaac into the image of the necessary readiness for martyrdom, a requirement for all true Israelites. Fateful though that development undoubtedly was, it proved to be only one step in the deepening impact of Abraham's curse. What Judaism portrayed as a requirement for people, Christianity would transpose into the very nature of God.

Part Two

BLOOD OF THE LAMB

III

The Son's Eternal Sacrifice

In all Jesus' teaching, nothing is more challenging than his insistence that human suffering is necessary, meaningful, and sometimes to be welcomed. He didn't teach the specific theology that came from the Maccabees, but spoke personally as a martyr. Internalizing the Judaic ethos of his time, he grappled with his own fate, and his disciples', in terms of martyrdom. Although many believers today resist this strand of Jesus' message, it is central to understanding him and what his followers taught about him after the crucifixion. For that reason, we have to deal here with Jesus' call for self-sacrifice, and also to identify—and correct for—the maneuvers commonly deployed to circumvent his meaning. In the case of Christianity, as in the cases of Judaism and (as we will later see) Islam, the defensive tendency to deny the underlying theology of martyrdom, however understandable, leads only to an inadequate understanding of the religion, which shows itself defenseless and clueless in the face of the implacable imperative to follow in the footsteps of Abraham and Isaac.

Jesus never spoke of the Aqedah in so many words, as far as the Gospels show us, although they do give an indication, which we will come to shortly, that he might have referred to it allusively. Yet after his death, his followers overtly compared Jesus' fate to the sacrifice of Isaac. By the end of the first century c.e., Christians had produced a new and powerful theology that extended and intensified the Maccabean program of martyrdom, even though the persecutions Christians faced were only sporadic and inconsistent as compared to what the Maccabees confronted. In effect, preparing to become a martyr emerged as a requirement of Christian faith for all believers, no matter what their political circumstances.

Christianity today prides itself on framing its religious identity in terms of Jesus' endorsement of the commandments, expressed in the Torah, to love God and love one's neighbor. Those are unquestionably vital dimensions of Christian faith, but they are not the only dimensions. In addition, Jesus risked his life, and ultimately paid with his life, for his prophetic vocation, and he expected his followers to act in the same way. The faith that grew up around Jesus portrayed him as fulfilling the role of Isaac in Genesis 22, and urged all Christians to take on Isaac's identity, as Jesus did, by accepting the cross of suffering. The mysticism of self-sacrifice has been a formative impulse within Christianity from its beginning, and although that devotion has sometimes proven so dark as to provoke aversion, it is as vital to appreciate as Jesus' teaching of love, if the movement that he founded and the faith he inspires are to be understood.

As Jesus faced death in Jerusalem, his insight into the significance of the ordeal he would undergo was precise, although he confronted a complex and volatile political situation that he was in no position to understand fully. He conveyed his teaching on martyrdom to his disciples in their own language, Aramaic, and they memorized it. After his death in 32 C.E., his words eventually made their way, following forty years of oral transmission, translation, and written editing, into the Gospels in Greek, among which Mark, probably written in 73 C.E., is the earliest.

Prior to his arrest in Gethsemane, Jesus insisted that suffering was not to be denied, but embraced. Jesus acted as a prophet, announcing his spiritual wisdom for the people of God, wisdom he described as "the kingdom of God." This Aramaic phrase (*malkhutha' d'Elaha'*) referred in first-century Judaism to the divine power behind and within the universe, which one day, Jesus and other rabbis of his time taught, would overwhelm and transform every human regime with biblical justice.

When you act on God's behalf, Jesus said, resistance to you from the defenders of the unjust status quo is both inevitable and a sign of the kingdom's advance—and therefore no cause for despair. "You are favored, when men hate you and when they exclude you and censure you and put out your name as evil for the son of man's sake: rejoice in that day and skip, for look, your reward is great in heaven, because their fathers did the same things to the prophets" (Luke 6:22–23). He spoke of how encountering persecution could link a person intimately to God, so that he or she could enjoy the same familiarity with the divine that the prophets did, and he demanded that his disciples follow his example.

Jesus' words were precisely remembered; sometimes the Greek of the Gospels is so literal that they can be rendered back into the first-century Aramaic that Jesus and his disciples spoke. Retranslated into his original language, his most basic teaching about martyrdom in the earliest Gospel recovers its force and even its original rhythm (Mark 8:34; with stresses here marked with the sign "/"):

'In/ man detsa/dah
   m'atah/ batray/,
yitnacham/ veynasa'/ yat tseliy/veyh
—veyeyteh/ batray/!

If anyone wants
   to come after me,
He will self-deny, take up his cross,
   —come after me!

No wonder the Gospels refer to the fear of the disciples, not only at the time of Jesus' arrest, but during the whole period leading up to the crucifixion. Their rabbi not only took risks; he also saw death as the likely outcome of his actions, and expected his disciples to follow his lead. Worse, he demanded, *as a condition of discipleship*, that they join in his willingness to suffer. Life to Rabbi Jesus was a prophetic vocation to transform this world according to the design of God's kingdom by every means necessary. He asked each of his disciples to seek the life beyond this life, to which even a death as public and humiliating as crucifixion could be the gateway.

Christian interpretation during the modern period has flinched in the face of these words. Believers routinely worship Jesus in his dying, or at least venerate him, but Christianity (especially in America since the end of the Second World War) has contrived to ignore Jesus' plain call to suffering discipleship. The desire to qualify Jesus' vocation to suffer is natural enough among believers, and perhaps inevitable, but even scholars who claim not to be engaged theologically have supported views of his teaching that play down or eliminate his demand for self-sacrifice. Denials of this kind need to be overcome in order to make any real progress in assessing the role of Christianity among the Abrahamic religions in the promotion of violence under the guise of martyrdom.

Interpreters since the Enlightenment have deployed two conventional arguments to avoid the clear meaning of Jesus' teaching about taking up one's cross; both have been around so long that they have picked up the aura of reliable approaches to the historical Jesus and the Bible. But, in fact, as soon as you consider the logic of these arguments, you see they are desperate, flawed gambits to evade Jesus' meaning.

The first gambit is to treat the whole saying as a hyperbole, as if it were just a vivid way of telling people to do their duty and try their best. Jesus did use metaphors frequently—in his parables, peppered among his aphorisms, and in his discursive teaching. The term "cross" in this saying about self-denial, for example, is obviously not a literal reference, requiring every single disciple to seek actual crucifixion at the hands of the Romans. The phrase "his cross" refers to any eventual trial that a *disciple* will face, rather than the unique personal fate that awaited Jesus in Jerusalem. The cross symbolizes the burden that a disciple takes up in his life, despite the risk and pain involved, in order to join Christ in transforming the world to accord with God's design.

The cross in Jesus' saying stands for the possibility of crucifixion, but for other possibilities as well. Yet the use of this metaphor within the aphorism obviously does not make the whole saying metaphorical or hyperbolic. Jesus is talking about actual self-denial, up to and including Roman execution, the most painful end imaginable to a disciple's mortal existence. If there is a passage in the Gospels where Jesus alludes to the Aqedah, it would be this saying, because it is possible that Jewish teachers in his time taught that Isaac carrying the wood up Mount Moriah was "like a man carrying his cross on his shoulder" (Genesis Rabbah 56:3). The date of this Rabbinic teaching remains uncertain, but the possibility emerges that Jesus used a proverbial simile, not a completely original metaphor, in his saying and demanded that his disciples learn from Isaac's obedience, which went well beyond conventional good behavior.

In recent years, scholars have acknowledged that trying to read Jesus' imperative as completely figurative is an unconvincing expedient, designed to evade the force of his challenge. But the metaphorical evasion still echoes in popular discussion, demonstrating the power of wishful thinking, and the constant desire in the modern period among Christians and non-Christians alike for a gentle, non-threatening Jesus, rather than the prophetic insurgent who appeared in history and changed history forever.

Some scholars, instead of denying the saying means what it says, simply deny that Jesus actually said it. The "Jesus Seminar," for example, argued in its published results that Jesus never said the words attributed to him in this case, but that the early Church put them into his mouth. In general terms, it is indeed wise to be alert to the possibility that early Christians projected what they wanted to hear from Jesus back into the Gospels. But that possibility needs to be tested by sifting the evidence. Otherwise, scholarship can invent any image of Jesus it likes, by dismissing inconvenient parts of his teaching as inventions of the Church. I was a member of the "Jesus Seminar" for a number of years, albeit in frequent opposition to its findings. Some of their work was sound, and some of it original as well. But for a number of reasons this is an example of a particularly bad decision.

This saying is found not only in Mark's Gospel, but in a source commonly used by Luke (14:27) and by Matthew (10:38), and in a different form in the noncanonical *Gospel According to Thomas* (saying 55): the teaching about carrying one's cross is obviously not any single author's projection onto Jesus. The "Jesus Seminar" acknowledged this fact, but countered with the weak argument that the saying could not be authentic, because the symbol of the cross had "strong Christian overtones." But the saying's stringent demand on Jesus' followers to accept, if necessary, the status of criminals on their way to crucifixion makes no sense as part of the general policy of the Church, reflected in the Gospels and early Christian literature, as it tried to make peace with authorities of the Roman Empire. That kind of stringency *is* typical, however, of Jesus' prophetic demands on his disciples. Finally, this decision typifies a profound and persistent weakness in the work of the "Jesus Seminar": it functioned by the equivalent of push-polls. Different members were present to vote on sayings at different times, and the director of the seminar, Robert Funk, insisted on retaking votes on authenticity until results appeared that he felt he could approve. The strange outcome in regard to Jesus' teaching about self-denial could only be obtained after two rounds of debate and voting.

The weakness of the finding of the "Jesus Seminar" in this case is underlined by the complete disagreement of John Dominic Crossan, who was billed as cofounder of the enterprise along with Robert Funk. Instead, Crossan agreed with me that the appearance of the saying across a wide range of literature, from Mark to *Thomas,* tells against taking it as later teaching projected back onto Jesus. Crossan's disagreement with the "Jesus Seminar," and his agreement with me, is unusual for him, because he has formed a dislike for my analysis of Jesus as a prophetic and rabbinic teacher. To avoid moving too close to my view, Crossan compared Jesus' statement to the philosophy of the Hellenistic teacher Epictetus: "If you want to be crucified, wait and the cross will arrive" (Epictetus, *Discourses* 2.2.20). Because Epictetus was born some twenty years after Jesus died, and justified his stance with an appeal to the Stoic imperative to maintain "reason" (*logos*) in the face of adversity, it involves more than a stretch of the imagination to claim that Epictetus is the source of Jesus' image. A better comparison is with the Rabbinic statement, already mentioned, that Isaac carrying the wood was like a man carrying his cross. In any case, although Crossan and I are not likely to agree any time soon on the balance of Greek and Aramaic influences on Jesus, we can and have found accord in finding that Jesus truly did demand self-denial of his followers.

The second conventional gambit to evade the meaning of Jesus' words is to say that they applied only to his disciples, restricting their applicability to select followers alone. This feeds into the romantic view that the first generation of Christians was uniquely heroic. A variant of this gambit holds that the teaching applies only to those who have completely devoted themselves during the history of the Church to Jesus' way of life: monastics, clergy, high functionaries in the Church, and the like. The latter attitude is by far the one I have most frequently encountered in more than thirty years of teaching the Gospels, in colleges, universities, and churches. People look dismayed in any of those settings when I point out that Jesus' saying demands suffering from "anyone" who would follow him, not just from select followers in his own time or later from followers ordained to a special status or rank. "Anyone" means "anyone," in as unqualified a way in Aramaic and in Greek as in English; the meaning cannot be limited to Simon Peter in Jesus' time any more than it can be limited to Mother Teresa in our time.

Although a variety of means have been developed, from popular paraphrase to scholarly deflection, to sidestep Jesus' demand for self-sacrifice in the life of discipleship, the hard fact of his teaching remains. His focus on martyrdom, and the subsequent comparison between the crucifixion and the Aqedah in Christian theology, have deeply affected the history of the Church as well as the nations and institutions that have been influenced by Christianity. Once Jesus' focus on martyrdom is appreciated, many crucial elements of his teaching that otherwise seem inexplicable find their natural meaning.

The sense of a common vocation to martyrdom, shared by Jesus with his disciples, comes through clearly in another key saying: "For even the son of man did not come to be served, but to serve, and to give his life: redemption for many" (Mark 10:45). Two expressions in Aramaic govern the meaning of this teaching. Jesus speaks of "the son of man" (or "the one like a person": *bar 'anasha'*) referring to any human being, including himself, but not limiting the statement to himself. No matter what the rank or status or circumstance of a person, service is the proper aim of life. Each person is to give his life as *redemption* (*purqana'*), a sacrificial term that refers to how an offering given to God brings all who participate into the circle of forgiveness, celebration, and divine favor that sacrifice creates.

Jesus' insistence on his disciples' readiness for martyrdom animates the basic meaning of Eucharist, the most characteristic sacrament of Christianity. In his meals with his disciples toward the end of his life, not only at a single "Last Supper" but also at gatherings on many occasions in Jerusalem, Jesus spoke of sacrifice with ever-increasing precision.

By that time Jesus had entered the Temple in Jerusalem in order to clear out the commercial transactions that in his view, inspired by the prophet Zechariah, polluted worship there. In order to effect the operation, and expel animals for sale and their owners in an area of some twenty-five acres, I have estimated he needed to be joined by around two hundred followers. Although Jesus' action amounted to no more than a temporary incursion, because the priestly authorities had armed forces at their disposal, it aroused the mortal enmity of the high priest Caiaphas and those allied with him. After all, Jesus had intervened directly in the Temple to change the way sacrifice was offered at its divinely sanctioned altar. He stood for banning traders from the sanctuary, removing profits from the priesthood that permitted that trade, opening worship in the Temple to those beyond the borders of Israel according to the prophecy of Zechariah, and demoting Caiaphas from his position as the supreme Jewish authority in favor of his own prophetic vision. The antimony between Jesus and Caiaphas was deep; neither side would or could concede.

Now banned from the Temple, Jesus imputed a new and revolutionary meaning to the significance of the meals he had long enjoyed with his disciples. Jesus said that the wine was his "blood," the offering usually poured out on the altar, and that the bread was his "flesh," the sacrifice that God consumed in flame while favoring his people. Jesus did not originally refer to his own personal blood and body in these meals, because in the Judaism of his time and place, human flesh could neither be eaten nor sacrificed; that meaning came much later, in the Hellenistic environment of John's Gospel, c. 100 C.E.

Within Jesus' own setting, immediately after his occupation of the Temple, his prophetic symbolism in his meals with his disciples directly contradicted the priestly practice of animal sacrifice. In his view, wine and bread had become *superior sacrifices* to the usual offerings, because worship in the Temple had been defiled by commerce. As far as Caiaphas and his colleagues were concerned, Jesus was setting up an altar to rival the Temple's, and they reacted with the powerful resources at their command.

Jesus responded to the controversy he caused, and exacerbated that controversy, by crafting a liturgy for the practice of his communal meals with his followers, which had been part of his movement since the time of its origins in Galilee. As he shared meals after his failed occupation of the Temple, he said to his disciples, "Do this for my remembrance" (1 Corinthians 11:24, 25; Luke 22:19). This phrasing in Aramaic (*'aviydu dena' ledukraniy*) is not a banal request to be remembered as if Jesus' disciples might forget him. Rather, the phrase refers in the tradition of Judaism to the remembrance *before God* that a sacrifice brings for all who participate. Every time they eat the sacrificial meal he taught them, they bring his remembrance before God, even as they prepare themselves to follow his example.

Jesus taught that suffering is an aspect, not only of our human nature but also of our capacity to live a life that goes beyond the grave. Taking up your cross, serving others as a redemption for their estrangement from God, and remembering both Jesus' meal of sacrifice and his readiness to give his life are all intertwined in a single message: your life is not limited to mortal existence, but extends from the present into eternity. Suffering involves the happenstance of being mortal, but also marks the painful yet spiritually necessary transition from living a self-centered existence to entering into a life in which God and neighbor take their place along with a concern for one's self.

Many forms of modern Christianity, in their facile equation of faith with material prosperity, have obscured that way of the cross, of service, and of sacrifice. In this respect, the modern Church has reversed the stance of its ancient inheritance, which not only celebrated martyrdom, but also expected every believer to imitate the virtue of Jesus and the martyrs. This primitive theology, developed from the background of Judaic antecedents the Gospels do not name—including the Aqedah—became central to the teaching of the Church and permeated the cultures that Christianity has influenced, including our own. The direction this demand for martyrdom took after his death, however, might well have surprised Jesus.

By the time the New Testament writings as known today emerged near the end of the first century, martyrdom featured as a requirement for believers with a powerful new motivation, beyond even what Maccabean interpreters had asserted. One writer in particular, the author of the Epistle to the Hebrews (c. 95 C.E.) produced a focused yet sweeping vision of Jesus and his significance that gathered up earlier theologies and included a universal requirement of martyrdom. The writing is called an epistle rather than a letter because it is a formal, theological treatise, not an occasional message. Hebrews explicitly portrays Jesus' death for the Church as a whole as a sacrifice, borrowing the model of Abraham and Isaac, and that sacrificial theology has been with Christianity in one form or another ever since.

In Hebrews' portrayal, Jesus' sacrifice was unlike any previously known, whether of an animal in ritual or of a human being in martyrdom. Jesus was God's Son, his death a divine offering from God to God, and therefore the only perfect sacrifice, untainted by mortal weakness, that there ever had been or ever could be. The sacrifice of the divine Son became the fulcrum of Christianity, balancing human actions on one side and divine action on the other.

Jesus' death on the cross, in the presentation of Hebrews, accomplished everything that the ritual sacrifice of animals had tried to achieve but could not, because the only offering God had truly desired, from before time existed, was his own Son. Following out that line of reasoning, the author of Hebrews argued that, since Jesus had transcended sacrifice, ritual was a thing of the past. This modern-seeming theme of the transcendence of sacrifice was not accompanied, however, *by any reduction whatever* in the imperative toward martyrdom. In fact, Hebrews made willingness to become a martyr a requirement, not only during periods of persecution, but for as long as the life of faith endured, under any conditions. The paradoxical story of how theologically eliminating ritual intensified, rather than reduced, the role of martyrdom in Christianity begins with the Epistle to the Hebrews, and its argument illuminates a profound impulse within the Church and the cultures Christianity inspired, including our own, over the centuries.

Although Jesus became the only offering that mattered in the Epistle to the Hebrews, at the same time that only believers who accepted the vocation of martyrdom were worthy of him. The old Maccabean image of the willing victim, comparable to Isaac, is repeated, but also altered crucially, so that martyrdom becomes an eternal as well as a universal requirement in Christianity, and not only in times of deadly persecution—a fateful change from Judaism.

In a famous summary of its message, Hebrews proclaims that the reality of Jesus as the Christ is "the same yesterday and today and forever" (13:8), signaling a crucial development that made Christianity a religion distinct from and autonomous of Judaism. By insisting upon Jesus as the embodiment of a divine and eternal principle rather than simply as an important prophet in history, early Christians began to measure all the institutions of Judaism in the light of Christ, instead of the reverse. Christ became the enduring standard of all revelation in every age, and Hebrews presented his crucifixion as the moment in time that disclosed him as the one sacrifice God had always wanted. No document in the New Testament voices this perspective as clearly and trenchantly as Hebrews. By the standards of a later time, this epistle might seem to be making routine statements about Christianity, but that is only because it has exerted a deep and enduring influence.

By establishing Jesus' eternal identity in his sacrifice as a martyr, Hebrews also made the imperative of becoming a martyr central to Christianity. Martyrdom was the very substance of faith (Hebrews 11:1–38), and believers gave proof of their own commitment to Christ by framing their lives so that they were ready for the call of martyrdom. This explosive requirement of permanent martyrdom is elegantly expressed in the Epistle to Hebrews in a style that is so rich in allegory, rhetorical flourish, and imagery that commentators have often taken its call to martyrdom figuratively. But that is unwarranted: Hebrews means what it says. The style of this writing is complex and—because it breaks new theological ground—sometimes so detailed that it becomes convoluted. Our concerns here are not at all stylistic, however. What demands our attention is how Hebrews articulated a sacrificial theology that made martyrdom central to Christianity, feeding its requirements into some of the most basic dogmas of the Church.

The author of the Epistle to the Hebrews wrote in Paul's name, but around thirty-one years after Paul's death. During the prolonged crises and disruptions that followed the deaths of Paul and Peter in Rome in 64 C.E., including the Jewish War with Rome, the Roman persecution of Christians, and the gradual but painful separation of Christianity from Judaism, teachers such as the author of Hebrews attempted to awaken an authoritative voice from the past to deal with acutely painful issues that no Christian leader alive during the 90s of the first century could resolve.

Everything about the structure and contents of Hebrews shows what the most pressing issue for its author was. With the Temple lying in ruins in the wake of the Roman campaign against Jerusalem and the fire that followed the final siege, he needed to know: What was the meaning of sacrifice, and of all the ritual prescriptions set out in the Scriptures of Israel, if they could no longer be put into action? Once, Christians had sacrificed in the Jerusalem Temple, whether personally, as Jews living in or near Jerusalem or making pilgrimage there, or indirectly if they were non-Jews, by providing offerings that were sacrificed on their behalf in Jerusalem by teachers such as Paul. Did the end of the Temple mean that God had abandoned his covenant, breaking the covenantal chain between himself and his people that had existed since the time of Abraham?

Because Paul was the greatest covenantal thinker in the Christian tradition, the author of Hebrews naturally looked to Paul's thought, applied in a radically new context, to deal with what Hebrews presents as the most critical problem of its time. The Epistle to the Hebrews addresses the problem by insisting that Jesus, as the Son of God, was the willing, innocent sacrifice that took the place of all other sacrifices. Jesus and his divine Father actually did what Abraham and Isaac almost did, surpassing the devotion depicted in the Aqedah. Each move in Jesus' journey to the cross fulfilled the prescriptions of ritual in the Temple completely, so that no further offering in the Temple could please God. In fact, according to Hebrews *all* the rituals of ancient Israel pointed forward to the crucifixion, the one moment of sacrifice that God really desired: the offering of his own Son.

What Abraham and Isaac did on Moriah was no more than a foreshadowing of the reality that Jesus revealed, God's desire to immolate his own child in a single, supreme, all-forgiving sacrifice. The Eucharist, which commemorated that moment and joined believers in Jesus' offering of his eternally valuable sacrifice, replaced the animal sacrifices of the Old Testament with the one form of worship God had desired from all eternity. The Epistle to the Hebrews, with studied elegance and powerful rhetoric, proclaims Christianity an eternal religion independent of Judaism, and lays out the Christian claim to understand the mind and heart of God.

Hebrews pioneered in Christianity the approach of Plato's philosophy called typology: any apparent reality on earth was a "type," a rough, transient copy in the material world of a true reality in heaven, the world of ideal and permanent forms. Christian Platonism made Jesus' sacrifice the single, true reality of heaven; Israelite worship, including the Temple, was only an approximate replica of the divine Son's immolation. Before and after Hebrews, Christians found various ways to speak of Christ's eternity in poetry and hymn and prayer; Platonic philosophy was by no means always their idiom. But when analytic theology was involved, Christians turned as instinctively to Plato as they did to the Scriptures of Israel for purposes of worship.

Within this view Jesus in his death on the cross takes the place of any value that other forms of sacrifice in the history of Israel once seemed to have possessed. As far as the author of Hebrews was concerned, Jesus as the Son of God not only emerged as the standard by which every major institution of Judaism was to be measured; Jesus actually replaced those institutions, the Law given by Moses and the high priesthood, as well as sacrifice. On this view Jesus gave all humanity a new and better covenant (Hebrews 8:6–13) compared to the covenant with the patriarchs and with Moses. The author of Hebrews needs to insist that Jesus died without cause and in line with sacrificial procedures to make this argument, praising Jesus and challenging the authorities who condemned him at one and the same time—and he does so relentlessly.

Jesus in Hebrews is so innocent that he is perfect and sinless (Hebrews 7:28), which he personally never claimed to be. This perfection as compared to the weakness of Israelite high priests implies what Hebrews will later say in so many words (in its tenth chapter): that daily offerings in the Jerusalem Temple—or anywhere else, for that matter—are beside the point. When human beings other than the divine Son offer sacrifice, according to Hebrews, their action is self-interested: they know very well that they are sinful, and they anticipate the benefit of forgiveness from performing ritual acts. That means that conventional priests wind up perpetuating sin when they offer sacrifice, because the memory of wrongdoing is propagated at the same time an offering is brought. This consciousness of sinfulness, inextricably connected with ritual sacrifice, demonstrates that Jesus' innocent death has transcended all ritual.

Hebrews' way of thinking has contributed directly to how sacrifice has been conceived in the West over the centuries, whether within or outside the Church. Typically, the ritual of offering an animal is assumed to acknowledge guilt for the purpose of acquiring forgiveness for wrongdoing; apart from that, the person who sacrifices is not supposed to enjoy any benefit. The celebratory feast, which had been dominant in the ancient conception of sacrifice, has been eclipsed in the thinking of the West by the issue of sin's connection to sacrifice. This represents a revolutionary development, which permitted the author of Hebrews to portray the destruction of the Temple in Jerusalem by the Romans as proof that it belonged to a passing, imperfect age. By a stroke of Platonic logic, he marginalized the ritual act of sacrifice that had been irreducibly important within Judaism, and continued to be characteristic of Greco-Roman worship.

By claiming that Jesus transcended sacrifice, Christianity minimized ritual sacrifice as a marginal activity that was not a life-sustaining form of worship at all, but just a faulty remedy for sin. According to Hebrews and the line of thinking it set in motion, ritual makes people feel ever more guilty in their attempts to rid themselves of sin by means of ceremonies that only exacerbate the consciousness of sin.

Although Hebrews' dismissal of ritual sacrifice has become an axiom of Western culture, that is only one step—and a fairly straightforward, Platonic step—toward the goal of its argument. The second step is more radical and original. For Hebrews, God only takes pleasure in what is perfect, and that perfect offering is not anything a conventional priesthood could offer, but only God's own Son. Apart from that perfection, more ritual and more sacrifice just amounts to more sin. That is why Hebrews is the fountainhead of the theological claim—still embraced by many Christians, although disputed by others, and rejected by many non-Christian thinkers—that Jesus was in all ways perfect. The author even risks making Jesus seem not quite human, when he describes Jesus as the unique high priest, "tempted in every way in our likeness, apart from sin" (Hebrews 4:15). For Hebrews, Jesus was not merely divine: he also had to be faultless to be accepted by God as a human sacrifice for human sin.

Why this fixation on sin, and its projection onto the whole system of Israelite sacrifice? The conflation between sin and sacrifice is today so strong that many people cannot imagine sacrifice as a celebration, and cannot think of sin as anything but an irremovable shame, endemic to all human beings (except for Jesus in the view of those who agree with Hebrews). When the Epistle to the Hebrews identifies ritual with sin, it does so in order to argue that Jesus takes the place of what the Temple priests once tried and failed to do. The author's desire to prove that Christ fulfills and transcends ritual requirements causes him to restrict his attention to just one kind of sacrifice, offerings for sin. The argument presents a choice to the reader of the Epistle: either feel more and more guilty by means of conventional ritual, or finally wipe sin away on the basis of Jesus' ideal sacrifice.

Although Hebrews' portrayal of Jesus as the ideal high priest is not accepted universally (even within Christianity), Hebrews did succeed over the long term—with considerable help from other Christian authors—in portraying sacrifice as inherently sinful and backward. In regard to the relationship between sin and sacrifice, the claim of the modern world to be more civilized than the ancient world—doubtless justifiable in some respects—appears shaky. When sacrifice was practiced in Antiquity, the joy and sharing that was the dominant mood shines through countless texts across cultures as well as in the images of music and dance and festivity on the walls of ancient temples. Is the conviction that all sacrifice must be lugubrious and bloody really an advance?

Augustine's teaching of Original Sin during the fifth century C.E. claimed that sexual intercourse, flawed by the very nature of human desire, inevitably produces sinful children. Whether sin is viewed as Original in Augustine's sense or as ambient in Hebrews' sense, Christianity represents a marked departure from other ancient cultures. The Scriptures of those cultures—Israelite and Greek, Persian and Egyptian, Chinese and Mayan—deal with sin in terms of specific errors that people learned how to correct, rather than as an inexorable burden of guilt passed on by nature or by procreation. The latter view, derived from Saint Augustine, has driven the association of sacrifice not only with sin, but also with sexual sin in particular. Understanding how that has happened in the West helps explain modern attitudes toward ritual, sacrifice, and related issues, attitudes that need to be taken into account in assessing the impact of the Epistle to the Hebrews, even though the ideas concerned were not articulated in Hebrews. The conflation between sin and sacrifice, and the eventual addition of sexuality to that conflation, was set in motion by this Epistle, and has shaped behavior, taste, and culture until the twenty-first century.

Why should Augustine's conception of inherited sin have proven perennially popular in Western thought (among Christians, non-Christians, and post-Christians)? It appeals across the board of religious and philosophical thinkers, no matter their persuasions, because Original Sin and the belief that the present world and all within the world are corrupt reaches deep into an ancient wellspring of thought that has influenced every religion, every philosophy that it has touched. Augustine focused on the ambient suspicion in the ancient world that evil, which afflicts human beings, derives from their flesh rather than their spirit, and that flesh is the principal medium of sin's contagion, especially in sexual acts. His unparalleled capacities to analyze human emotions and behaviors, and to see the connections of cause and effect that convey evil from one generation to the next, make Augustine's teaching of Original Sin powerful and effective in poetic as well as theological terms.

From a time prior to the sixth century B.C.E. (how long prior has proven extremely difficult to pin down) the Persian prophet Zarathustra taught that opposite a good, supreme god, Ahura Mazda, an evil counterpart, Angra Mainyu, deliberately corrupted this world. Zarathustra's powerful system of belief challenged the moral value of the material world, and his dualism profoundly influenced the later Persian empire, and—as a result—both Greek and Israelite literature. A third-century C.E. Iranian prophet, named Mani, took up this dualistic approach, and Mani's teachings directly influenced Augustine, who was a committed Manichaean before he became a Christian. It was Mani who taught Augustine, and Christianity after Augustine, that sexual intercourse introduced evil into the world. At the same time, Mani also saw external rituals as sinful devices. Augustine wrapped ritual sacrifice, sexuality, and sin up into a single package, all the lures of the devil in a fallen world, by claiming that sexual intercourse transmitted sin, and that because of sin people offered sacrifice to false gods in self-deceived rituals.

The triad of blood sacrifice, sin, and sex became a favorite horror of medieval Europe. When Christians went to war against Muslims, retreated before Mongols, razed Jewish communities, and killed alleged witches, their propaganda often portrayed their enemies as guilty of sacrificing and even eating Christians while engaging in orgiastic worship of their false gods. Anti-Semitism has been rife in the West, not only because guilt was imputed to Jews as a race for the death of Jesus, but also because they embodied the alien counterimage of Jesus' perfect sacrifice: like Muslims and witches, only weaker than the former and more numerous than the latter, they brought perverse sex, bloody sacrifice, and a false god into the heartland of Europe. To this day the genre of horror films shows that the bloody triad continues to work its symbolic power. Sin, sacrifice, and superstition form a fearful image of what might corrupt culture and civilization in an endless slide into perversity.

To the author of Hebrews, sin could not be limited to a sexual definition, as it has tended to be limited as a result of Augustine's influence. But the Epistle to the Hebrews does focus on another single issue, in a way that amounts to limitation of another kind. Along with other writers in the New Testament, Hebrews saw the catastrophe of the Temple's destruction, a fearful event for Judaism and Christianity alike that put God's desire for sacrifice in doubt as well as the covenant with Israel, as the consequence of Israel's sin in particular, specifically the killing of Jesus. Hebrews even portrays the Temple's replacement as coming when Jesus died and entered into the true sanctuary in heaven and revealed that the sanctuary on earth was only a provisional copy of the heavenly archetype (Hebrews 9:11–28). The author's mind was so fixed on eternity, he ignored the chronological fact that nearly forty years separated Jesus' death from the destruction of the Temple, an indication of the author's fully Platonic rather than historical thinking.

To his mind, the covenant mediated by Jesus is better than Israel's, the "second" replacing the "first," the "new" taking over from what is now "obsolete" (Hebrews 8:7–13). With the Epistle to the Hebrews, Christianity claimed not simply to represent the best or purest form of the covenant with Israel, but to offer the world the new covenant or "New Testament" (the Greek term *diatheke* referring to a will or testament, as well as translating the Hebrew *berit*, "covenant") that God had always intended for humanity as a whole.

From Hebrews on, it became a truism—repeated with variations by generation after generation of thinkers in the West, whether from a Judeo-Christian perspective or not—that "the blood of bulls and goats is incapable of removing sin" (Hebrews 10:4). But if ritual slaughter no longer amounted to effective sacrifice in the mentality of the West, that by no means brought the end of sacrificial behavior. Among Christians, the theology of Christ's eternal sacrifice remained, as well as the incentive for martyrs to emulate his ennobling death. Perhaps even more powerfully, modern nations captured the rhetoric of Hebrews in a secular form, offering young soldiers the immortality of national remembrance in exchange for their willingness to shed the human blood that alone made sacrifice effective.

Without sacrifice, how could sin be forgiven? Christ's death, the supreme sacrifice, had since the time of Paul (Romans 6:1–11) been understood to offer access to forgiveness at baptism, but what about thereafter? Side by side with its portrayal of Jesus' death as the climax of all sacrifice, Hebrews obsesses over the problem of Christians who sin after they have converted to Christ. Jesus had "offered for all time a single sacrifice for sins," which believers accessed when they were baptized (Hebrews 10:12). But that brings with it a consequence (Hebrews 6:4–6, italics added), that it is *"impossible (adunaton)* to renew to repentance" those who have been baptized and then fallen into sin. In Hebrews and in the early Church, "impossible" meant just what it said: once you were baptized, the way to repentance after a serious sin was forever barred. By contrast, the medieval teaching, which required confession and absolution after the commission of a "mortal" sin, appears lenient. The life of faith involved following the way of a perfect example during the first centuries of the Church.

Even the emperor Constantine, during the fourth century, delayed his own baptism until the time of his death. Since it was impossible to achieve the benefit of baptism more than once, those whose professions implicated them in mortal sin—for example, sending soldiers to certain death, as any emperor must sometimes do, and ordering political assassinations which, necessary or not, Constantine had arranged—often put off receiving this sacrament and the promise of eternal life until they could promise to sin no more. Constantine's delay did not signal any cynicism on his part; there was no question but that he made Christianity the preeminent religion of the Roman Empire long before his baptism. Yet in practice, delaying baptism was open to abuse and uncertainty. The unbaptized might use the time before perfection would be demanded of them to multiply their sins, while death in the early centuries of the Common Era came more unpredictably than it does now. Hebrews anticipates these problems, establishing ethical precedents as powerful in their own ways as the sacrificial depiction of Jesus' death.

In extending the Maccabean teaching on martyrdom, Hebrews is startling, and to many readers, gruesome. Modern Christianity blanches at the thought that the Epistle to the Hebrews insists upon: that all Christians should be potential martyrs, prepared to face up to the world and take their stand "until blood" (Hebrews 12:4), the pivotal phrase on which the ethical teaching of Hebrews turns.

This idea so disturbs modern readers that it has become routine to describe Hebrews as "symbolic," "abstract," "deep," "mysterious," "complicated," and the like, when in fact it is among the most articulate (if somewhat baroque) documents in the New Testament and early Christian literature. Ancient Christianity prided itself on its martyrs and incorporated the language and thought of Hebrews within its whole system of belief and practice. Unless you understand the theology of martyrdom, like it or not, you can never comprehend early Christianity, or the capacity of Christians in every age to seek martyrdom, whether on the mass scale of the Crusades and the First World War, or on the personal scale of Sir Thomas More, Dietrich Bonhoeffer, and Martin Luther King Jr.

How could the author of Hebrews insist that Jesus personally accomplished all the requirements of sacrifice, while also demanding further sacrifices from believers? In the answer to that apparent paradox lies a clue to the pervasive influence of Christianity within the West. The paradoxical embrace of both Jesus' death as the one effective sacrifice *and* the way of martyrdom for every believer developed in circumstances of deep turmoil after the death of the first generation of Christian leaders and the destruction of the Temple. The author of Hebrews complains that his community has forgotten "the former days, when enlightened you endured a great contest of sufferings, by being exposed to both revilings and tribulations" (Hebrews 10:32–33). Suffering is a mark of true faith, proving the believer does not convert for expediency's sake. But what happens after conversion, when—within a group of the faithful—believers might enjoy preference in view of supposedly superior faith? Then, says the author, is the time to encourage one another—literally to a "paroxysm (*paroxysmos*) of love and good works" (Hebrews 10:24). And this author leaves no question of how the paroxysm is best displayed: it is by means of martyrdom.

As in the case of the Maccabean theology of martyrdom, the theology of Hebrews was also articulated in the context of persecution, and persecution on a gruesome scale. In 64 C.E. fire broke out in Rome and decimated the city. Rumors abounded that claimed the emperor Nero had ordered the arson and forbidden efforts to fight the flames. The modern cliché of his "fiddling" while Rome burned understates his depravity: he floated down the Tiber on a barge with his prostitutes during the blaze (Tacitus, *Annals* 15.37). The prospect that he could rebuild Rome along any lines he wanted no doubt enhanced the emperor's pleasure. He even had building plans ready to go. All Nero needed—to complete his enjoyment and to avoid pesky rumors that he was responsible for the arson—was to find someone else to blame for the fire. The emperor deflected suspicion from himself by pinning responsibility for the disaster on Christians. Their marginal status, neither Jewish nor non-Jewish, and numbering only a fraction of 1 percent of the population of the Roman Empire, must have seemed to him a gift from the gods. They were rounded up, interrogated, often subjected to elaborate torture, and then slaughtered. Nero's excesses were obvious even to those who despised Christianity. Tacitus, the Roman historian who lived during the period, represents an aristocratic perspective on these atrocities (*Annals* 15.44): "First those who avowed were arrested; and upon their information a vast number were condemned, not so much on the charge of arson as for their hatred of the human race. Their death was turned into a diversion. They were clothed in the skins of wild beasts, and torn to pieces by dogs; they were fastened to crosses, or set up to be burned, so as to serve the purpose of lamps when daylight failed. Nero gave up his own gardens for this spectacle; he provided also circus games, during which in the garb of a charioteer he mingled with the populace, or took his stand upon a chariot. But guilty as these men were and worthy of extreme penalty, pity arose, since they were being destroyed not for public good, but for one man's savagery."

Although Nero's anti-Christian pogrom was thirty years in the past by the time Hebrews was written, the emperor Domitian initiated a new persecution, aimed at those who refused to offer a sacrifice of wine and incense before his image as a divine ruler. Jews could escape that obligation, because their religion was legal, a *religio licita*, and it prohibited such acts of idolatry, but Christians represented a modern cult, a *superstitio*, and could be faced with death if they refused this civic obligation. The Epistle to the Hebrews, written during the last year of Domitian's reign (95–96 C.E.) reflects the fear that Nero's excess would provide the precedent for anti-Christian witch hunts on a massive scale.

In this context, there is no mistaking Hebrews' message, and the model of Christian life and virtue this Epistle promotes (11:1–2): "Faith is the substance of the hoped for, the conviction of things not seen, because by this the elders were martyred (*emarturethesan*)." Examples of the "elders" follow, so that it is plain the author has in mind the heroes of faith from the time of ancient Israel until the recent past, and he privileges examples of violent martyrdom above all.

First on his list is Abel, whose sacrifice pleased God more than Cain's, and who died at his brother's jealous hand (Hebrews 11:4). Abraham figures three times, because he left his native land for the inheritance that was to come (Hebrews 11:8–10), believed God could give him a son (11:11–12), and then offered Isaac (11:17–19). This is reminiscent of the tradition in *Jubilees* that Abraham passed through seven tests, and scholarly opinion remains divided over an intriguing question: Does Hebrews presuppose Judaic interpretation in which Abraham actually sacrificed Isaac, and God brought him back to life? That might or might not be the case (and I remain undecided, as I am in the case of Judaic literature of this period), but it remains certain that Hebrews sees Isaac as a foreshadowing of Christ, particularly saying that Abraham "reasoned that God is capable of raising even from the dead, whence—by analogy—he also secured him" (Hebrews

11:19, referring to Isaac). Those qualifying words, "by analogy" (*en parabole*), show that Hebrews is not at all concerned to speak of what actually happened on Mount Moriah, or of what interpretations of the story might lie in the background. That is why we don't quite have enough evidence to decide whether the author thought of Isaac also as returning from the dead. The driving concern in Hebrews is not what happened to Isaac or Abraham, but the *meaning*, in terms of Jesus' perfect sacrifice, of what they did and intended to do. Event, intention, possibility, and promise are all mixed together, because the significance of Genesis 22, in Hebrews' conception, is that the Aqedah was only truly completed in the crucifixion and resurrection of Jesus.

In Hebrews' vision, Abraham's offering of Isaac stood both for the supreme sacrifice of Christ and for the mysticism of suffering that linked every believer to Christ. The heavenly reality, revealed to Israel since the time of the Aqedah, was the eternal sacrifice of Christ, the Son offering to the Father the sole worship the Father ever wanted. Once, this reality could only be discerned by means of "types." That is why Abraham and Isaac, Abel, and the whole sacrificial system of Leviticus can be seen as foreshadowing Christ's sacrifice in Hebrews.

Connections by means of types do not end there, because believers are called to imitate Christ in Hebrews, and to imitate him in his suffering. Believers understand clearly and fully what the patriarchs and prophets of the past could only dimly perceive or intuit, and for that reason they themselves live in the world as types or examples of Christ, manifesting his power. Because his revelation was consummated in death, believers are also to embrace martyrdom. Coming to the climax of his argument, the author details the methods of execution inflicted by the Romans on Christians, as on the Maccabean martyrs of the past: "they were subjected to stoning, sawn apart, died murdered by sword, went about [the gladiatorial arena] in sheep pelts, in goat-skins, destitute, afflicted, ill-treated" (Hebrews 11:37–38). Such deaths and agonies are seen to be the imprint of Christ in the world (Hebrews 12:1–2): "Therefore let us also, having such a cloud of martyrs around us, putting off every impediment and distracting sin, run with endurance the race set before us, looking to the founder and perfecter of faith, Jesus, who for the joy set before him endured a cross, despising shame, and sat at the right of God's throne." This is why resistance in Hebrews must be "until blood" (12:4). By his own blood, a believer cannot secure the forgiveness of sin, because he is guilty himself. But believers' blood, their willingness to endure martyrdom, demonstrates their dedication to the eternal sacrifice of the one whose "blood speaks better than Abel's" (Hebrews 12:24). Jesus is the same "yesterday and today and forever" (Hebrews 13:8) because his sacrifice is the fulcrum of eternity. Martyrdom itself does not remove sin, but it opens the martyr to the sacrifice of Christ, which alone effects sin's removal.

Armed with this thought, that shedding their own blood for Christ made them worthy to benefit from the sinless blood of Christ, Christians were prepared to face down the threat of death at the hands of persecutors. Their blood would convert the Roman Empire to Christianity, but to a form of that faith which, once it had tasted the benefits of blood, would never lose its ambition to produce martyrs. A persistent stream of deliberate suffering has twisted and turned through the violent history of the West, often—as we shall see—turning Abraham and Isaac into ideals of warriors in battle rather than martyrs in the classic sense, but always pressing the claim that they represent Jesus, the one sacrifice that God desires. The model of martyrdom derived from Abraham and Isaac has been even more pervasive within Christianity than within Judaism, because the pattern is understood to reflect, not just what believers should do, but the very action of God offering his Son, a divine activity that all Christians are called in every time, in war and in peace, to emulate.

IV

Martyrs, in the Flesh

Early Christianity's keenest minds, collectively known as "the Fathers of the Church," explored the connection between Christ and Isaac once it had been established. These teachers evolved entire philosophies out of their faith, in active dialogue with other Platonic thinkers in their time—Christian, non-Christian, and anti-Christian. Intellectual ferment during the whole Patristic period (that is, the time of the Fathers, *pateres* in Greek, until around the eighth century C.E.) was second to none in the history of the Church, and theology constituted a principal preoccupation of the Roman Empire generally in Late Antiquity.

Following out the logic of the Epistle to the Hebrews, the Fathers, whose numbers included priests and bishops, prophets and poets, taught that Jesus' crucifixion represented the culmination of all sacrifice, ending the need for the ritual slaughter of animals or people, even as it motivated Christians to embrace the ethos of martyrdom. During the course of the second century in particular, the entire conception of martyrdom shifted irrevocably in emphasis, from being a proof of Christians' personal faith (as depicted in the Epistle to the Hebrews) to becoming the *necessary means*, providentially appointed, to enable non-Christians to come to faith in Christ. In effect, the power of the cross to inspire faith in God was delegated to those whose martyrdoms replicated Jesus' crucifixion. Each martyr, in the unique circumstances of his suffering, became the personal incarnation of Christ for a new community of people drawn to his example.

Both the momentum of earlier Christian beliefs and the peculiar attitude of the Roman Empire toward Christians produced this shift. Although Patristic literature provides the best evidence for this momentous change, it is also apparent that the new face of martyrdom was not the Fathers' invention. Rather, longing for martyrdom welled up from within the Church, and Christianity's intellectuals did their best to make sense of this development.

At the close of the first century, shortly after Domitian's persecution of Christianity ended, Clement—the influential bishop of Rome, later referred to as the pope—taught that Isaac personally acted as he did "with confidence, knowing what was coming" (1 Clement 31.3). The phrase "what was coming" (*to mellon* in Clement's Greek) referred both to the immediate future in the story, the release that would come to Isaac by angelic intervention, and to the ultimate completion of Isaac's sacrificial offering by Jesus' crucifixion. With the subsidence of the threat of persecution, Clement focused more on the sacrifice that Jesus replaced than on the sacrifice demanded from disciples, but both features of the Christian Aqedah would prove extremely influential in the decades that followed.

The typology that the Epistle to the Hebrews pioneered, which saw events and characters in the Old Testament as analogies to realities in heaven, was so basic to Clement that it became instinctive to him. Patristic thinkers as a whole followed the same impulse, which also inspired the behavior of thousands of Christian believers. Christians saw figures such as Isaac as "types" of Christ, who completed or fulfilled the rudimentary, provisional example that Isaac or another patriarch or prophet provided. The true sacrifice was Christ, eternal in heaven, and that heavenly reality—called the "antitype" in the neo-Platonic language of early Christianity—left its imprint, its "type," on the course of human events even before the time of Jesus.

Early Christianity can only be understood when its belief in the eternity of Christ is fully taken into account, along with Christ's capacity, through types such as Isaac, to make himself known to people who could not possibly have known Jesus in history. Christian faith evolved on the basis of timeless principles, comparable to the Torah in Judaism. The Fathers and their congregations saw the world from the perspective of eternity; historical events, however dramatic, were incidental in comparison. For that reason, the Fathers could adopt Plato as one of their own, as the philosopher who made the best sense of their own faith and the sensibilities of growing numbers of Christians in the Mediterranean world.

The second-century theologian from Samaria named Justin, usually known as Justin Martyr, because the Romans executed him for his faith, believed that the Prophets of Israel and the philosophers of ancient Greece were in dialogue about the same eternal principles of creation, redemption, and immortality (*Apology* 44.9). Classic Christian theology, as taught by the Fathers, was not a ghetto for believers only, distant and antithetical to philosophy and science, as is all too often the case today. Rather, all those fields were combined in the various theological syntheses of the Patristic age, Christian, Gnostic, Stoic, and neo-Platonic.

Justin's picture, which became that of the Christian Platonism that dominated the theology of the Church until the Middle Ages, made the Prophets of Israel into the agents of true philosophy, and Christ the source of prophetic inspiration. Medieval Europeans unfortunately learned more from the Fathers about ignoring the importance of history than they did about the role of philosophy in the quest of faith. But medieval distortions of Patristic theology cannot conceal its central insight, that Christ had always been available, an eternal reality that could and did reveal himself to sages such as Socrates as well as to patriarchs such as Abraham.

The Fathers conceived of Christianity as breaking through the divisions between Greek philosophy and the Judaic Torah, to form a powerful synthesis of all that was best in human thought, insight, sensibility, and ethical action. The partial comprehension of Christ that had been possible in the past had been succeeded, they argued, when Jesus—the true "word" or principle (*logos*) of God himself—entered human history. Just as he brought an end to ritual sacrifice, so Jesus replaced every other partial reflection of the truth that he alone fully revealed and embodied.

The Fathers' dedication to ideas already developed in the Epistle to the Hebrews meant they could never agree to any continuation of ritual sacrifice. But it would be mistaken and superficial to imagine that, for this reason, early Christianity simply banished the sacrificial reflex that the Aqedah expresses. The exact opposite is the case.

Patristic theology insisted upon the importance of the martyrs' self-sacrifice, including very young martyrs, to an extent unprecedented among the major religions in Antiquity. That happened because, alongside their development of Hebrews' claim that Christ replaced all ritual sacrifice, the Fathers also ratcheted up the ethical imperative found in Hebrews—its demand that believers be willing to pursue their devotion to Christ "until blood" (Hebrews 12:4), that is, to the death.

The insistence that you needed to be willing to shed your own blood in order to access the power of Christ's supreme sacrifice resulted in one of the most profound dichotomies in the history of Christian thought. By the second century, Christianity's principal teachers had long argued that ritual sacrifice was useless, but they also required that believers should prepare themselves to give their lives for the sake of Christ and his message. The death of a believer was not the same thing as Christ's crucifixion, of course, but self-denial—including the ultimate self-denial of giving up one's life—was presented as the way that leads to union with Christ, dying with him so as to be raised with him into the heavens. Patristic theology tied that personal benefit of martyrdom to the distinctive claim, current from the second century onward, that martyrdom was necessary to bring Jesus' crucifixion alive to new generations of believers.

In proudly claiming to transcend ritual sacrifice, Christianity made Jesus' ultimate sacrifice perpetual. For that reason, the sacrificial moment of his crucifixion became continuous, primary, and suffused in the heart of every believer. Christ was forever on the cross, the axis of spiritual orientation, so that every Christian needed to be willing to offer himself or herself as a sacrificial victim by following the ritual pattern of holy martyrs. Without that willingness, the Fathers argued—and without literal martyrdoms to make that willingness real—Christ's crucifixion would have been in vain. The reversal of polarities, from *denying* the requirement of sacrifice to *insisting* upon it among all believers, generated far-reaching consequences, setting up patterns of behavior that have been repeated even by people who have no idea of the theological roots of their actions.

Countries with a deep history of Christianity have, over the centuries, displayed a capacity to mobilize their youth on a massive scale in times of crisis, and to put them in harm's way. This reflex—which seems powerfully impressive or appalling, depending upon whether one is a victor or a victim in conflict—feeds into a culture of bloodshed. In their haunting book on World War I, Stéphane Audoin-Rouseau and Annette Becker remark: "As in Hiroshima, where the long-term physical, psychological and political after-effects of the bomb were infinitely more destructive than its immediate impact, the inter-war generations failed to see how irradiated the post-war world had been by the Great War's culture of violence." Accurate though that observation is, it does not account for deeper cultural forces. For centuries, Christianity's view of sacrifice has released impulses in the lives of nations which have proved more powerful than the technological and political developments that in the end only serve cultural purposes.

Christianity's turn to martyrdom as a principal expression of its identity emerged as a consequence, not only of the theology of the Fathers, but also of the policies of the Roman Empire as set out during the second century. Compared to Nero and Domitian, the emperor Trajan (98–117 C.E.) seemed tolerant in dealing with the question of what to do with Christians, but his attempted policy of moderation only provoked Christian martyrdom over the long term.

In a correspondence in 112 C.E. with Pliny, governor of Bithynia and Pontus in Asia Minor, Trajan framed his policy in reply to a question from Pliny. Pliny had written, in some confusion, that when people were denounced to him as Christians, he did not know whether just being a Christian was cause for punishment. Neither did he have precedent to decide whether he should actively search out believers in order to correct their "atheism," as denying the gods of Rome was called. Doing so meant resorting to torture, the preferred method of dealing with atheism, but Pliny gives no indication of having a troubled conscience over inflicting pain, provided Trajan authorizes the procedure. Trajan replied that recognition of the gods of Rome (specifically by means of divine honors of incense and wine offered to the emperor's image) was all that should be required of those denounced as Christians. The ultimate issue was not their beliefs or their practice as such, but whether they were loyal to the Roman Empire and emperor. For that reason, Christians were *not* to be sought out, but only reprimanded on the complaint of reliable witnesses and corrected. When it came to Christianity, Trajan set out a deliberate policy of "don't ask, don't tell."

Christians were given several chances—if necessary, with the incentive of torture—to renounce their former atheism, the perceived danger in the Christian refusal to worship Roman gods. They were killed for their "obstinacy" if they repeatedly refused to accede to the offer of clemency in exchange for their repentance. Trajan took the separation of Christianity from Judaism for granted, in effect treating Christianity itself as an innocuous superstition, provided its members could be prodded to desist from their atheism and their nocturnal meetings. Pliny is obligingly optimistic in this regard, reporting back to Rome that the sale of sacrificial animals increased after his persecution of Christians, and that by torturing a couple of women slaves, he was able to determine that he was dealing only with a bizarre *superstitio* that did not have the likely prospect of exerting much influence.

Trajan had nothing to do with the indiscriminate persecution that Nero had indulged in, and insisted only upon the equivalent of an oath of loyalty from those accused of being Christians. Interestingly, Trajan does not comment on Pliny's report that he had tried to compel Christians to curse Christ in the course of interrogation; presumably, he left that practice to the discretion of local rulers.

Yet even without the curse, the loyalty oath was to the gods of Rome and to the emperor with his divine spirit as God's son. That requirement directly led to the phenomenon of Christian martyrdom. In good conscience, many Christians could not comply with the policy:

swearing allegiance to the emperor was an act performed before his image, with an oblation of wine and the burning of incense. It was an imperial sacrifice, and an obvious example of idolatry. This patriotic devotion to the divine ideal of the Roman Empire sometimes led to the use of the loyalty test to denounce Christians out of malice and to encourage pogroms (a welcome opportunity for riot, looting, rape, and murder for thugs in every age and place) despite the apparently tolerant policy established by Trajan.

Trajan himself did not anticipate that his plan of "don't ask, don't tell," like its modern counterpart in President Clinton's policy in regard to homosexuals in the military, would inflame, not only local opponents who denounced their victims to give a cloak of legality to their hatred, but also the victims themselves, who took pride in announcing their identity rather than concealing who they truly were.

Christians responded to the execution of Trajan's policy by portraying their martyrdom explicitly as a sacrifice, modeled on that of Isaac, and as a sacrifice necessary for salvation itself—not simply for the salvation of martyrs themselves, as in the Epistle to the Hebrews, *but for the salvation of believers generally and even of humanity as a whole.*

Martyrdom emerged as a requirement of salvation because the Fathers as well as Christians in their thousands internalized the logic of Hebrews and pressed on to a conclusion that was emotional, practical, and logical, although dissonant with modern sensibilities. They maintained that ritual offering was a thing of the past, because Christ's death alone provided for the forgiveness of sin; yet self-sacrifice in their minds became essential—in the form of martyrdom—to prove that Christ's sacrifice lived on in the hearts of believers and guided their actions, and to propagate new believers through the exemplary suffering of the martyrs.

Today the logic of martyrdom seems abstract and foreign, but the suffering of the martyrs provoked an effective, simple form of literature with a rhetorical blunt force and style of defending Christianity that contributed directly to the conversion of the Roman Empire by the fourth century C.E. Martyrdom helped to turn what had been a marginal sect into a world religion whose power and influence became incalculable. Martyrs did not merely put into action the intellectual theology the Fathers loved; each martyr seemed like a directly new revelation of Christ, and the heroism of those who suffered for their faith drew new adherents to Christianity, even during periods of persecution by torture. Long before Patristic writers had fully thought through their views, popular literature from the second century and later glorified martyrdom viscerally—by means of vivid evocations of the bleeding flesh and broken bones of famous martyrs.

Building upon the Maccabean tradition as well as the example of Jesus, an entire genre of praise for heroic martyrs, each of them a personal recapitulation of Christ, shaped Christian faith for centuries. This hagiography (that is, writing about holy people) filled the calendars of ancient, medieval, and modern churches with commemorations of those who suffered and died for the faith, and hagiographic portraits persist to this day, not only in the liturgical practice of commemorating saints' days, but also in popular accounts of the last days of Pope John Paul II, for instance, or the assassination of the Reverend Dr. Martin Luther King Jr. The suffering saint endures as an icon of faith, even among those who do not profess belief in Christianity. Martyrologies have held a secure place in folk literature and popular imagination in every century since the time of the Maccabees, and Christians intensified and developed the genre.

The depth of the influence of these portraits can scarcely be overestimated, because hagiography connects the suffering of the martyr directly to Christ's sacrifice, as if this connection were an obvious fact rather than an argument. The transparency of Jesus' passion within the martyr's ordeal, however the particulars of the stories might differ, makes martyrdom into a redemptive act. The cult of the martyrs in Antiquity, as well as the reverence for victims of assassination today—the Kennedy brothers as well as King, Che Guevara and Salvador Allende as well as Yitzhak Rabin and Anwar Sadat—expresses the profound although often inchoate conviction that their deaths were redemptive. The "sacrifice" of the fallen leader—language often used to describe the deaths just mentioned and many others, even when accidental—not only recollects the death of Jesus by invoking the myth of martyrdom, but implicitly claims to move Christ's work of redemption forward by taking us nearer to realizing the dream of peace or progress the hero articulated for his followers.

This veneration of the martyred dead, ancient and modern, gives expression to the sacrificial reflex that the story of Abraham's offering lays bare. In its detail, in its persistence, in its long-lasting effects for centuries after Roman persecution came to an end, and above all in its capacity to be retooled in the service of nationalistic propagandas of martyrdom that encourage sacrifice on behalf of country, the Christian veneration of martyrs has proven to be the single most influential incentive to self-sacrifice among world religions over the centuries.

Among the many stories of martyrdom recounted in ancient Christianity, two men in particular, both of them gifted, charismatic bishops active in Asia Minor with large followings during the second century, emerged as models of the ideal martyr well before the Fathers had fully articulated their theology of martyrdom. By force of personality and tenacious heroism, they enacted the teaching of the Church before anyone had fully expressed it. Ignatius of Antioch and Polycarp of Smyrna set out what the martyr must do by their own actions, shaping their deeds with constant reference to the rough-and-ready resources of a barely emerging New Testament and, with all its variations, the Greek form of Israel's Scriptures. They laid the foundation for the Christian teaching that the suffering of every believer perpetuates Christ's redemption. They did so within an understanding of the Church that was increasingly "catholic" (*katholikos*), a term referring to the whole movement throughout the Mediterranean world, and a view of the Aqedah that internalized it within Christianity.

Ignatius disdained Trajan's compromise. He refused to offer sacrifice to the Roman gods or to acknowledge the emperor as divine when he was denounced as a Christian. Other Christians no doubt did so, but Ignatius, as third bishop of Antioch (the first being Jesus' preeminent disciple, Peter, who was active in Antioch before he traveled to Rome) was not about to comply with the rule of "don't ask, don't tell." He was sentenced to die in Rome by being fed to wild animals, a form of punishment that enabled the Roman Empire to satisfy the demands of its justice and provide entertainment all at once.

On his way to his death in 107 C.E., Ignatius wrote letters to a series of six churches that lay along the route that he and his military escort followed, as well as a letter to his fellow bishop, Polycarp. Ignatius's Greek is solid and correct; while not in a literary style, his rhetorical power is self-assured, and he used his rudimentary eloquence to fashion a new genre of literature. Paul had made the letter form into a familiar category of Christian Scripture, but Ignatius took that form and reshaped it into an advance announcement of his own death and the reasons for it. No other topic truly concerns him; he does not even defend himself against the Romans' accusation. Instead, he focuses on the fact of his upcoming death as an opportunity to offer sacrifice with his own body.

The most touching of his letters pleads with Christians in Rome itself not to interfere with his offering: "Furnish me with nothing more than to become a libation to God, while an altar is still ready" (*Letter to the Romans* 2.2). The ease with which he moves into the sacrificial language of becoming a libation (*spondisthenai*), his blood like the wine that was offered to deities in the Hellenistic world and the wine shared during Eucharist, is as striking as his anxiety that the window of opportunity for his offering might close. Ignatius was an acute observer of his world; he fully understood that the Romans might change his sentence in response to public pressure and skillful intercessions on his behalf, or to suit the winds of bureaucratic change.

Once Ignatius thinks of his own death as a sacrifice, he engages in a metaphor of his own flesh becoming comparable to the flesh of Christ that was available in Christian worship (*Letter to the Romans* 4.1–2):

Let me be prey of beasts, through whom indeed to attain to God. I am God's wheat and ground by the beasts' teeth, that I might be found pure bread of Christ. Rather, incite the beasts, so that they become a tomb for me and leave nothing of my body, that I might not become a burden to anyone when I die. Then I shall truly be a disciple of Jesus Christ, when the world shall not even

see my body. Entreat Christ for me, so that through these means
I might be found a sacrifice.

Ignatius's body is to be like wheat milled by suffering to become
"bread," the sacrament of Christ's presence in the Eucharist.

Ignatius's equation of himself with Christ inevitably seems im-
modest, but it was in no sense inadvertent. He believed that, as a martyr, he replicated the suffering of Christ: "Permit me," he pleads, "to
become an imitator of the passion of my God" (*Letter to the Romans*
6.3). Ignatius signals the contribution of second-century Christianity
to the ideal of martyrdom that was the inheritance of the Maccabees
and the Epistle to the Hebrews. To Ignatius, the "birth pangs" (6.1)
of martyrdom opened to him, not merely the prospect of his own
salvation, but the status of offering a sacrifice like Christ's—for the
salvation of others. Those who see him die nobly on behalf of his
faith, Ignatius believed, would themselves turn to the worship of God
through Christ. Martyrdom was now not only proof of genuine belief,
but the necessary method of spreading salvation in the world.

However ambitious for glory Ignatius might have been, he was not
merely a narcissist, grandiose though his claims were. He spoke of
himself in exemplary terms, so that many martyrs, learning from him,
might earn their own eternal glory as well as the prospect of salvation
in heaven for others by means of martyrdom. When he refers to the
tortures that Rome might inflict, his purpose is not simply to call his
own fate to mind, but to articulate the vocation to suffering to which
any martyr might respond by enduring various torments (*Letter to
the Romans* 5.3): "Let fire and cross, struggles with beasts, dissections,
slicings, rackings of bones, cutting up of limbs, grinding of the whole
body, cruel tortures of the devil come upon me, only that I attain to
Jesus Christ." Without a fully articulated theology, but with enormous
rhetorical power, Ignatius crafted his final journey to Rome into an
exemplary paradigm that made martyrdom a means of salvation for
others and glorification for oneself to any believer willing to follow
that bloody path.

Especially for those Christians who were slaves, a substantial proportion of the Church's demographic, Ignatius's example was inspir-

ing. Christianity promised to liberate people from the gods of this world; with the uncovering of the divine Son within them, even the oppressed could hope to share in the ongoing, spiritual life of Jesus, God's Son raised from the dead. And with that life, they got their own bodies back from the world around them, whatever the demands of their worldly masters. Ignatius was a man who despised the effort to break his body, because his spirit was already free. Ignatius was focused so completely on the result he was after, his martyrdom, that he did not fully articulate the reasons for the imperative to sacrifice himself that he put into action. But the man Ignatius wrote one of his letters to, Polycarp of Smyrna in Asia Minor, revealed how deeply the imperative to become a martyr was rooted in the Aqedah.

The special power of *The Martyrdom of Polycarp* lies in its articulation of the martyr's own motivation as well as of how his sacrifice was viewed by dedicated believers. The Aqedah features at the center of attention in both regards. Ignatius's letters founded and fed a Christian movement of sacrificial martyrdom, but his letters were not followed up by a contemporary description of his death (although later legend filled in that gap). The first known contemporary account of a martyr's actual death with an articulation of his theology of martyrdom was written in order to glorify Ignatius's fellow bishop, Polycarp.

Written by an unknown hagiographer in Smyrna, and dating from shortly after 156 C.E., when Polycarp died, *The Martyrdom of Polycarp* portrays the events leading up to the bishop's execution as providential, and makes its hero into a replica of Christ: "For almost all the proceedings happened in order that the Lord from above might show us martyrdom according to the Gospel" (*Martyrdom of Polycarp* 1.1). Just as Ignatius's sacrificial language from early on in his *Letter to the Romans* highlights the meaning of martyrdom as he refers to it in the letter as a whole, so *The Martyrdom of Polycarp* shows in its initial, thematic statement that it sees its hero as fulfilling the specific example of Jesus in the New Testament.

Polycarp's own experiences and actions reinforce the theme of his inevitable suffering. After acceding to his community's urging to flee from Roman persecutors in the city of Smyrna proper into the surrounding countryside, a vision convinced Polycarp—now eighty-six years old and no doubt weary of the constant effort involved in evading soldiers—that the time for flight had passed. During prayer in a farmhouse he fell into vision, and in that state he saw the cushion he was lying on in flames. This made Polycarp realize that his death by fire was God's will, and he decided to give himself up when the Roman police at last caught up with him. After they could not convince him to relent in his refusal to sacrifice to Caesar as to a god, they conducted him back to Smyrna (*Martyrdom of Polycarp* 5.1–8.3) and to the stadium, where he would have to choose between apostasy and death.

There Polycarp confronted the proconsul, who urged the old man to be prudent and follow along with general custom: "Swear by Caesar's spirit, repent, say, 'Destroy the atheists,'" the proconsul urged. This follows a frequent motif in martyrologies, which probably reflects what sometimes really did happen: the persecutors show their victims pity and argue that the demand to acknowledge the emperor's divine status is more pro forma than a demand for personal belief. But in the end (*Martyrdom of Polycarp* 9.1–9.3), Polycarp simply asserts that he is not about to abandon Christ after eighty-six years of discipleship.

The martyr's concern is not with self-defense, or even with convincing the magistrate that Christians should not be tortured in order to turn them from their faith. In fact, Polycarp issues a flat refusal of the opportunity to defend his beliefs before the crowd, saying that if the proconsul really wanted to learn the truth about Christianity, he would do so on a private occasion, not in front of the rabble gathered in eager expectation of a public killing (*Martyrdom of Polycarp* 10.1–10.2). With aristocratic aplomb, Polycarp goes on to say that he does not consider such a mob "worthy for a defense to be made to them." Democratic debate is made to seem beneath contempt, when compared to the persuasive power and salvific effect of a martyr's death.

Instead of arguing for his life to be spared or for toleration of Christianity, Polycarp uses what bargaining power he has to influence how he would be killed. He is bound on his pyre, and then the executioners prepare to nail his limbs to stakes, so that once the cords burn through he will not be able to escape the flames. But Polycarp asks them not to do so, explaining that his vision of the flaming pillow had assured him of his ability to remain in the fire without being fastened (*Martyrdom of Polycarp* 11.1–13.3): he is to die as a *bound* victim. The executioners oblige, and this means that Polycarp dies in a way that accords not only with his vision, but also—and specifically—with the ram in Genesis 22 (*Martyrdom of Polycarp* 14.1): "So they did not nail him, but they bound him, and he put his hands behind him and was bound, just as a ram distinguished from a great flock for an offering, a sacrifice by fire prepared, acceptable to God."

Following the example of Christ, Polycarp is more like the ram that was actually sacrificed on Moriah than he is like Isaac, who was redeemed by the ram. The ram prefigured Christ, and Polycarp's death brings the reality of Christ's sacrifice as well as its symbolic type in Isaac directly into the experience of all who saw him die according to the *Martyrdom*. In that way, the redemption of Christ is extended by this exemplary death, and Polycarp thanks God for letting him accomplish that (*Martyrdom of Polycarp* 14.2), having "received a share among the number of the martyrs in the cup of Christ."

Unlike the case of Ignatius in his letters, Polycarp's *Martyrdom* moves beyond the intention of the martyr into the response of those who witnessed the death, weaving visionary insight into a portrayal of literal events, so that it is impossible to disentangle actual happenings from collective vision. The value of the text does not reside in its accuracy as a chronicle of events, but in its portrayal of what people who committed themselves to becoming martyrs, and encouraged others to become martyrs, believed was possible when faith was strong. The *Martyrdom* describes a disembodied voice addressing Polycarp as he entered the arena (*Martyrdom of Polycarp* 9.1), and then later, with ferocious detail, the shape of the fire around the martyr forming a chamber.

What the witnesses see within the flaming chamber amounts to a religious vision that is at the same time recounted as a literal description (*Martyrdom of Polycarp* 15.2): "He was in the midst not as burning flesh, but as baking bread or as gold and silver refined in a furnace. For we also apprehended an aroma such as scenting incense or some other of the precious spices." Now the ram is fully sacrificed, complete with the incense that normally accompanied ancient rituals, and bearing the image of Christ, down to the smell of baked bread, another allusion—as in Ignatius's imagery—to the flesh of Christ in the Eucharist.

The executioners, horrified by his miraculous transformation at the moment of what was supposed to have been a disgraceful death, stab Polycarp's burning body to hasten his demise. That, however, only compounds their dilemma, because a dove—the primal symbol of the Holy Spirit that also appears in Jesus' baptism—issues from Polycarp's breast in the account (*Martyrdom of Polycarp* 16.1). That forms an elegant and powerful symmetry: the same Spirit that descended upon Jesus to guide him in the way of the cross returns to its divine source whenever a martyr dies. Finally, as the martyr's blood flows out of him, its potency and its abundance are so great that it quenches the flames of execution. Although the executioners in their fury go on to reduce Polycarp's corpse to its bones (*Martyrdom of Polycarp* 16.1–18.3), he had already taken his place as an angel among the angels (cf. 2.3); his martyrdom assured his own place in heaven and opened the way for others to follow. Here both the martyr himself and those who witness the martyrdom are accorded a vision on earth, in the midst of suffering, which links them to the sustaining power of Christ in the heavens, where his sacrifice secured a place for all who follow him.

The *Martyrdom of Polycarp* glorifies the martyr as a completed sacrifice, and specifically as the ram that redeemed Isaac and foretold the crucifixion of Christ. But the *Martyrdom*'s aim goes considerably beyond the praise of a single person, although the curmudgeonly character of Polycarp does provide one of the singular attractions of this work. In the end, Polycarp merely illustrates what is supposed to be a much wider program for Christian behavior. He exemplifies "martyrdom according to the Gospel" (1.1) so that others will take up his pattern of discipleship. Near the end of the work, the *Martyr-*

dom praises Polycarp as a distinguished teacher and eminent martyr, "whose martyrdom, happening according to the Gospel of Christ, all desire to imitate" (*Martyrdom of Polycarp* 19.1).

Despite his idiosyncrasy, Polycarp became an exemplary case of the aspirations of all who face martyrdom rather than a unique instance. The *Martyrdom* states in its general praise of all Christian martyrs (2.3):

> And attending to the grace of Christ they despised worldly tortures, purchasing eternal life in one hour. And the fire of the brutal torturers was cold to them, because before their eyes they had escaped from the eternal and never-quenched fire. And with the eyes of the heart they looked up to the good things kept for those who have endured, which neither ear has heard nor eye has seen, nor has arisen in the heart of man, but which have been shown by the Lord to those who were indeed no longer men but already angels.

Framing the martyrs' reward in the terms of the avoidance of hellfire, the *Martyrdom* signals the early Church's appeal to its followers to trade sin and suffering in this world for glory in the next. Every person who dies for his faith follows Jesus and Isaac, and is transformed into the angel that Jesus promised each resurrected disciple would become (Mark 12:25), the same kind of being that delivered Isaac from his father's hand (Genesis 22:11–12) on Mount Moriah.

The Martyrdom of Polycarp incites younger men in particular to become martyrs. As in the case of Eleazar in 2 Maccabees, the bishop's age is emphasized to give an example to the youth, to shame them—if necessary—by showing what the old man could do, in contrast with any tendency they might have to flinch from suffering. The *Martyrdom* refers to specific cases of young people who either followed, or failed to follow, Polycarp's realization of Jesus' passion.

When the proconsul and his minions attempted to convince Germanicus, a youth who had been arrested, to betray his faith by threatening him with wild animals, Germanicus "violently pulled the beast to himself, wanting more quickly to be released from their unrighteous and lawless life" (*Martyrdom of Polycarp* 3.1). Here martyrdom is an end that is aggressively sought once the arrest has been effected, and the martyr's cooperation in death consummates his glory, as in the case of Polycarp himself. The *Martyrdom* pursues the connection with Polycarp, because Germanicus's heroism makes the crowd yell out in fury, "Destroy the atheists! Polycarp must be searched out!" (*Martyrdom of Polycarp* 3.2). The crowd understands, as the reader is supposed to, that Bishop Polycarp inspired self-sacrifice in his people well before his arrest; his own eventual death put into action the pattern he had long taught.

In tragic contrast, "one, named Quintus, a Phrygian recently come from Phrygia, cringed when he saw the beasts" (*Martyrdom of Polycarp* 4.1). Quintus had come forward voluntarily, and his pride in wishing to make himself a martyr went hand in hand with the eventual proof of his cowardice. The same self-regard that can make a person seek the glory of confronting danger might in the end unhinge him in the face of danger. That is the reason, the *Martyrdom of Polycarp* explains, that "we do not commend those who deliver themselves over, since the Gospel does not teach so." Although the zealous pursuit of martyrdom is criticized, that is not only because recommending suicide is wrong, but also because experience had shown that courting death in this way betrayed a self-interest that might easily dissolve any real willingness to die for Christ into craven acquiescence to the demands of Roman authorities.

This program for the Church during the second century later proved extremely effective. Although the total number of martyrs between Stephen's death in 32 c.e. and Constantine's Edict of Milan (which ordered the toleration of Christianity) in 313 c.e. probably came to only a few thousand, they eventually changed the religious policies of the Roman Empire. Even more deeply, the memory of the martyrs endured in the Christian tradition as the heroic ideal of how accepting agony and death could bring a taste of heaven to oneself and to others.

An acute philosophical mind, second-century emperor (and noted philosopher) Marcus Aurelius already knew that the persecution of

Christians was creating a problem for Rome: the deaths of the martyrs aroused admiration among some spectators, winning the *superstitio* new recruits. In practical terms, martyrs reinforced the claim of an Ignatius or a Polycarp that martyrdom did not merely imitate Christ's redemptive work, but extended his redemption to others. Marcus Aurelius was himself dedicated to Stoic philosophy, and his *Meditations* mark an important moment in the popular influence of Stoicism. One of the Stoics' ideals was a good death, which could include committing suicide in order to avoid the kind of shame that would destroy one's reputation or life's work. The great philosophers and statesmen Cicero and Seneca (from the first centuries B.C.E. and C.E. respectively) exemplified the nobility of heroic suicide when faced with political ruin. But if death for one's principles is noble, how could anyone deny that Christians also embodied that same nobility?

This was an especially vexing matter for Marcus Aurelius, since he had permitted persecutions and pogroms against Christians to take place, notably in 177 C.E. in the Rhone Valley in modern France. Marcus had to confront an irony: he was arranging for Christians to do what a Stoic might find noble, and to win more Christian converts in the process. Christians had already internalized the very Stoic virtues, including a noble, disciplined death, which Marcus promoted. This process had begun long before Marcus or the rise of the ethos of martyrdom in Christianity, and is already reflected within the New Testament in concepts such as the "word" (*logos*) of God in John's Gospel and the corporate, divine "body" of enlightened believers in Paul's letters. But during the second century, Christian thinkers went on to craft the view of martyrdom they had inherited from Judaism to suit Greco-Roman fashion. Marcus responded by accusing Christians of exhibitionism.

The *Martyrdom of Polycarp* had actually answered Marcus's objection before he voiced it. Sobriety in the face of persecution, and a refusal to seek death out, had been clearly taught as the virtues Polycarp instilled and embodied. During the whole of this period, Christianity saw a steady growth, as a result of both births to already Christian parents and conversion. Martyrdom did not interfere with this growth. In fact, the noble resistance of Christians to persecution, even when it resulted in death, sowed the promise of faith in others.

By the end of the second century a widespread conviction among Christians held that Christ and Isaac together defined the heavenly paradigm of sacrifice. Both were victims, both bore the wood of the offering, and the aim of both was to shed blood for the redemption of others, leaving an example to the followers of Christ.

To the Fathers of the Church, the combined examples of Christ and Isaac offered Christians the equivalent of a weapon to defeat an unjust empire. In a brilliant attack on Roman policy, written in North Africa around 197 C.E., Tertullian of Carthage excoriated the imperial policy of "don't ask, don't tell" as applied to Christianity. Judges *should* punish crime, he said, but their behavior in the case of Christianity is bizarre, because they do not punish Christians who confess their faith, provided they then renounce it by acknowledging the gods of Rome. How can Christianity be a crime, when you are released instead of punished when you confess? And what kind of judge would believe both the confession of Christianity and the renunciation of Christianity by the same person in the same trial? As if answering Marcus Aurelius directly, Tertullian went on to write (*Apology* 50.1–50.2): "Certainly we wish to suffer; but in the way of the soldier and war. No man readily suffers the inevitable fear and danger, but he battles with all his powers and, victorious in battle, he rejoices . . . ."

By this time Tertullian could simply allude to the motif of Christ bearing the cross being like Isaac carrying the wood, because the sacrificial typology of the Aqedah had been repeated many times during the second century. Tertullian argued that martyrs "sowed Christian blood" on promising soil (*Apologeticus* 21.25). "The blood of Christians is seed"; its potency was such that its growth and flourishing was only hastened by persecution: "We are made more whenever mown down by you" (*Apology* 50.13), so that martyrdom is a kind of "lure" (*inlecebra*). The more the Romans took the bait, the more believers were captured for Christ.

Although the Fathers used the example of Isaac and careful reflection to urge martyrs on, martyrdom never ceased to be a folk movement. The mysticism of death as communion with Christ became increasingly insistent during the Patristic period. Melito, the second-century bishop of Sardis, is of particular interest because his writing *On the Pascha* was popular, intended for public recitation at the time of the paschal celebration of Easter. He argued, in an eloquent but inaccurate folk etymology, that the Aramaic term *paskha* (that is, Passover, when Christians celebrated the resurrection of Jesus) derived from the Greek verb meaning to suffer, *paskhein.* Melito expressed the idea with a poetic eloquence that won him many admirers in his own time and later.

Melito's evocation of the suffering of Christ as the true meaning both of the crucifixion and the Scriptures of Israel helps explain why the image of the Suffering Servant from Isaiah and of Isaac on Moriah was so easily identified with Jesus in early Christianity (*On Passover* 46–69):

What is the Pascha?
It obtains its name from its characteristic:
    from "suffer" comes suffering.
Learn therefore who is the Suffering One,
    and who shares the suffering of the Suffering One,
    and why the Lord is present on the earth
    to clothe himself with the Suffering One
    and carry him off to the heights of heaven.
It is he that delivered us from slavery to liberty,
    from darkness to light,
    from death to life,
    from tyranny to eternal royalty;
    and made us a new priesthood
    and an eternal people personal to Him.
He is the Pascha of our salvation.
It is he who in many ways endured many things:
It is he that was in Abel murdered,
    and in Isaac bound,
    and in Jacob exiled,
    and in Joseph sold,
    and in Moses exposed,
    and in the lamb slain,

and in David persecuted,
and in the prophets dishonored.

Recitations of this kind made the image of Jesus being bound with Isaac so well known that the Fathers could refer to it in passing with the assurance that the image would be understood and appreciated. Melito had already taught Christians so well to "Learn therefore who is the Suffering One, and who shares the suffering of the Suffering One," that they could readily understand they were to be new Isaacs, following the example of the One who had completed the sacrifice of Isaac. That was key to his argument that, while Jesus was bound by his executioners as Isaac was, and carried his cross as Isaac had brought the wood for sacrifice, Jesus suffered and completed the paschal offering, while Isaac did not.

Believers who witnessed martyrdoms actually thought the martyrs *looked like Christ* as they suffered after the example of the one who completed the sacrifice of the Aqedah. During the persecution under Marcus Aurelius, a young woman named Blandina gave an example, as a later Father of the Church said, to show "that all who suffer for Christ's glory have fellowship forever with the living God" (Eusebius, *History of the Church* 5.1.41). So close was her identification with Christ, when she was hung naked on a stake for beasts to eat, onlookers thought it was the crucified Jesus, and at her death her martyrdom states that she was "sacrificed."

That imagery of women becoming male, visually identified with Jesus in their valiant witness to Christ, became persistent. The most famous example comes from Carthage, during a period of renewed persecution early in the third century C.E. The noblewoman Perpetua recorded her dream prior to her execution (*Martyrdom of Perpetua* 10):

And as I knew I had been condemned to the beasts, I was amazed that they did not send them out at me. And an Egyptian with a vicious look came out against me with his seconds to fight me. And handsome young men came out to me as seconds and supporters. And I was stripped naked, and became a man, and my supporters began to rub me down with oil as they do before combat.

Because Perpetua had at this stage recently given birth, the imagery is all the more striking. Despite her weakness, she is to do battle with a monstrous Egyptian, probably a symbol of the Roman emperor Severus, who coiffed his hair and beard to look like the Egyptian god Serapis. No matter what his apparent power, the martyr's faith proves stronger.

Early Christian literature repeats many such stories, often so gruesome modern readers prefer to believe they could have nothing to do with actual events, and some modern historians play them down, much as they try to explain away human sacrifice in Antiquity. It does not suit the modern stereotype of the Romans as tolerant pagans to remember their torture of Christians, and many Christians today are reluctant to own up to the veneration of martyrs that is part and parcel of their faith. Martyrdom was central to Judaism before Christianity emerged, but Christianity is the first religion ever—and so far the only religion in history—to make martyrdom a permanent demand of faith, even absent persecution. Coming as they did during Christianity's formative period, Rome's policies helped give permanent shape to this dimension of Christian faith. From the time of the Epistle to the Hebrews, the classical Christianity developed both by the Fathers of the Church and by their less educated, anonymous contemporaries who told countless stories of martyrdom emphasized that giving one's life in testimony to the truth of Christ sealed one's true identity as a Christian. That demand has been inherent in Christianity since it emerged in the Greco-Roman world, for believers to realize in their lives or to finesse.

Carthage proved to be the city that put martyrdom at the very center of the Christian faith, and linked it irrevocably to the Aqedah. After the time of Tertullian, and Perpetua's martydom, the third-century bishop of Carthage, Cyprian, taught that every time the priest offers the Eucharistic bread and wine, he repeats the sacrifice of Jesus on the cross. This theology of sacrifice, long dominant in the history of the Church and still current today, was developed with a conscious comparison in mind between Abraham offering Isaac and God permitting Jesus to be crucified. As Bernhard Lang has written, "Eating the sacred bread and drinking the sacred wine, Christians were assimilated with their Lord and thus made ready to follow him even unto death." Isaac prefigured the sacrifice of Christ, Christ completed the offering on Moriah, and every Christian both witnessed that death every time he or she took part in the Eucharist, and prepared to follow the example of Isaac's patience and Christ's, to the ultimate sacrifice if necessary.

Through the changes and chances of Roman imperial policy, some of them surreal in their violence, martyrdom remained a fixed virtue among early Christians, who saw martyrs as people who enjoyed eternity with God in Christ and whose remains and memory conveyed the power of salvation as well as healing. Eusebius, the Christian historian who lived through the last period of persecution under the emperor Diocletian (303–305 C.E.), speaks of women hung naked and upside down for their flesh to be scraped off (*History of the Church* 8.9.1), and of an imperial servant named Peter who was scourged to the bone, had vinegar and salt put in his wounds, and then was slowly roasted in a failed effort to get him to take part in idolatrous sacrifice (*History of the Church* 8.6.2–8.6.4).

Yet the exalted status of these heroes by no means required that Christians across the board should become martyrs: Pliny explicitly says that most of those he interrogated confessed and repented. In fact, from the *Martyrdom of Polycarp* on, Christian teachers warned *against* seeking to be martyred. Eusebius relates that, after his father was killed in Alexandria during the persecution under the emperor Severus, a young man sought martyrdom (Eusebius, *History of the Church* 6.2.2–6.2.6), but his mother forced him to remain at home by stealing his clothing.

The young man was Origen, arguably the most gifted theologian in the history of the Church. Among his many attainments, he was the first of the Fathers to provide an answer to the question: How could martyrdom be effective enough to redeem humanity, when so few people actually were martyrs? He had every reason to provide a cogent answer to that question, and his response set in motion a theological explanation for martyrdom that, as we will see in the next chapter, lives on to our time.

V

Gnostic Laughter, Roman Pornography, Blood Payment

Blood has featured prominently in the West since the Middle Ages as the price that must be paid for serious wrongdoing. Nations have demanded it from one another in war; courts have required it of criminals; blood feuds have taken countless lives in factional fighting. Through centuries of contention fueled by increasing technological expertise, the sufferings of the innocent—and the capacity of a guiltless person to give his blood as a vicarious offering to resolve violence—have run like a red thread alongside the price of blood in the dark story of human relations. To this day, bloodshed seems to many people the price of history, with the death of innocents a collateral necessity.

But just as the necessary sacrifice of children was a myth of the Stone Age, the medieval idea that blood needs to be shed in order for conflict to be resolved reflects a mythological conviction more than an insight into human nature. By understanding the connections between these two myths, each requiring young blood to be spilled for its own reasons, we will be able to see why modern conflicts are still propelled by cultural forces of which the antagonists are barely conscious. Those connections, in turn, linking primordial impulses of sacrifice with nationalistic ideologies, were forged by the inheritance of the cult of the martyrs in Christianity between the Patristic period and the Middle Ages. The logic of martyrdom, fascinating and deadly, lives on in a reflex that is no less potent for being thousands of years old.

Christians celebrated the nobility of their martyrs in stories that describe human pain in literally loving detail, rejoicing in the capacity of their heroic deaths to spread faith. But they also had to ask: Why did God choose such a course for his people? If God guided the paths of the faithful, in his mind what purpose did the pain and the mess and the humiliation of their gruesome executions really serve? Christians' desire to know why God permits evil to happen in the world went beyond the usual human perplexity in the face of disease, famine, and natural disaster. They saw the most powerful empire on earth torture and kill virtuous people who believed in God: Why God allowed that was a grievous existential issue.

In engaging the issue, early Christians associated the blood of martyrs so closely with Christ's blood that they made them virtually identical. The Fathers described the value of the collective blood of Christ *and* his martyrs in sacrificial terms. Animal blood had been viewed in the Jerusalem Temple, as well as at altars all over the known world, as the most sacred element in sacrifice. When blood was poured out before a deity, that symbolized life itself returning to its divine source, so that life might issue forth from the god again, multiplied by divine blessing. Priests—whether Israelite or not—sometimes spattered blood on participants in sacrifice, to purify them from any pollution and confirm their mutual festivity as being more than a communal gathering, but a sharing of the divine world and its life-giving power. Blood invoked sacrificial power in two dimensions: pleasing God, and readying human beings to take part in offerings. For Christians, Isaac, Christ, and blood joined to form the perfect sacrifice that God desired, and at the same time gave believers the model of true martyrdom.

Alongside Isaac, the Suffering Servant—a mysterious figure from the Book of Isaiah (chapter 53)—found a permanent place as a type of Christ in Christianity during the second century. In the Hebrew text of Isaiah, this servant of God is not specifically identified: he personifies humiliation and rejection, with his suffering and death described as a sacrificial offering for the benefit of others. After Jesus' humiliating death by crucifixion, many of his followers came to see Isaiah's Suffering Servant as a reference to Jesus.

The apostle Philip first made this connection near the time of the crucifixion in 32 C.E. (Acts 8:26–40), and it became axiomatic among Christians a hundred years later. In the pseudonymous *Epistle of Barnabas*, the Servant in Isaiah becomes a type of Christ, one of many that show—*Barnabas* insists—that the true meaning of the covenant with Moses belongs now to the Christians, not to Jews. *The Epistle of Barnabas* fatefully maintains (5.2) that in addition to Jesus' offering of blood, still more blood—the blood of his true followers who prove they are true by their suffering—also needs to be shed.

Isaiah's Suffering Servant is celebrated in *Barnabas* as a sheep or a lamb brought to be slaughtered, an image that links Isaac, the Servant, and Jesus as the paschal lamb together with the fate of every believer. Payment in blood for the fact of being mortal was sooner or later to be demanded of absolutely everyone, because Jesus' death showed the significance of *each* human being's death as a transition to being raised from the dead. The last chapter showed that by the end of the second century, Christians widely claimed that Jesus was actually bound along with Isaac at the time of the Aqedah, and that Isaac was a type of every believer, as well as of Christ. That confident assertion reveals the deep extent of belief that Jesus represented an eternal reality that could not be limited to historical data about the teacher from Nazareth.

Although the Fathers of the second century insisted on making a strong connection between Jesus' death and believers' deaths, their argument proceeded more by metaphor than by logic. The Suffering Servant of Isaiah as the type of Christ showed, along with Isaac on Moriah, that Jesus' sacrifice on the cross superseded Jewish worship in the Temple with its literal, physical sacrifices, and at the same time mandated offerings in the future by means of martyrdom in Christ's name. This argument operates by metaphor, image, analogy, and allusion, yet comes up short of giving a convincing, logical explanation of *why* martyrdom should be theologically necessary, when Jesus' death had superseded sacrifice.

The connection of Isaac, Jesus, and martyrdom remained more metaphorical than logical until the third century. Yet the connection was forged with a poetic urgency and a command of imagery that assured its wide acceptance, and its contribution to the ethos of martyrdom in Christianity during the ancient period and later.

By no means, however, did all Christians agree that the readiness to be a martyr was a requirement of faith. The willingness to follow Isaac and the way of suffering seemed natural to those believers who were moved by the metaphorical power of the Aqedah, but a more analytic perspective favored another approach altogether. After all, anyone with real knowledge understood with little difficulty that the Roman emperor was not really a god, and that the idols that soldiers tried to force Christians to worship did not truly represent divinity. Because this point of view was based on an argument from knowledge (*gnosis* in Greek) of the divine, and was associated with groups of people who explicitly quested for this divine *Gnosis*, it has been recognized from Antiquity until the present as a Gnostic alternative.

The most direct way to deny that martyrdom was necessary, a way some Gnostics pursued, was to claim that Jesus himself had never truly suffered or died on the cross. What if someone else had suffered in his place, for example as a result of mistaken identity? The ancient Gnostic teacher Basilides, in Alexandria, made that suggestion according to his opponents. Basilides claimed that, at the crucifixion, the physical appearance of Simon of Cyrene (the man commandeered to carry Jesus' cross; Mark 15:21) changed, so that he was mistaken for Jesus and executed instead of Jesus.

This theory, originating in the second century, found its way into the Qur'an as well as a revisionist scholar's work that was published in 1965, and still finds adherents today. Basilides added insult to injury in his portrait of the crucifixion, according to Irenaeus, the Catholic bishop and scourge of Gnostics during the second century, by claiming that while Simon of Cyrene was crucified and dying, Jesus—an incorporeal power who could change his forms at will to disguise himself—stood by and laughed outright.

That laughter has long perplexed modern commentators, and some of them have dismissed the image as being deliberately blasphemous. On this view, either Basilides was mocking Christ or Irenaeus was mocking Basilides. Yet as a matter of fact, the laughing Savior who cheats death—not necessarily making Simon a stand-in double at the crucifixion, but because the true Savior is spiritual and incorporeal, suffering only in flesh, not spirit—is well known from the writings found at Nag Hammadi (in a fourth-century Gnostic library discovered in 1945) as well as other documents. A related portrayal from the second century distinguishes between Jesus as a physical being and the Christ as an entirely spiritual reality. The two were joined during Jesus' life in this theology, but went their separate ways when he died. At the crucifixion, Jesus feels no pain, but then shouts from the cross that his divine power has left him. Physically, he died at that point, but the spiritual reality of the Christ was taken up to heaven, his natural home.

Even though the picture of the laughing Jesus that Irenaeus scorns may seem bizarre, this image represents a definite theology shared by Catholics as well as Gnostics during the second century and relates directly to Abraham's offering on Mount Moriah. In their theology of Jesus' death as fulfilling the example of Isaac, Gnostics and their sympathizers could actually adhere more closely to the biblical text than their Catholic colleague Irenaeus could. After all, the name Isaac *means* "he will laugh" (Genesis 17:16–21; 21:1–7), which is exactly what the boy Isaac must have done when Abraham found the ram to replace him on Moriah. An early Christian representation of the offering of Isaac, from the third-century c.e. catacomb of Callixtus in Rome, shows father and son after the divine intervention, both of them standing with arms lifted high to rejoice in prayer, a proud-looking ram to their right. Their faces are slightly indistinct, but their mouths are open wide with joy, praise, and—it is reasonable to surmise—laughter.

Intrinsically, the "laughing Christ" that has puzzled and shocked modern scholars, who have dismissed the image as a Gnostic parody of the Gospels, derives from the dedication of ancient Christians generally, both Gnostic and Catholic, to see the reality of Christ in Isaac. Basilides' Jesus laughs because a replacement is found for him, while a subtler form of the same thought pictured Jesus as laughing because his suffering was only superficial, a matter for transient flesh rather than eternal spirit. This was a strong image, which Catholics could not—and did not—ignore. Catholics did not reject Christ's laughter; they rather found their own reasons for Christ to laugh, just as Abraham and Isaac had.

A prominent Catholic thinker at the end of the second century drew on the metaphor linking Isaac carrying the wood and Christ bearing his cross, and on the etymological meaning of Isaac's name: "Isaac laughed for a mystical reason, to prefigure the joy with which the Lord has filled us, in saving us from destruction through his blood" (Clement of Alexandria, *Paidagogos* 1.5.23). This interpretation aims to get the last laugh on the Gnostics, by insisting that it is precisely *in suffering* that Christ shows his divinity. Yet this laughter comes at the expense of accepting the basic point of the Gnostic laughter of Jesus: at the end of his ordeal, Jesus suffered to show how suffering is transcended, and that pain is laughable. What has been falsely characterized as a purely Gnostic and derisive image carried Catholics as well as Gnostics along to see that spiritual identity could not be crushed by the death of their mortal bodies.

In debate with their Gnostic counterparts, and in their desire to understand why martyrdom was necessary, Catholics at last found an answer in the work of Origen of Alexandria during the third century. To Origen's mind, there is complete transparency between Christ's suffering and that of the believer, in that both bring about a union between God and humanity: "Just as those who served the altar according to the Law of Moses thought they obtained forgiveness of sins for the Jews by the blood of goats and bulls, so also the souls of those who have been beheaded for their witness to Jesus do not serve the heavenly altar in vain but mediate forgiveness of sins to those who pray." Martyrdom literally brought salvation, just as Christ did.

Origen cited 2 Maccabees at length, and emphasized the example of the mother who saw her sons die before her eyes, driving home his overarching ethical point: piety and love for God, in the face of the most painful agonies and the severest torments, is far more powerful than any other emotional bond. He even insists that true love of God and human weakness cannot dwell together in the human heart.

Origen asserts that some people are redeemed by the precious blood of the martyrs, just as the Church had been redeemed by the precious blood of Jesus. The martyr is united so thoroughly to Christ that his blood and Christ's become one. Origen pursued his metaphorical understanding of the link between Christ and each martyr through their mutual connection with the Aqedah in what were by his time classic images. Origen also seems well aware of the principles behind the portrait of the laughing Savior. He alludes to these previous traditions with masterful economy, while tying Jesus' death to the title "lamb of God," attributed to him from the time of John's Gospel:

So Christ suffers [like Isaac], but in his flesh, and he underwent death, but in the flesh, of which the ram is here the form. John said, similarly, Look—the lamb of God, who takes away sin from the world. The *Logos* [Word], however, which is Christ according to the spirit, of whom Isaac is the image, remained in incorruptibility.

Origen's influence lies not only in his capacity effortlessly to synthesize earlier approaches to this theme together with his own fresh, innovative extensions. Endlessly curious and inventive, he persistently pushed into an investigation of God's ultimate reason for choosing the way of the cross.

Frequently, later theologians of the Church wished that Origen could have resisted his own speculative curiosity. He once posed the question to himself, for example: What would God do, were the devil to repent? Unlikely though that event may seem, Origen reflected on the issue and concluded that God, to remain true to his nature, would of course forgive Satan.

The idea was so scandalous that three centuries later, when the doctrine of an eternal hell with infinite punishment and endless vengeance for evil had become canonical, the emperor Justinian convened the Second Council of Constantinople in 553 to consign to hell anyone who "says or thinks that the punishment of demons and of impious men is only temporary, and will one day have an end." This is the last "anathema," or condemnation for heresy, that the emperor Justinian sought against Origen and "Origenism."

Yet even as the increasingly literalistic Church found less and less time for Origen and finally turned him into a heretic, it embraced one of his most daring and speculative flights. Origen could not leave open the issue of God's purpose in permitting the death of his Son. The metaphor of a sacrifice, linked with the offering of Isaac, gave his mind what he needed in order to pursue the matter to a logical outcome, an outcome that ultimately included an interpretation of the Aqedah as well.

Although Origen was a subtle, wide-ranging thinker, he came up with an awkward conception of the significance of Christ's death, by imagining God handing over his Son to the devil in order to pay a fine. Origen taught that, by means of the crucifixion, God paid a ransom to the devil for the sins of humanity as a whole. The notion of God striking a deal with the devil at the cost of his own Son may seem ludicrous, until you remember that, in Origen's view, God and Satan might still come to an accord with one another on the other side of history. The crucifixion began that epochal reconciliation, by literally giving the devil his due.

How Origen came to this conclusion, and how his suggestion was embraced with uncritical zeal up until and through the Middle Ages, centrally involves the interpretation of the Aqedah, which he wove into his picture of a transaction between God and Satan. In a catalog of places in the Bible where, according to Origen, the devil appears, first place goes to the serpent in the Book of Genesis who beguiled

Eve. But the very next case from Genesis, unexpectedly, is the Aqe-dah. The angel who speaks in Genesis 22:12 says, "Now I know that you fear God, and for my sake have not withheld your beloved son whom you love"; since God knows all in every moment of time, Origen concluded that God himself could not have been speaking here. It must have been an angel with less knowledge than God—in short, the devil!

Because this angel is really the tempter, the divine intervention comes in the form of the ram, which Origen had learned from Melito was a type of Christ. Like Melito, Origen also linked Christ with the lamb of Passover, yet also emphasized the sacrificial imagery of the scapegoat (Leviticus 16). As the scapegoat was driven away into the wilderness on the Day of Atonement (Yom Kippur) to carry off the sins of Israel, so, said Origen, Christ descended into the underworld to free all generations from the consequences of sin. The idea of Christ as the scapegoat, which modern scholars associate with the theory of René Girard (or his predecessor, James Frazer), in fact reaches back to Origen, and—as we are about to discover in the next section—to a surprising source prior to Origen.

By associating Christ with the lamb of Passover, the scapegoat of the Day of Atonement, and the ram discovered by Abraham on Moriah all within the typology of Isaac, Origen had produced a rich, baroque, and at the same time lucid expression of the eternal sacrifice that Christ offered. By portraying that sacrifice as a ransom paid to the devil, Origen also explained the eternal value of that sacrifice: in principle, every sin ever committed, or ever to be committed, had been compensated for by the crucifixion, because after the payment of Jesus' life, the devil could expect no further recompense.

In framing this theology of atonement by Christ's blood, which compensated for the sins of humanity as a whole, past and present, Origen was extending a line of thought that, somewhat like the typology of Isaac, had already been partially developed. Christian thought, once it had conceived of Christ as replacing sacrifice, as it had done since the Epistle to the Hebrews, had difficulty conceiving of why God would really be pleased with sacrifice in any case. Every ritual operation seemed to have resulted from Jewish misunderstanding and literalism, while the spiritual meaning of the Israelite Scriptures pointed to Christ's sacrifice alone. From the time of the Epistle to the Hebrews, and through *The Epistle of Barnabas*, as well as the writings of Justin Martyr, Irenaeus, Clement of Alexandria, and Origen, this approach to the whole question of sacrifice became more and more entrenched. That ancient Christian attitude helps explain why today many people assume that a devotion to "ritual" rather than to "spirituality" is a sign of religious immaturity, why Judaism is often dismissed as a throwback form of faith, and why it is widely supposed that ultimately the only true test of belief is the willingness to die for one's faith in the way Christ did.

This deep-seated paradigm in Christian sensibility—which involves attitudes toward ritual, Judaism, sacrifice, the "spiritual" interpretation of Scripture, martyrdom, and Christ's purpose all at once—left theologians of the Church bereft of means to appreciate why the Israelites had ever conceived of God as enjoying sacrifice in the first place. The divine pleasure that resulted in God deciding not to flood the earth again after Noah's offering and to permit people to eat meat for the first time, to preserve Jerusalem after King David's offering, as well as to save Isaac's life from Abraham's knife, is not a part of Origen's sacrificial equation.

Because Origen deliberately replaced anything approaching a historical evaluation of texts with his typological approach, fixated in the fashion of his age on eternity rather than happenstance, he was in no position to recover the underlying purpose of sacrifice in Israel's Scriptures. Indeed, he thought the aim of theology was to transcend any such earlier belief with faith in Christ. The stage was set for Jesus' sacrificial offering to be mistaken as a crude commercial transaction, ironically with the justification that this corresponded to the spiritual meaning of Scripture.

By the time of Origen, the primordial logic of sacrificial redemption had been largely lost in Christianity. "Redemption" had meant more than merely paying money in the Hebrew Bible, although payment also was sometimes involved. At base, sacrifice spared one life as a result of divine enjoyment of another life. In Exodus, for example, Israelites are commanded to offer the firstborn males of all domestic animals in commemoration of their liberation of Egypt, but to redeem every firstborn son (13:11–16). Each is "redeemed" by the offering of an animal. A person could be neither sacrificed nor killed, and so firstborn human males needed to be redeemed.

There are alternative customs of redemption reflected in the Torah, which correspond to differing sources. By a priestly reckoning, the life of each Levite belonged to God (Numbers 3:44–51), and so redeemed the life of an Israelite firstborn son. In this case, each Levite is literally a living sacrifice. Confronted with the problem of firstborn sons over and above the number of Levites, the same passage demands payment in "the shekel of the sanctuary." The latter provision makes it unmistakably clear that, within the ancient practice of Israelite sacrifice, the meaning of ritual offering was not merely a payment or bribe handed over to the deity. When the issue of payment does arise, the transaction in money or kind is not the aim of sacrifice, but deals with cases in which sacrifice cannot be performed in the classic manner. It would be truer to say that in the Scriptures of Israel commercial exchange was the substitute for sacrifice rather than the reverse.

By the time of Origen, however, that equation had been turned backward. For centuries Jews had been mocking Greco-Roman sacrifices as vain attempts to bribe the gods, Hellenistic philosophers had ridiculed the superstitious attempts of their contemporaries to curry divine favor with gifts from the human world, and Christians had been attacking both Jews and Greeks as literalists, idolaters, and more often than not both.

It did not help that, in Greek, a single word, *lutron*, might mean "redemption," "rescue," or "ransom." Linguistic imprecision has long plagued the translation of a saying of Jesus (Mark 10:45): "For even the son of man did not come to be served, but to serve, and to give his life, *lutron* for many." The sacrificial sense of these words has been twisted for centuries into the image of a commercial transaction by commentators who are out of touch with the Semitic environment in which Jesus taught, where the Aramaic term *purqana'*, which the term *lutron* represents, clearly means "redemption" rather than "ransom." Origen probably did not fall victim to this linguistic confusion; after all, biblical language was one of his major interests. Rather, he truly believed that sacrifice was so much a matter of the mistaken past that, when it came to explaining the efficacy of Jesus' sacrificial death, only the commercial model of a payment made sense to him, even if that involved God paying off Satan at the price of his own Son, and handing over what Abraham had not been required to give.

In embracing his picture of God paying ransom to Satan, Origen introduced into Christian theology a conception that originated, not with the teaching of Catholics, but with a Gnostic thinker. In second-century Rome, Marcion, a bishop from Sinope in Asia Minor, established a radical new form of Christianity, portraying the god of the Israelite Scriptures as false, a demiurge compared to the true God, the Father of Jesus. Predictably, this led him to eliminate the Old Testament from use in his communities, and to cut out what he considered Jewish materials from the New Testament. That textual surgery is what scholars usually discuss when they consider Marcion. They also argue about whether or not to call Marcion a Gnostic. But although his system of thought is not as complex as in many of the writings of Nag Hammadi, his approach to the whole issue of God by means of the false demiurge makes it apparent the term "Gnostic" can be used with caution to characterize him. In fact, however, Marcion's most enduring contribution is not to the ancient debate about the true content of Scriptures or to Gnosticism, but to the Christian understanding—both Catholic and Gnostic—of how Jesus' death freed humanity from sin.

According to Marcion, who was not inclined to attribute even provisional value to the sacrificial system of ancient Israel, the crucifixion liberated people from the demiurge who had created the physical world and produced the Hebrew Bible. According to his theory, the ancient equivalent of René Girard's, the demiurge was compelled to acknowledge that he had arranged to kill an innocent man, and in compensation he had to free all those who believe in Christ. Jesus becomes the ransom that buys believers out of their slavery to the demiurge and frees them for the true God. If you put Satan in place of the demiurge, this is Origen's conception. Before the "ransom" theory was a Catholic doctrine, it had been a Gnostic teaching for a century.

———

Once the transfer from Gnostic teaching to Catholic dogma had been made, it became a resource for putting Christ at the center of a cosmic drama. In the unforgettable image of Gregory of Nyssa, Origen's fourth-century disciple, the devil was so greedy and ignorant, he took the bait of a helpless victim so that the fishhook of Christ's divine nature captured him. By this train of thought, every innocent death further pushed back the devil's power, demon by demon. Christ had broken Satan's hold on humanity, but it was the vocation of each believer to free himself and his world from whatever residual forces of evil remained. That is why, in the end, Origen's dramatic portrayal of Satan's defeat did not mark the end, but only an enhancement, of the incentive toward martyrdom.

In the theology of the fourth century, by which time the emperor Constantine had legalized Christianity, effectively making it the state religion of the Roman Empire, the martyr was not only a passive victim. *Roman soldiers* who fought the non-Catholic enemies of Rome were praised in hagiographies alongside those who had died under the persecutions of the previous centuries. These new martyrs were warriors as well as victims, and their blood dispelled the host of Satan even as their brawn shored up the Roman frontier. During this same period, Christian artists did what Maccabean interpreters had earlier done: they armed Abraham with a sword rather than a knife.

Gregory of Nyssa speaks of weeping whenever he saw an icon of Isaac, and that is not surprising, because in Isaac's image shone the reflection of the past passion of Christ, and the future sufferings of countless others in Christ's image and likeness. Gregory marks a key turn in the portrayal of the Christian Aqedah from the fourth century that reaches until our time: the deeply emotional connection between the father and the son put their acts beyond moral reproach, and they were celebrated for their affections not only in sermons and hagiographies, but in plays, music, and poetry during the Middle Ages, the Renaissance, the Reformation, the Enlightenment, and the modern period. From Søren Kierkegaard to Jerry Falwell (who was devoted to a version of Origen's theory), the righteousness of Abraham's actions in the Aqedah became a virtually unquestionable axiom. Isaac combined in himself the suffering that linked Jesus and the believer in paying ransom for the sins of others.

Gregory was wise enough to see Abraham's curse and to weep, but deceived enough by his emotional response to mistake the curse for a blessing. Fiercely criticized in his time, Gregory's ideas nonetheless entered the vernacular canon of Christianity. Blood had been assigned its value, and would never stop being shed in Christ's name to defeat the demons and their surrogates.

The cruel detail that characterizes scenes of torture in the stories of martyrs derived from actual conditions, but also from embellishment, reflecting the aesthetics of Christianity, which came to value bloodshed and to see its beauty as well as its necessity. Jesus was the perfect image of how a human being could enter into an intimate relationship with God, providing an incentive to follow the path of his suffering. Christians were literally to walk in his footsteps (1 Peter 2:21), and they were baptized, in their liturgies, into his death so that they might arise to a spiritual form of life (Romans 6:3–4). The story of Jesus' Passion, recounted at the time during the year when new believers were baptized, provided a dramatic opportunity for Christians to identify with the suffering of their Messiah. In addition, Origen's theology of ransom, which swept aside other fashions in Patristic thought, gave each believer reason to offer human life more readily than even Abraham had. No wonder Christians, like the Maccabees long before them, embraced a well-established genre in the Hellenistic world: they resorted to tales of violence in the Roman fashion in order to make moral claims.

The seal of Rome's power—capital punishment for criminals of most classes, especially slaves and noncitizens—might include throwing victims to beasts, setting them afire, forcing them to drink molten lead that burned out their insides, crucifying or beating them to death, sewing them into sacks with carnivores prior to drowning, hurling them from the height of a cliff, or condemning them to become gladiators in the arena. Rome coveted the display of pain, humiliation, and death as much as the punishment of death itself. Citizens and respected persons enjoyed gentler prospects of execution, with decapitation and the opportunity to commit suicide to look forward to, when the prospect of exile was not on offer.

Execution inscribed Roman hierarchy and class structure in the bodies of the victims; each victim contributed by his or her death to the order of the empire as a whole. The role of extending the reach of hierarchical authority into the moment of death itself accounts for the particular satisfaction Roman narratives took in stories of non-aristocrats who overreached themselves. When Sejanus, praetorian prefect of Rome, was strangled by imperial order on October 18, 32 C.E., his corpse was dismembered by a mob, and various members of his family were killed. Roman historians repeated this story frequently enough, down to the depiction of his young daughter being gang-raped by soldiers prior to being killed, to suggest they enjoyed it. Rome relished its pornography of violence, tales that titillated by detailing the brutality they ostensibly condemned.

At times, tales of this kind became surreal, as when an aristocratic matron is said to have forced a freed slave to cut off his own flesh bit by bit, roast the pieces, and eat them. Plutarch's doubts about the story's veracity do not prevent him from repeating it; in fact, by expressing skepticism, he gives himself license to take pleasure in giving the gory details. Like pornography, the tale needn't be true to titillate, any more than Thomas Harris's Hannibal Lector has to be an actual person for novels and films about his gruesome exploits to provide entertainment.

Rome's pornography of violence formed a precedent for stories of martyrdom, whether Judaic or Christian. It is no accident that the most explicit tales of martyrs' varied tortures appear in biblical literatures most influenced by Greco-Roman culture during the period of the Roman Empire. Both Judaism and Christianity absorbed the Roman fascination with pain and the Stoic praise of noble death, transforming them into narratives that ennobled victims of violence when they perished in testimony to the one true God.

Martyrdom, both as actual event and as literary form, played into the cultural attraction of spectacle throughout the Roman Empire. The prospect of mutilation, humiliation, and death drew the attention of the market for violent pornography, whether in the arena or in literature. By changing the focus of even a small proportion of those gathered to see the event or hear the story, away from enjoyment of the victim's pain and toward his or her transcendence of pain by means of faith in the single God who was master of both the spiritual world and the world of experience, the martyr indeed sowed the seed of faith, as Tertullian had said.

Long before Constantine embraced Christianity as the faith most compatible with the Roman Empire, Christians had absorbed Rome's violent pornography within their deep commitment to martyrdom. Even after Constantine's conversion, that commitment remained, at the same time as the martyr's persona was transformed from passive victim to active warrior. Spurred on by Origen's teaching of the metaphysical necessity of the martyr's suffering, narratives of martyrdom continued to be produced well into the Middle Ages, long after the age of the Roman persecution of Christianity had come to an end. Indeed, to be perceived as nobly resisting enemies who incarnated evil, Christians did not shrink from inciting and inflicting violence.

As the Roman Empire became Christian, Christians introduced a fateful shift in the identity of the martyr. Once the Roman Empire could call on Christian soldiers for its defense, the benefit of martyrdom could accrue even to those who risked their lives by engaging in violence, military or otherwise, on behalf of faith in Christ. Martyrs became executioners as well as victims, while laying claim to the virtue of victimhood the whole time, as Christianity made its way into the Middle Ages. Increasingly, the risking of one's life in physical combat, even when that risk was relatively minor, took the place of giving one's life in procuring the benefits of martyrdom. By telling the martyr's tale, joining in the story, and courting risks for their faith, Christians of modest (or even theoretical) heroism felt they had some part in the noble death and could lay claim to its virtue.

Constantine, whose mother Helena was a Christian, met his principal rival for imperial power in battle at the Milvian Bridge in 312 C.E. Legend has it that, as a result of a religious vision, Constantine permitted his soldiers to display crosses as their standard. His victory at Milvian Bridge, and his eventual emergence as sole emperor of a once again united Roman Empire, reversed policies of persecution; Christianity became privileged, and it had every reason to find a justification for the militant form of faith that Constantine had brought to power. In this new age, according to Eusebius, the principal Christian historian of the period, not only Christ, but the Church as a whole, had lived the pattern of Isaac, whose name means "laughter" and who was saved by divine intervention.

Power now meant something new. It could be noble and even serve the supernatural realm while commanding attention and respect on earth. The sanctioned violence of Rome no longer repressed the Catholic Church, but instead mandated its teachings in a credal form that was more clear-edged and categorical than ever before after the Council of Nicea in 325 C.E. Prominent Christian leaders embraced this model of state-sanctioned religion, and they sanctioned the use of force, including violence, to permit Orthodox Christians to attack their competitors. The term "heresy" now denoted not only a school of thought, the original meaning of the word, but a heterodox creed that needed to be expunged. Roman power had been baptized; martyrs no longer needed to be passive victims of oppression; the soldier fighting a noble cause could wear the martyr's crown as well as Roman laurels.

The institutions of Judaism as well as Jews themselves became favorite targets of martyrs turned warriors. Later in the fourth century, in Callinicum on the Euphrates, a local bishop had encouraged the plunder and arson of a synagogue by a mob of unruly Christians. Concerned that such behavior was a breach of public order, and mindful of the importance of law and decorum throughout his empire, the emperor Theodosius directed that the bishop rebuild the synagogue at his own expense. Bishop Ambrose in Milan—a city that had surpassed Rome in importance in Italy with the removal of the capital to Constantinople—confronted Theodosius personally.

Ambrose clearly expressed the emergent attitude toward Judaism, which he wanted to have treated as if it were heresy, while he argued that the mob consisted of overly enthusiastic but good-hearted people, "the least of Christ's disciples," childlike martyrs in their immature but vigorous faith. Ambrose got his way. Mob violence had become virtuous, on the argument that Christ was witnessed in these acts as martyrs had once witnessed Christ. Having made his case to Theodosius, Ambrose described himself as feeling as if he had entered into Paradise.

For the Orthodox and Catholic Church, the very existence of alternative religions, conceived of as heretical options, was at best to be tolerated only until the work of history eliminated them. "The Jew" now becomes a standard figure of speech, referring to an alien element in the progress of human history. So the Jew without (in the form of the synagogue) and the Jew within (in the form of any nostalgia for Jewish practices among Christians) were objects of zealous resistance.

Once Abraham's shepherd's knife was replaced by a soldier's sword, that new weapon came to dominate in Christian iconography of Abraham's offering of Isaac, both artistic and literary. In his sermon on Abraham (written c. 390 C.E.), Ambrose portrays the patriarch as the spirit of the believer, called to leave behind land, family, and house, to detach himself from the body, physical sensations, even the call of human emotions in devotion to God. The sword represents the patriarch's cutting away from the world of appetites as he prepared to sacrifice his son.

But the sword that cut men away from human affection and appetite still had more work to do, and became a metaphor of combat with sexual passions. Ambrose also interpreted Isaac's bride Rebecca as a figure, not of fertility but of virginity, completely ignoring her role as the mother of Jacob and Esau in order to concentrate on her as a metaphor of the marriage between Christ and the human soul. Fully in accord with the trends of his epoch, Ambrose became a principal champion of the virtue of lifelong virginity. As the persecutions of Christians ended, the private choice of virginity replaced the choice of public martyrdom as the dominant mode of self-sacrifice in the early Church. Stories of virgin-martyrs resisting the sexual assaults of pagan princes and consuls accordingly gained conspicuous prominence in fourth-century martyrologies, and Ambrose's portrait of Isaac made him the ideal of both martyrdom and virginity.

Christian mobs rioted against pagans in Alexandria in 415, encouraged by Cyril, the local bishop; they dragged the neo-Platonist philosopher Hypatia from her chariot, stripped off her clothing, and flayed her—and then burned her alive. Alongside his militant campaign of religious cleansing in Alexandria, Cyril developed distinctive, influential ideas in his interpretation of both Christ's death and Abraham's offering. When it concerns a Christological reading of Genesis 22, Cyril concludes that "the child being led to the sacrifice by his father indicates through symbol and outline that neither human strength nor the greed of the conspirators led our Lord Jesus Christ to the cross, but the desire of the Father." This turns around Origen's theory of Christ's death as a ransom paid to the devil. Now it is God's active desire, not Satan's, that is the hidden hand behind the story.

Cyril of Alexandria here signals a determinative shift in the understanding of the Aqedah and of Christ's death, which came to light fully during the Middle Ages and continues to shape how, in the modern period, readers of Genesis 22 see God as thirsty for human blood. In making the crucifixion God's active desire, Cyril posed a stark contrast between the sacrifice that God (rather than Satan) wants and the Old Testament scene, when Cyril says that Isaac, "having been placed on the wood, is stolen away from death and suffering." Isaac and his Jewish progeny had cheated God of what he most desired on this reading: the Old Testament "type" was so faulty, it effectively inverted the reality that Christ accomplished. Despite the popular teaching, defended on Origen's authority, that the devil accepted Jesus' death as a ransom, the view steadily gained ground that violence for the sake of God, including the death of his own Son and the destruction of Jewish and pagan "heretics," fulfilled the Father's pleasure.

Cyril's God *wanted* human sacrifice, in Isaac's time, in Christ's— and beyond. The Old Testament and the Jews had denied God what he wanted most, Christ had accomplished God's will, and it was left to Christians to pursue Christ's sacrificial action to its logical conclusion by eliminating heresy, whatever the risks involved. Cyril used the Aqedah in its spiritual meaning, as applied to Christ and to Christians who were willing to offer the "sacrifice" of themselves in mob action, and in its literal meaning, as applied to Isaac and to the Jews who tried to escape Christian mobs. He converted the Aqedah into a justification for the Christian equivalent of the *cherem*, the total destruction of non-Israelites, set out as early as the Book of Judges.

Once God was seen as the true inspiration for the sacrifice of Isaac as the paradigm of Jesus' death, some of the Fathers radically reshaped their view of the Aqedah. In fact, when Augustine came to the text "Now I know that you fear God and have not withheld your son, your cherished one, from me" (Genesis 22:12) he laconically transformed the text into "Now I have made known." Without any justification whatever, Augustine altered the text of Scripture in order to accord with his view that God had done just what he had planned to do from the start. On his reading, even "Abraham is worthy of praise, because all along he believed that his son, on being offered up, would rise again": the patriarch put belief ahead of human emotion. Abraham simply stood in for the kind of heroism that Christians should be even more ready than he to demonstrate, since they lived in an age that had come to know the power of martyrdom and resurrection.

Augustine also indulged, like his contemporary Cyril of Alexandria, in an anti-Jewish reading of the ram that was caught in the thicket: "What, then, did he represent but Jesus, who, before he was offered up, was crowned with Jewish thorns?" Given Augustine's ferocious perspective on "the Jews" as enemies of God and Christ, it comes as no surprise that Ambrose had baptized him. Convinced that the Lord was crucified by Jewish cruelty and impiety, Augustine even—as we have just seen—describes the mockery of the *Roman* soldiers in the Gospels (see Mark 15:16–18) as giving Jesus a crown of "Jewish thorns."

Augustine believed that he was living during the *Christiana tempora*, corresponding to the millennium promised in Revelation 20, the thousand years of temporal rule exerted by the saints of Christ.

This age of dawning power, released in flesh by Jesus and conveyed by the Church, simply awaits the full transition into the city of God, complete with flesh itself. In his millennial expectation, as well as in his commitment to sacred violence and its use against "heretics, Jews, and pagans," Augustine represents a crucial transition to medieval thought in the West. He articulated a rationalization for violence on the grounds that forced conversion was improving for its victims, thus refining the anti-Semitic polemics of his age and providing a moral opportunity to inject zeal into persecution. But one further development was needed to complete the transition to the medieval Aqedah, and to make holy violence and self-sacrifice, complete with appeals to Isaac and to Christ, standard within popular devotion during the Middle Ages.

Even as Origen's theory of Christ's death as a ransom paid to the devil was increasingly replaced by Cyril's view of the crucifixion as payment to God, literal payment grew as a method of righting wrongs within early medieval Europe. This was an inheritance of customs of Europe prior to the Roman conquest that later passed into Common Law. Whether for divine forgiveness or to assuage a desire for vengeance, paying in money or in kind for crimes, even murder (for which *weregild*, "man-coin," was demanded), became widespread. As a method of justice, the approach of enforceable recompense clearly had advantages, offering benefits to victims of crime and inflicting palpable losses on offenders without the enormous social costs associated with incarceration and execution. Because arrangements in society were projected onto humanity's relationship to God during the Middle Ages, often with little reflection, sins also came to be compensated for specific amounts, which were duly published in penitential manuals.

Amounts paid to compensate for sin could obviously not be thought of as being paid to the devil, as in Origen's theory of the ransom. Even the thought of compensating God for sin required explanations of gymnastic proportions; making the concept work with Satan seemed hopeless. So Anselm, the archbishop of Canterbury who died in 1109, converted Cyril of Alexandria's suggestion into a fully renovated ransom theory, and deliberately refuted Origen. In Anselm's analysis, it must be God who receives the recompense for human sin, with Christ's death the gift of a blameless and noble life in recompense for the guilt of others. Among educated readers today, Kierkegaard has made Anselm's interpretation canonical, while Christian Fundamentalists have made his ransom theory a *requirement* of belief, apart from which salvation is impossible. As a direct consequence of medieval theology, bloodshed has become a divine imperative in modern thought.

Although the devil had been banished by Anselm's scheme, a new twist was introduced into the logic of atonement that proved diabolical. Blood became precious, either as the innocent payment one might offer in imitation of the sacrifice of Christ, or as the compensatory punishment that virtuous people could rightly inflict on evildoers. This was a theology ideally suited to the Crusades, whose origins and interactions will occupy us once we have opened the subject of Islam. For now, however, it is worth bringing to mind Raymond d'Aguilers's famous image from the Crusades of 1099 c.e., that of the blood on the Temple Mount reaching up to the bridles of the Crusaders' horses as they slaughtered their Muslim enemies. That picture is literally apocalyptic, drawn from the Book of the Revelation (14:20), but it is also bathed in the twofold efficacy of blood: to cleanse the fault of the guilty, and to offer a pure sacrifice by the innocent.

In a fourteenth-century play depicting Genesis 22 that was frequently produced during the Middle Ages for audiences that could not read but avidly followed dramas, Isaac asks for a kerchief to cover his eyes, so that he does not flinch, and to be beheaded in a dignified, soldier's death. His father and he then exchange the following dialogue, exemplifying the virtue of the father as soldier-martyr and the son as victim-martyr:

O Isaake, sonne, to thee I saie:
God hath commaunded me to daye

Sacrifice—this is no naye—
  To make of thy bodye.

Father, I praye you hyde my eyne
That I see not the sorde so keyne;
Your stroke, father, woulde I not seen,
Lest I againste it grylle.

Locked in a common commitment to the virtue of shedding blood, the medieval Abraham and Isaac, the biblical types of God and Christ, set the stage for ennobled violence for generations to come. There is no mere coincidence in the fact that the professions of those who staged the Chester play, just cited, were barbers (that is, bloodletters) and candle makers, the masters of blood and fire. Rome's pornography of violence has been incorporated into Christianity, mistaken for virtue, and acclaimed by countless causes as the road that alone leads to progress.

Part Three

TAKING LEAVE OF MORIAH

VI

Ibrahim's Sacrificial Vision

A braham's curse insinuated itself through the development of Judaism and Christianity, linking them—even when they were locked in argument and opposition—in a common devotion to the ideal of giving one's own life, and at times the lives of one's children, in order to preserve faith. The Aqedah exemplified the martyr's zeal in both Judaism and Christianity, while Christianity took the additional step of having God carry out the sacrifice of the son that Abraham did not complete in Genesis 22, making martyrdom a central virtue, literally a divine activity that believers were to imitate.

Despite classic expressions of martyrdom in their canonical Scriptures, Jewish and Christian theologians today typically play down the image of the martyr in their religions, a denial belied by the continuing power of the call to martyrdom in political as well as religious settings in the West. The gambit of denial has proven even more transparent in the case of Islam. Any number of liberal scholars insist, with some justification, that the Qur'an teaches moderation, but the simple fact is that the popular Muslim counterpart of the Aqedah today galvanizes believers to commit violent acts under the name of martyrdom. Like the interpretations of Genesis 22 in Judaism and Christianity, the Islamic Aqedah is a living tradition that pushes past the limitations of any single text to convey a burning vision that glorifies the martyr's sacrifice.

In a vivid sermon, widely disseminated on the Internet as a resource for preachers and practitioners of Islam, the moment of the patriarchal sacrifice in the Qur'an becomes an example for all believers to emulate. Both father (called Ibrahim, as in the Qur'an) and son (not Isaac, but Isma'il, Ibrahim's older son, born of Sarah's slave Hagar) stand for what Muslims everywhere are called to do. The preacher paraphrases and interprets the Qur'anic text with vehement mastery:

> How could Ibrahim take his beloved son, the fruit of his life, the joy of his heart, the meaning of his living and staying, his Isma'il, and hold him on the ground, put a knife to his throat and kill him?

> If it were only the slaughter of Ibrahim at the hand of Isma'il, how easy! But no! The young Isma'il must die and the old and aged Ibrahim must remain!

> Ibrahim, the steel-like idol-smasher must have felt torn apart!

> Within him, there must have been a war, the greatest jihad. Which war? The war between Allah and Isma'il! The difficulty of choice!

> Which should Ibrahim choose?

> Love of Allah or love of self? Prophethood or fatherhood?

> Loyalty to Allah or loyalty to family? Faith or emotion?

> Truth or falsehood? Conscience or instinct?

> Responsibility or pleasure? Duty or right?

The preacher pursues his theme as relentlessly as any appeal in Maccabean literature or Bishop Ambrose's sermons: this is rhetoric at the service of faith, pushing the faithful to dedicated action.

Isma'il also finds his particular role as willing victim and proto-typical martyr in this sermon:

> But Isma'il also had faith. He submitted to Allah's will. Realizing his father's distress, Isma'il gave him these comforting words: "O my father! Do as you are commanded. You will find me, if Allah so wills, patient and constant" [here quoting directly from *Al Saffat* 37:102 in the Qur'an].
>
> *Allahu Akbar! Allahu Akbar! Allahu Akbar!*
>
> Ibrahim consulted his son, who willingly offered himself to Allah's command. The choice of Ibrahim was sacrifice. That of Isma'il was self-sacrifice, martyrdom.

Having forged the link between Isma'il and a true martyr, the preacher calls on all who listen to or read his words to take the sacrifice to heart: "Brothers and sisters, the Isma'il of Ibrahim was his son. But for you, who is your Isma'il? What is it? Your degree? Your reputation? Your position? Your money? Your home? Your car? Your beloved? Your family? Your knowledge? Your title? Your dress? Your fame? Your soul? Your spirituality? Your beauty? Your strength? Your career?"

Then comes the answer, with a certitude that anticipates no contradiction, and urges any listener or reader to consider militant action on behalf of Allah:

> Whatever is in your eyes that holds the place of Isma'il in the eyes of Ibrahim!
> Whatever weakens you on the way of faith!
> Whatever stops you in your movement!
> Whatever brings doubt to your responsibility!
> Whatever has enchained your freedom!
> Whatever leads you to compromise and justification!
> That very thing that deafens your ears before the Message of Truth!
> Whatever calls you to remain with yourself!
> Whatever causes you to flee from your duty!

Whoever or whatever keeps you behind in order to remain with her, him, or it!

Brothers and sisters, these are the signs of our Isma'ils. Let us search for them in ourselves and let us slaughter them to move towards Allah (Glorified be He) and to remove the real knife from the throat of oppressed Muslims all over the world, particularly in Palestine, Chechnya, Iraq, and Kashmir.

In this powerful presentation, listeners who are afraid of warfare and death are encouraged to confront their fears, as if each of them were Ibrahim and Isma'il so that the preacher induces recruits to engage in conflict without an overt mention of that purpose. This is Abraham's curse, no mere museum piece, but living and influential within Islam and in conflicts throughout the world, an example not of history repeating itself, but of a primordial reflex that has never died, and continues to shape the behavior of individuals, societies, and nations.

Even Islam's fiercest critics estimate that Muslim militants account for only between 10 and 15 percent of the faithful, a lower proportion than Fundamentalists in America, voters for the far right in France 2002, or Jewish Israelis who believe Arabs should be expelled from Israel. Yet many observers evaluate Islam according to its most extreme expressions rather than according to its classic teaching or the behavior of the majority of believers. Muslim militancy is a reality, but those who mistake it for Islam as a whole will never understand the challenges that commonly confront nations and religions around the world.

Western interpreters have distorted Islam more than any other religion over the centuries. Their treatment may not seem deliberate for the most part—until factors such as propaganda for the Crusades and slanders by generations of colonial adventurers are taken into account. Even aside from deliberate distortions, misunderstanding inevitably arises in the study of religion when scholars project their notions of the exotic onto others' beliefs, as well as when they attempt to reduce what others believe to some variety of their own doctrines. Islam is far from unique in being subjected to such treatment.

For centuries, Christian scholars in Europe, and later America, treated Hinduism and Buddhism with a combination of linguistic curiosity, in regard to their little-known languages, and orientalizing fantasy, over their alleged indulgence in both idolatrous worship and unusual sexual practices, while Judaism was typically dismissed (following the lead of Augustine) as a heretical form of Christianity, a tribal restriction of the universal truth of the Bible. Permitting a religious perspective to define itself in its own terms has proven especially difficult in the case of Islam, and programmatic distortions inherited from the past have persistently reemerged to complicate the effort. For reasons of geography as well as of history, Islam has suffered from *both* kinds of distortion, as exotic cult *and* as narrowly heretical sect.

The endlessly repeated and embellished exoticism of *The Thousand and One Nights* stands as a classic example of orientalist projection and thrives in the popular marketing of stories about Ali Baba and Aladdin. In this vein, since September 11, 2001, journalists have made the number of virgins that terrorists hope for in the Islamic paradise prepared for martyrs into a repetitive trope in their portrayal of Muslims as religious maniacs.

Yet newspapers *also* routinely report on Islam as a reactionary and puritanical religion, highlighting executions, examples of physical punishment, and prosecutions for sexual transgressions. Selective reporting equates Islam with the Western religious repression portrayed in Nathaniel Hawthorne's *The Scarlet Letter* and Arthur Miller's play *The Crucible*.

Allegedly both profligate and puritanical, the caricature of Islam in popular culture in the United States greatly diminishes the probability of genuine insight into what Muslims think, believe, and feel. Although the press cherishes clichés for most religions—so that Christians generally are caricatured as right wing, all Buddhists become ethereal followers of the Dalai Lama (who in fact heads a minority sect), Hindus seem inveterately premodern, and Jews never have a problem with money—the simultaneous distortion of Islam as both dissolute and repressive is uniquely oxymoronic.

———

The equivalent to the Aqedah in the Qur'an itself, an allusive invocation of vision and resolve, is spare—unlike the militant sermon just excerpted, which quotes from the Qur'an. The son is not in fact identified, either as Isma'il or Isaac; the call to arms against oppression is quite absent; mystery subsumes all the action in an evocation of sacrifice.

The original Aqedah of Islam, as revealed to Muhammad, is set in the midst of a narrative and uses language that I have translated afresh, to represent how economical the Qur'anic style is, emotionally charged in its understatement (*Al Saffat* 37:84–111):

> Look: he came to his Master [that is, Allah] with a whole heart.
> Look: he said to his father and to his people, "What do you
>   worship?
> Falsehood—gods other than Allah that you desire?
> What is your idea about the Master of the worlds?"
> Then he looked once at the stars,
> And said, "I am indeed sick."
> They turned away from him, and departed.
> Then he turned to their gods and said, "Don't you eat?
> What is with you that you don't speak?"
> Then he turned upon them, striking with the right hand.
> Then his people advanced toward him in haste.
> He said, "Do you worship what you have carved?
> But Allah created you and what you make!"
> They said, "Build a furnace for him, and throw him in the blaz-
>   ing fire!"
> They tried a plot against him, but we made them low!
> He said: "I will truly go to my Master, who will guide me!
> My Master! Grant me a righteous son!"
> So we gave him message of a forbearing son.
>
> When the son grew to work with him, he said, "My son, indeed
>   I see in vision that I sacrifice you. Look, what do you see?"

He said, "My father, do what you are commanded! You will
find me, if Allah wills, among the steadfast."

And when they had both submitted their wills and he pushed
     him forehead down,
We called out to him "Ibrahim!
You have already fulfilled the vision!" So indeed we reward
     those who do right.
This was an obvious trial—
And we redeemed him with an immense sacrifice.
And we left for him among generations in later times:
"Peace upon Ibrahim!"
So we reward those who do right.
Indeed he was one of our believing servants.

Here Ibrahim is involved in conflict with his own people about idolatry, in the course of which the sacrifice of his son is a "trial" that he
must pass in order to hand on his peace to future generations and
leave his inheritance as a Prophet of God (Allah). How that trial is
understood, in its application to the lives of believers, has shaped
Muslim theology and ethics for centuries.

Although traditional interpretation emphasizes that Ibrahim and
the Prophets as a whole bore burdens far beyond the ordinary, he
remains an ideal type of faith in *Al Saffat*. Doesn't this story, literally
understood, mean that true belief might *need to* face such a test, and
pass that test in order to be confirmed, no matter what the cost, just
as the popular sermon insists?

Scholarship as well as popular commentary plays into the stereotype
that Islam is a ruthless religion, and that the Qur'an, in stories like its
Aqedah, represents a crude call to violence. Bernard Lewis and Daniel Pipes, two competent and widely published observers, in differing
ways echo the widespread but fallacious claim that, because Muslims
as a whole believe that the Qur'an conveys the actual words of the angel Gabriel to Muhammad, Islam is inherently a form of Fundamen-

talism. They conveniently fail to observe that the Torah claims that Moses personally conversed with Yahweh on Mount Sinai, and that in the Gospels Jesus not only heard and spoke to God, but also communicated with Moses and Elijah, prophets from Israel's past whom Jews during the first century believed had never died.

Critical scholarship shows that all three Abrahamic religions are rooted in the mystical experience of their founders, which they deliberately conveyed to their followers, whom they enabled and authorized to replicate that experience. Without reference to that experiential core of encounter with the divine, neither the content nor the power of Judaism, Christianity, and Islam will ever be understood. They are religions, not just collections of traditions and beliefs and attitudes, but also engagements with the world guided by insights into the supernatural reality of God.

Some modern historians, however, ill at ease with taking religious impulses seriously, try to reduce Islam to a radical ideology. As Bernard Lewis, a retired professor of Near Eastern studies at Princeton University, puts his case, the literal inerrancy of the Qur'an is a basic dogma of Islam, and that literalism helps explain why the majority of terrorists today are Muslims. Daniel Pipes, in his more political rhetoric as a partisan historian and analyst of the Middle East, similarly observes a natural affinity between Muslim political thought and "earlier totalitarianisms, fascism and Marxism-Leninism."

The prophecy of an inevitable "clash of civilizations" derives directly from this type of analysis. Bernard Lewis used the phrase in an article that appeared in 1990, as part of his portrayal of Islam as the extremist Doppelgänger of Western democracy, and the Harvard policy analyst Samuel P. Huntington then took up this wording in a book also called *The Clash of Civilizations*. Theorists who see Islam in this way, and as leading directly to "Islamo-fascism," have been severely criticized by scholars of Islam. Many commentators, as well as scholars and committed Muslims, argue that the portrayal of Islam as inherently militant and Fundamentalist is a purpose-built artifice to provide the West with an enemy to confront that can occupy the place once held by the Soviet Union.

Having reduced Islam to "Islamo-fascism," Lewis and his colleagues have in fact recommended the tactics of the Cold War—containment coupled with strategic intervention—until Islam matures in a way comparable to the Soviet Union's dramatic conversion to Western values. The rapid redeployment of rhetoric and then armaments at the end of the Cold War, from opposition to the Soviet empire to confrontation with the Islamic world, raises the question whether the desire to find a target for the West's verbal and literal weapons might have preceded any genuine threat from Islam. Which came first: Lewis's proclamation of crusade against Islam as a civilization that clashes with the West, or Osama bin Laden's declaration of jihad against the United States?

Questions of that kind, and the related issue of precisely when and by whom policies and tactics authorizing violence emerged, cannot yet be answered definitively: time and the disclosure of evidence will eventually tell. But until then, it is crucial to keep in mind that, because the West's confrontation with Muslim revival has been conditioned by the end of the Cold War and the rise of terrorism and other local, violent conflicts, public perception of Muslims is likely to include an exaggerated dimension of threat. The appeal of Cold War strategies that would treat Islam as intrinsically Fundamentalist, backward, and foreign—a religious successor to the broken Soviet threat—is as natural as it is likely to prove deceptive, since it is grounded in a false understanding of Muslim faith, and a failure to consider the religious impulses that it conveys to believers.

Trying to identify Islam with Fundamentalism—the fallacy that lies at the heart of these mistaken tactics—represents a profound confusion of completely different religious phenomena. Fundamentalism is a recent and thoroughly Western religious movement, centuries younger than Islam. The movement arose at the end of the nineteenth century in what was then emerging as the industrial power of the future, the United States of America.

The Fundamentalist movement first saw the light of day in Protestant America under the name "the Princeton theology." At Princeton, Professor Benjamin Warfield taught that the Bible conveyed five basic truths as immutable as, and more powerful than, Darwin's laws of evolution. These alleged truths—the inerrant accuracy of Scripture, Jesus' birth from a biological virgin, his literal miracles, his offering of his blood in payment for the sins of the world (in the way that Anselm, rather than the Bible, taught), and his physical resurrection in the same flesh in which he died—came to be called "the Fundamentals." These ideas are modern dogmas, not ancient teachings agreed upon throughout the Church, and at each point both the New Testament and Patristic literature offer alternative ways of conceiving of Christian faith.

But Fundamentalists mastered the modern media of radio, television, cable stations, and the World Wide Web, falsely claiming that their ideology was exactly the traditional, incontrovertible faith of Christianity. Many millions of Christians, particularly in the United States, have embraced these claims, making Fundamentalism the fastest growing religious influence in the country during the twentieth century, and confusing Fundamentalist dogma with what the Bible and Christian tradition actually say.

The idea, suggested by a living Princeton professor (Bernard Lewis), that we should interpret Islam in the light of a theological fad based on what a dead Princeton professor (Benjamin Warfield) said about Christianity a hundred years ago used to strike me as almost funny in its comic-book reductionism. But the stakes involved in coming to grips with Islam are too high for me to see any humor in the situation now. Attempts to stigmatize Muslim cultures have become as dangerous as they are persistent. Those who conflate Islam as such with reactionary, militant excesses within their own religious traditions not only stand in the way of genuine understanding; they also contribute—indirectly but inexorably—to the rising level of religious intolerance and violence that threatens civilized peoples all over the world. Understanding Islam, along with the other most influential religions in the flow of current events, has become a matter of civic duty, and perhaps of survival.

Islam fortunately does not need outside observers, whether academic or popular, to make sense of its teachings. Ancient and elegant traditions of commentary and interpretation—comparable to those of Judaism, Christianity, and other religions with extensive literary histories—articulate what it means to be a Muslim and suggest how

Islam relates to other religions (especially to Christianity and Judaism). The complex and fascinating connection between martyrdom and sacrifice, expressed in terms of Ibrahim's sacrifice of his son, has in particular been explored since the time of Muhammad.

In the Qur'an and the exegetical tradition that enriched that primordial text, a powerful set of impulses and reflections, in some ways comparable to Judaic and Christian readings but amounting to autonomous expressions of a distinctive faith, come to voice and provide access to a religious world we need urgently to understand and appreciate. Looking through the lens of the patriarch and his son on the mountain of sacrifice, Muslim sages explored the human impulse to sacrifice and the vocation to martyrdom.

These creative interpretations opened up dimensions of meaning and action familiar within Judaism and Christianity as well as radical new insights, full of passion and crucial for seeing how religions shape human actions. Just as Judaism and Christianity are better understood in terms of their mutual, sometimes complementary and sometimes countervailing readings of the Aqedah, so too does Ibrahim's sacrifice in the Qur'an offer indispensable perspectives into Muslim faith, the origin of Abraham's curse, and how that violent reflex can be reversed.

Muhammad claimed to receive divine messages in chapters (each called a surah) disclosed to him in a series of revelations between 610 and 632 c.e. by the angel Gabriel, a messenger from God. The result was the Qur'an. Muhammad began to receive the revelation of the Qur'an at the age of forty, first during the night, and then while he isolated himself near the end of the month of Ramadan in a cave on Mount Hira', near Mecca. There, his wife Ayesha later said, the angel Gabriel came to him as a man, physically seized him, and taught him to recite. Further revelations, as well as opposition from local authorities who supported polytheist traditions, came on the heels of this initial experience and led to Muhammad's *hijrah* or emigration from Mecca to Medina in 622 c.e., the start of the Muslim calendar. From that moment Muhammad turned his back definitively on any possible compromise with polytheist religion in all its forms and laid the groundwork for his victorious return from Medina to Mecca at the head of an army eight years later.

In the context of constant clan warfare among competing interests and local religions, Muhammad's monotheism proved to be a source of military discipline and political unity as well as of committed faith. By the time of his death in 632 C.E., Muhammad had destroyed the idols that in his view desecrated the sanctuary in Mecca, the Ka'bah, and had extended the reach of his revelation through much of the Arabian Peninsula by means of preaching and conquest.

The Prophet—as he is designated by his revelation—memorized the surahs and passed them on to his followers. In fact, the word "Qur'an" in Arabic means "recitation." The process of producing the Qur'an involved a shift from oral to written media, somewhat analogous to the case of Jesus and the Gospels. This transition was better organized in Islam's case than in Christianity's: it began during the lifetime of the Prophet, did not require translation from one language into another, and at a fairly early stage came under the control of effective religious and political successors to Muhammad, the caliphs.

Twenty years after Muhammad's death, 'Uthman, commonly counted as the third caliph, acted in response to the passing of many men who had been capable of reciting the Qur'an from memory, as well as to disputes in regard to accuracy, by ordering and supporting the redaction of the Qur'an. The written text therefore emerged from an interaction of written and oral sources. The process of Gospel-formation took longer, and didn't result in full, written documents until a generation after Jesus' death.

The transition to writing naturally left its mark in the organization of the Qur'an, but the aim of oral recitation continued to be served: the order of the individual surahs moves from the longest to the shortest, in order to facilitate memorization. As a result, the account of Muhammad's call, for example, comes near the end of the Qur'an. As in the case of the Hebrew Bible and the New Testament, it is a mistake to assume that the aims of the Qur'an are those of literal history. The Qur'an is a more coherent document than the Scriptures of Israel or of the Church, because multiple authors are not involved, but the focus of the whole is on revelation, not historical inquiry.

The Qur'an powerfully conveys its absolute commitment to revelation by what it says, and does not say, about the sacrifice of Ibrahim. The Qur'an does not explicitly identify the son whom Ibrahim sacrificed, or nearly sacrificed—another issue that is addressed allusively. Is this Isaac, son of Sarah, as in the biblical text, or his older half-brother Isma'il, son of Hagar? The Qur'anic text no more tells us in so many words which son was involved than it specifies how far Ibrahim went in his sacrificial intent.

This ambiguity produced a profound disagreement within the Muslim interpretive tradition, between those who identified the son as Isaac and those who said he was Isma'il. A useful monograph counts up to 130 medieval Muslim commentators who identified Isaac as the victim, and 133 who said it was Isma'il. In contrast, pious Muslim opinion today overwhelmingly goes with the second option. But by leaving open the question of the son's identity, the Qur'an indicates that other issues are more important. Before considering the age-old debate regarding the identity of the son, which in my judgment has become a distraction, we will focus on what the Qur'an does say openly, and with powerful force.

In the surah called *Al Saffat* (named after the angels ranged in their "ranks" in heaven and also around believers), Ibrahim appears first of all as defending the cause of Allah and resisting idolatry, as a *ghazi* or warrior, and only then in connection with the offering of his son. Here the spare style of Genesis is stripped even cleaner; wisps of phrases, economically crafted for ease in recitation, allude to a totally fresh construction of the patriarch's sacrifice and its significance. Muhammad's revelation transforms the story of Abraham's offering so thoroughly, it might seem to be a different narrative altogether. But in fact, this surah weaves together elements taken from cycles of tradition about Abraham outside the Bible with the biblical narrative, and produces a tapestry of a new shape and kind.

Because historical analysis in the West has often been applied to denigrate Islam and its traditions, many interpreters of the Qur'an have fiercely resisted any suggestion that Muhammad's visions derived from previous sources, whether biblical or extrabiblical. I can understand that reaction, as I understand the response among believing Christians who fear that the historical scrutiny of the influences that made Jesus who he was represents a threat to their faith.

Yet although I appreciate the root of this fear and acknowledge the sincerity of the concern, my commitment to historical analysis remains. Christian faith identifies Jesus Christ as the eternal Son of God, which means that—from the point of view of that belief—any and every historical insight concerning Jesus in his time illuminates a timeless truth. Similarly, understanding the distinctive quality of the Qur'an in comparison to earlier sources brings out its qualities as the final seal of prophecy, the uncorrupted message of Allah according to Islamic theology. Historical inquiry as applied to religion neither insists upon a particular faith nor denies that faith: it simply clarifies the focus and the logic of belief. The issue of what a person believes is for him or her to resolve; how people come to believe, and how their commitments relate to others', is a pressing, collective concern, involving all those—of whatever faith or denial of faith—who are concerned with how people of different religious orientations have reacted to one another over time and are likely to behave in the future.

Just as I have shown in the past that Jesus learned from John the Baptist's visionary teaching, and that Paul's thought was imbued with Stoic philosophy, I have to observe—and will show here—that Muhammad was influenced by the Judeo-Christian traditions of his time. An obvious example is that, according to the Qur'an, Ibrahim had to battle with his contemporaries about idolatry and was cast into a furnace of fire during the controversy. The surah *Al Saffat* refers allusively to that legend, but a much older Jewish text from the second century C.E. that we have already encountered, the *Liber Antiquitatum Biblicarum*, tells the story in detail.

No doubt, some readers will react with hostility to this observation, but a simple respect for history causes me to make it. In any case, negative reaction from Muslim critics is not likely to be any more extreme than my being branded "an agent of Satan" by a Christian Fundamentalist reader who was upset by what he read in my earlier book, *Rabbi Jesus*. Although I would happily dispense with personal attacks by ideologically driven opponents, their extremity often illustrates why historically based theological work is vital: only that approach addresses the increasingly sectarian character of religions since the beginning of the twentieth century, as the methods and attitudes of Fundamentalism have been embraced by extreme, or simply ill-informed, believers of many faiths.

In contrast to ideologically driven views of faith common today, the Abrahamic religions are all quite clear in their original languages (Hebrew, Aramaic, and Arabic) that faith—from the Semitic root *'amiyn,* one of the early nicknames of Muhammad—is a matter of placing complete confidence in God, not just agreeing to a proposition. They make a categorical distinction between faith and fantasy, faith and ideology, faith and wishful thinking—in fact between faith and anything that, as Ibrahim says in *Al Saffat* (37:95), human beings "have carved" for themselves. The worship of one's own desires is the idolatry that Ibrahim warns his people against, and that warning underlies the meaning of faith, not only in all the Abrahamic religions, but also in mature religions generally and in meaningful philosophical discussion.

Unless faith can confidently confront investigation, questioning, and doubt, the suspicion arises that it is not faith at all, not a confident reliance on the greatest truth an inquirer can find, but only a package of convenient opinions held in place by social convention. That sort of unexamined faith is not worth believing. No scholar can compel believers to inquire into the grounds of their faith, and I would not attempt to force the issue. Yet I can say to both believers and nonbelievers, on the basis of personal experience and the experiences of those I have taught, that probing the bases of their convictions will deepen their awareness of why they believe what they believe.

Of course, religious inquiry always carries the risk of conversion, and I have witnessed that as well. Inquiry commonly causes people to change their religious identification or switch from being believers to becoming atheists, or the reverse, or to banish what once seemed to them central beliefs to the periphery of their commitments, while the marginal concerns of the past acquire pivotal importance. Nothing is more predicable or healthier than the alteration of our beliefs over time, as new insights about the world, ourselves, and the past feed our sense of the values and truths that matter most. As a scholar and as a priest, my vocation is not to manipulate people into agreeing with me or with the creeds of Christianity that most appeal to me. My vocation is rather to enable people I encounter to become clearer about why they believe in the particular ways they do. Apart from a commitment to fully informed faith on all sides, no meaningful discussion of beliefs can take place. That is why I read about Ibrahim in the Qur'an in the way I read about Jesus in the Gospels, with appreciation and skepticism at one and the same time.

Near the time that Muhammad's surah *Al Saffat* wove together the stories of Genesis and the *Liber Antiquitatum Biblicarum*, an interpretation in Rabbinic midrash, Genesis Rabbah, also portrayed Abraham as threatened with death in a fiery furnace. The relatively late date of Genesis Rabbah should make us cautious of assuming it is an influence on the Qur'an. Yet while the issue of which precise texts were involved in a web of influence at a given time is a matter for further study, the fact of influence, as stories and their interpretations circulated both orally and in written form for centuries before and after the Qur'an was written, is a matter of certainty. Just as what the Hebrew prophets learned from their environment and Jesus' preaching was rooted in the Scriptures of Israel, so Muhammad and his successors reflect the biblical tradition and its interpretations as they circulated in oral and written form on the Arabian Peninsula during the seventh century C.E. and later.

Although saying that the Qur'an borrows from biblical and extra-biblical traditions may provoke controversy, it remains a fact to be explained. By tying Ibrahim's sacrifice to the story of his combating the use of idols and facing the threat of death by fire (an allusion to the tradition in Daniel 3), Muhammad associates the whole action of the offering of Ibrahim's son with the fundamental issue of martyrdom. Appreciating influences does not undermine the claims of the

Qur'an, nor does historical work prove or disprove claims to truth. Historical reading discloses only what was believed in the past, how it was distinctive in relation to influences upon it, and what that belief meant, not whether it should be believed in the present.

The uniqueness of Muhammad's revelation—whether it is embraced or not—becomes plain under critical analysis. Scholars can sometimes infer when during the course of his life Muhammad received particular revelations, and inference of that kind has become a normal part of scholarship. Muslim scholarship has assigned at least the initial composition of *Al Saffat* to Muhammad's first period in Mecca, when his conflict with the polytheist custodians of the Ka'bah, who came from his own clan, the Quraysh, was growing. Yet Islamic faith is grounded, not in Muhammad's personality or biography, but in what Gabriel (on God's behalf) revealed to Muhammad, the Qur'an. During the whole period the angel seized Muhammad, both Judaism and Christianity, with many varieties—orthodox and unorthodox—and a host of ancient religions and Gnostic innovations, were well ensconced in the Arabian Peninsula.

The richness of the relationship between *Al Saffat* and interpretations of Genesis 22 suggests that this surah was also to some extent composed during the period after the *hijrah* when Muhammad lived in Medina, where several Jewish communities thrived. By the time of Muhammad's revelation, stories such as Abraham's sacrifice had already passed through most of the Jewish and Christian interpretations we have encountered, reaching a stage of baroque controversy between and among Jewish and Christian interpreters.

Throughout his life, Muhammad maintained profound respect for "the people of the Book," whether Jewish or Christian, because he believed his revelation perfected the message of their prophets. Yet one principal purpose of the Qur'an is to cut through controversies over biblical exegesis and set out the true, underlying meaning of disputed texts and traditions. That program necessarily involved correction, and sometimes conflict. Debate with Christianity and Judaism is embedded as a principle in the Qur'an.

Well before the time of Muhammad, men typically settled their religious differences violently. Some commentators—although by no means all—have found in the Qur'an allusions to events in the cen-

tury prior to Muhammad, when the Jewish King of Yemen, Dhu Nu-
was, executed Christians by burning them to death on pyres set alight
in trenches in 523 C.E. (*Al Buruj* 85.4) and when Abyssinian Christians
mounted on elephants attacked Mecca (*Al Fil* 105.1–105.5). Whether
or not those precise references are in play, Muhammad's revelation
concerning Ibrahim evidently took place in an environment of religious controversy and violence, in which discord often brought the
outbreak of hostilities. Revelation required the backing of military
acumen if it was to survive, and Muhammad's strategic genius was a
seal of his prophecy. An otherworldly or pacifist perspective was not
an option, if faith was to survive.

Ibrahim features as a central character in Muhammad's inspired
reevaluation of the Bible and its interpretation, and as a model for
Muhammad himself. Ibrahim was completely obedient to God "with
a whole heart" (*beqalbin saleemin, Al Saffat* 37:84–85), so that he
and Isma'il can be called "muslims"—meaning people submitted to
God—even before Muhammad (*Al Baqarah* 2:128). The fullness of
Ibrahim's obedience motivates his rejection of the false gods (*Al Saffat* 37:85–98), the idols of his native land that distracted from the
worship of Allah, the one true God.

In the Qur'anic account of how Ibrahim left Ur of the Chaldees
(which is never named), the patriarch fought with his opponents, who
threw him into the furnace of fire. Then Ibrahim turned for guidance
to his lord, whom he addressed as his "Master," as I have translated
here, or "Rabbi" (*rabbiy; Al Saffat* 37:84, 99–100), a term common to
Arabic, Aramaic, and Hebrew, which means a "great" teacher.

Ibrahim's specific appeal to Allah is for a "righteous son." In the
Qur'anic context, the mention of this son—who is not named in this
story, although both Isaac and Isma'il are mentioned elsewhere—
intimates great obedience to Allah on the part of Ibrahim and the son
who is to be. The purpose of progeny is to promote greater submission to Allah and to provide allies in the combat with idols and their
partisans. The events involved with the sacrifice, in a place that also
goes unnamed, spell out what it means to be obedient.

The Qur'an is much more specific than any other text, Jewish or Christian, when it concerns the father's motives and the son's cooperation. In an unusually long line in the surah, Ibrahim speaks to his son, "My son, indeed I see in vision that I sacrifice you. Look, what do you see?" (*Al Saffat* 37:102), and the son eloquently urges his father—in the manner of Jephthah's daughter (Judges 11:36–37)—to perform the command. Both father and son "submitted their wills" to Allah. They were truly muslims, the victim pushed with his forehead down—with how much force is no more stated than what weapon Ibrahim used, and there is no reference to binding—to avoid any chance he would flinch at the sight of the knife (37:103). The image insists on the son's complete submission.

Then God himself called out, telling Abraham that he had "already fulfilled the vision" (*Al Saffat* 37:104–7), and redeeming the son with an "immense sacrifice." Muhammad could not be more emphatic in this revelation: Ibrahim sees what he will do in a vision, speaks of his action with his son, and God rewards him, as he will reward all who do right (*Al Saffat* 37:110). Vision and intention together bring divine blessing, and that process is possible because Ibrahim is attentive to revelation, not only before he acts, but also in the midst of actions more forceful than those portrayed in Genesis 22, to which Allah's command brings an end.

At one point in the Hebrew text of the Aqedah, the place name Moriah is given a cryptic explanation, "Yahweh saw" and "On the mount Yahweh was seen" (Genesis 22:14). In the Hebrew text, that refers to God seeing the ram, rather than Isaac, as the chosen sacrifice and to God being disclosed Himself. In the Qur'an this emphasis on vision is deepened, so that Ibrahim exemplifies such consistent devotion to the will of Allah that he is willing to change the course of his actions. By means of its economical, rhythmic presentation, the Qur'an shifts the center of balance of the whole story: because everything is a matter of vision and transparent openness to the divine, Allah at no point demands a literal sacrifice. As the text explicitly says (*Al Saffat* 37:106), "This was an obvious trial."

———

In the situation of Muhammad in Mecca, during a time of growing conflict with the Quraysh clan over appropriate worship in the Ka'bah, the meaning of the surah *Al Saffat* is especially resonant. Muhammad identified with Ibrahim, who confronted the gods of his ancestors, resisted polytheistic worship with a martyr's courage, asked Allah for the support of a righteous son to resist his opponents, and then had the vision that he was to sacrifice the very son that he had sought. Elsewhere in the Qur'an (*Al Baqarah* 2:125–29), Ibrahim and his son Isma'il established the Ka'bah together, so that Ibrahim's vision challenges the whole tapestry of the revelation of Allah on yet another level. In addition the deaths of Muhammad's own two infant sons during his first period in Mecca invests this challenge with emotional poignancy.

The motif of the patriarch being tested on multiple occasions that climaxes in this story, together with the portrayal of the son being turned away so as not to see the knife descend, reflects influences of the Judaic tradition that had been well developed by the seventh century. But those allusions are as oblique as the biblical text of the Aqedah itself, which in the Qur'anic manner is worked without being cited. That is the idiom of the recitation Muhammad learned from Gabriel: its purpose is to speak directly from heaven of what is only indirectly reported elsewhere by human agency, and to insist upon what matters to heaven, without preoccupation with incidentals. For that reason, the Qur'an moves with allusive subtlety, speaking through events scarcely described, to portray Isma'il as the warrior who cleansed the Ka'bah with Ibrahim and possibly as the martyr willing to be sacrificed at his father's hand.

The role of heavenly vision, of absolute importance within Muhammad's prophetic identity, is the fulcrum of the story of the sacrifice itself. At no point within the events does Ibrahim decide upon his own actions; his consultation with Allah as his Master by means of prayer and vision is constant throughout. For that reason, the course of the action, which produces mounting violence between Ibrahim and his contemporaries (reflecting the relationship between Muhammad and the Quraysh), is broken definitively when Allah calls out, "Ibrahim! You have already fulfilled the vision!" (*Al Saffat* 37.104–5). Human actions may well lead to killing, but Ibrahim, Muhammad, and anyone who recites the Qur'an learns that Allah does not require such a sacrifice (*Al Saffat* 37.106); beset by fraught circumstances, Ibrahim confronted "an obvious trial."

The Qur'an's emphasis upon the priority of vision throughout its version of the Aqedah conveys the distinctive character of Islam among the Abrahamic religions. All three take their bearings on Abraham, and all three portray him as a prophet in some sense, but Muhammad makes Ibrahim's prophetic identity the model for every single believer. Ibrahim's intimate response to Allah, reshaping his actions and relationships to others—his son included—from moment to moment, represents Muhammad's own biography, and calls those who hear the Qur'an to see the meaning of their lives in Ibrahim's obedience.

The readiness to submit, not to one's own ambition or to the convenience of convention or to the calculation of advantage, but uniquely and without compromise to the imperatives of Allah, lies at the heart of Islam, making it the most consistently prophetic religion, across all its adherents, that there has ever been. The prophetic character of Muslim faith contradicts all forms of materialism, which define human life in terms of measurable, empirical circumstances. Islam insists more vehemently than any other religion (Abrahamic or not) that the significance of our lives lies in the transcendent realm rather than in material considerations.

As the West has entered into its greatest period of materialism since the eighteenth century, it has all too naturally found reasons to fear the insights of Muhammad, who in his presentation of Ibrahim and his son pictured human life as an encounter with the divine rather than the outcome of material circumstance. Nothing within the Qur'anic presentation weakens the emphasis on vision or its visionary insight that appeals for divinely mandated violence, including child sacrifice, are cases of "obvious trial" rather than actual imperatives from Allah. Muhammad's revelation is that the threat to Ibrahim's son comes from human vision and will rather than directly from divine mandate.

The Qur'an elsewhere condemns the sacrifice of children and family (*Al Ma'arij* 70:11–14), as well as infanticide (*Al Isra'* 17:31), because they are sinful. That is why nothing takes away from the emphasis in the Muslim Aqedah that the test Ibrahim faced was "obvious." For that very reason, the son's identity falls into the background of allusion and becomes unclear, as a long tradition of discussion proves eloquently. But does the Qur'an, after all, suggest that identity to alert hearers and readers?

The run-up to the moment of sacrifice seems to suggest that Isma'il is at issue. Ibrahim asks for a "righteous" son, and that is a usual designation of Isma'il within the Qur'an. Moreover, the son is said to be of the age of work at the time of the sacrifice (*Al Saffat* 37:102), which implies the older Isma'il rather than the youngster Isaac.

But then, after the story of the visionary sacrifice, the Qur'an continues with a statement out of any apparent chronological order, "and we gave him the good news of Isaac—a prophet—one of the righteous" (*Al Saffat* 37:112). That means that the language of being the "righteous" son cannot be limited to Isma'il in this passage after all. More crucially, the close of the story, with its disregard of chronology in referring to Isaac's birth, opens up the possibility that the whole presentation is designed to look ahead in time, from the visionary perspective of eternity, and prior to the literal birth of *any* son, who might as well be Isaac as Isma'il.

The visionary idiom that Muhammad insists upon throughout lifts the story free of any specific association with the chronology of either son's life. Because this surah of the Qur'an may be connected with either son, in the history of Muslim interpretation it has been associated with both. An interpreter who died in 923 C.E., Al Tabari, gave a substantial list of the authoritative commentators who favored one view or another, and made his own preference clear: he was for Isaac. Yet whether citing authorities for one view or another, Al Tabari shows how the distinctive, visionary element of the Qur'anic story was enhanced over the centuries by embellishing on the original surah in a way analogous to the development of interpretations of Genesis 22 within Judaism and Christianity from the time of the Maccabees.

This visionary enhancement was achieved by introducing Satan into the story, so as to make Ibrahim into a Job-like character—as he had been since the time of the *Book of Jubilees*—who struggles between his devotion to Allah and the promptings of Satan. In the version of Muhammad's follower Ka'b Al Akhbar, a rabbi who converted from Judaism (dying between 652 and 654 C.E.), the son involved was Isaac. Satan realizes that he has a golden opportunity to convince Ibrahim and his family that Allah has not truly been revealing himself to the patriarch.

As Satan says in this version of the story, derived by Ka'b Al Akhbar from Judaic tradition, "If I cannot deceive the people of Ibrahim with this, I shall never be able to!" So Satan goes to Sarah, asking her why Ibrahim has left his home early. She replies that he has an errand. Not true, says Satan, "He took him out early to sacrifice him." "And why would he sacrifice him?" asks Sarah. Then Satan sets up his trap: "He claims that his Lord ordered him to do it." With this statement, Satan impugns the origin and purpose of Ibrahim's revelation, and therefore Muhammad's.

Here is Satan's glory, the suggestion that Ibrahim's vision is inauthentic if not made up, and in any case likely to be self-serving. If Satan's line were accepted, then Ibrahim's submission to Allah would be considered as just one more instance of idolatry among many, and, as Satan said at the beginning of the story, his work would be crowned with success. But Sarah defeats Satan with her direct reply, echoing what Ibrahim's son says in the Qur'an itself at the time of the sacrifice: "If his Lord ordered him to do that, it is best that he obey."

The simplicity of this statement conveys the full power of the insistence upon following the will of Allah, come what may. To underline this reading of the whole event, Satan's discussion with Sarah is repeated with Isaac, and then with Ibrahim himself: all insist upon the integrity of the vision, and the purity of their obedience becomes manifest.

When Allah then redeems Ibrahim's son, that is because Ibrahim and his family have persisted in their commitment to vision, until its truth has been revealed. They have not denied vision, as Satan wanted them to, but have permitted Allah alone to specify the content and meaning of vision. When Allah promises Isaac in this interpretation that he will grant him any prayer, Isaac replies: "My God, I pray to you that I be granted this: that you grant entry into Paradise to any worshiper, past or present, who encounters you and does not make anything a partner with you." Isaac here evolves into the primary symbol of the promise of Paradise to all who remain true to Ibrahim's vision, no matter what the cost. As Al Tabari goes on to relate, this refusal to consider anything equal to God characterized the patriarchs generally, so that Allah is indeed the God of Ibrahim, and of all the prophets and patriarchs, with the sacrifice in *Al Saffat* featuring as the greatest proof of the obedience of Ibrahim and his son.

Ibrahim's sacrificial vision came neither from Satan nor directly from God—who had never wanted a sacrifice when he set up this "trial"—but from Ibrahim's and Isma'il's devotion to God. Ibrahim has a vision, in the midst of his contention over idolatry, which leads him to see himself offering even his own son, and Isma'il consents. In the surah *Al Saffat*, unlike in the Book of Genesis, Allah does not personally command the sacrifice, but does personally intervene to prevent the sacrifice. The Qur'an removes the Bible's ambiguity in regard to divine intent, as later Muslim interpretation shows.

Because Ka'b Al Akhbar fully incorporated references to Satan within the visionary resolution of what the sacrifice meant in the Qur'an, and his reading proved powerful within the history of Muslim interpretation. He was known as a rabbi who had converted to Islam while Muhammad was in Medina, and his previous experience proved vital in his exposition of the Prophet's teaching. Like other rabbis of his time, Ka'b Al Akhbar portrayed God as opposed to any human offering, even as the devotion of the patriarchs would have permitted that sacrifice, and he enhanced that sensibility within Islam.

The promise of Paradise for Ibrahim's son at the close of the Muslim Aqedah finds a distorted echo in some of the most harrowing events of our time. According to one of his former students, testifying at the time of his capture at fifteen years old, a mullah named Hamidullah in Pakistan promised the adolescents he trained as suicide bombers that "if we blew ourselves up, we would go directly to Paradise." Many events in successive centuries were necessary to reduce the Muslim Aqedah to that lethal formula, which effectively reverses the sense of both the Qur'an and its authentic interpretation. Just as in the cases of Judaism and Christianity, however, the development of that reversal needs to be understood before it can be adequately addressed.

Contact and competition with Judaism was one reason Muslim interpreters insisted the son involved in the Aqedah was Isma'il. Al Tabari tells the story of the second Caliph 'Umar and his discussion with a Jew who had converted to Islam. 'Umar asked the man, "Which of the two sons was Ibrahim commanded to sacrifice?" The man answered:

> Isma'il, by God, prince of the believers! The Jews know that, but they are envious of you Arabs because it was your father who was named in God's command and to whom God ascribed such merit for his steadfastness in obeying God's command. They reject that and claim that it was Isaac because Isaac was their father.

This discussion might well reflect the growth of the interpretive tradition in Judaism, according to which the Aqedah was preceded by a dispute between Ishmael and Isaac, in which Ishmael boasted of his greater sacrifice in being circumcised at the age of consent rather than as an infant, and Isaac replied that he was prepared to sacrifice all his members for God's honor.

On the other hand, it is also conceivable that the Islamic teaching is what prompted this midrash: the dating of the sources concerned is not always refined enough to tell which interpretation is the earlier. In any case, dating the literary sources would not settle the issue of where and when the intriguing competition between the two sons took hold in the oral tradition. Yet Al Tabari does clearly show why the identification of the son as Isma'il became attractive to Muslims, and especially to Arabs among them.

Al Tabari also demonstrates that, even when the identity of the son changes, the theme of the story remains the same. He transmits the version of Ibn Humayd, in which Iblis, an evil demon, tries to convince Ibrahim, Isma'il, and Isma'il's mother, Hagar, that the command to sacrifice was made up and really came from Satan. That leads to the succinct moral of the whole saga, which agrees with Ka'b Al Akhbar's:

So the enemy of God returned enraged, for he had not achieved anything with the family of Ibrahim. They had all refused to deal with him by God's help, and they had agreed with God's command, saying, "To hear is to obey."

That emphasis on obedience transcends the controversy over the son's identity. Because of Ibrahim's steadfastness, Allah "took him as his friend and appointed him a leader for all those of his creatures who were to come after him." Through all the twists and turns of legend and the embellishment of controversy, the theme of the story remained the same from Muhammad to Al Tabari and beyond: Islam was born in vision, and in the willingness to be corrected by vision, even in the heat of action.

For Ibrahim's visionary obedience to be complete, two conditions needed to be met. The Muslim interpretive tradition explores these intrinsic necessities, which flow from the theological message of *Al Saffat*. First, Allah cannot be the source of the command to sacrifice: the redemptive offering of an animal has to have been Allah's wish all along. And second, although vision is the medium of the sacrifice, Ibrahim needs to be understood to have followed through thoroughly until the moment of God's intervention. Whether applied to Isaac or Isma'il, Muslim interpreters spelled out the inherent logic of the Qur'an to the point that it became unmistakable.

Al Tabari offers the penetrating insight that Ibrahim had asked Allah for a righteous son, and when the angels told him his wish had been granted, then Ibrahim rather than Allah said, "Then he is a sacrificial victim." In other words, Allah does not originate the imperative; it only becomes a divine command when Ibrahim is told, "Fulfill the promise which you made to God." It is the fact of the promise freely made by Ibrahim, not its content, that requires Ibrahim's obedience. Al Tabari is quite clear, in line with the Qur'an, that from the divine point of view everything that happened was "an obvious trial" from the outset, and so he adds a dimension of analysis: the impetus for the sacrifice came from Ibraham's atavism, not from Allah's will.

Once Ibrahim shows that he will obey, the sacrifice itself is revealed to be unnecessary. But how far does he have to go? In one story that Al Tabari records, after father and son had wept until a pool of tears gathered, Ibrahim drew the knife so forcibly across Isaac that his son was saved only by a sheet of copper God had put on his throat. In the equivalent story involving Isma'il, God turned the knife backward in Ibrahim's hand; he attempted to kill his son again, but God stops him with the words, "You have carried out the dream; this victim is yours as redemption for your son, so sacrifice it instead of him."

The sacrifice Allah truly desires—an animal offering that demonstrates that Allah alone is God and alone is righteous—takes the place of what Ibrahim was willing to give, but ultimately did not need to sacrifice. In Al Tabari's reading, the Muslim Aqedah proves that no believer should ever again offer to sacrifice a human being. The redemptive sacrifice of the ram rather than the child had been the divine intention, and remains so forever, not only for Ibrahim but also for every Muslim.

As the interpretations of the Muslim Aqedah made Ibrahim more and more aggressive, to the point that Allah could only prevent the slaughter of Isma'il by miraculous means, so also the insistence that the son was truly Isma'il, and not Isaac, became more categorical. He was the same son who helped build the Ka'bah in the Qur'an, and who as an infant was saved from death with his mother, Hagar, by an angel digging a miraculous well for them at Zamzam, much as a ram miraculously appeared from Paradise to redeem Isma'il when Ibrahim was in the act of sacrificing him. Over the course of interpretation, the true son also became a willing martyr, redeemed by supernatural power.

The redemptive offering, the "immense sacrifice" of a ram Allah disclosed to Ibrahim, is recollected to this day every year at the close of the *hajj* pilgrimage, when rams and other animals are offered at Mina near the Ka'bah. This ritual involves the greatest sacrifice in a single day in our time, and probably in any time, because the ram or sheep (or—for larger groups—the cow or camel) is to be slaughtered by Muslims all over the world, not only by those on the *hajj*. What is offered near the Ka'bah represents the practice of Islam as a whole.

Believers are to remember what Ibrahim and Isma'il did, and slaughter an animal, on the *Id al-Adha*, the Feast of Sacrifice. Each year, responsible news sources estimate that 700,000 sheep are sacrificed in Mecca alone, along with cows and camels. Slaughterhouses specially commissioned by the Islamic Bank handle the killing; nearly 30,000 butchers have to work around the clock in shifts for days, because the *Halal* method—involving a single stroke of a knife, as in the Israelite laws of *Kashrut*—is followed. Families living far from Mecca also offer sacrifice, eating one-third of the animal, sharing one-third with family and neighbors, and giving away one-third to the poor.

Muhammad offered sacrifice in conscious awareness of the sacrifice that Ibrahim and his son make in *Al Saffat*—and that is the pattern that Muslims today emulate during the *Id al-Adha*. Prescribed rituals include drinking from the waters of Zamzam and throwing stones at pillars, in the same spot where Ibrahim, Hagar, and Isma'il stoned Satan when he attempted to lure them away from their duty. Ritually, Islam inscribes Ibrahim's action in the practice of each believer, and has done so for over thirteen hundred years.

As the range of Muslim conquest extended into Asia, North Africa, and Europe, Isma'il emerged as the true son of the Aqedah, displacing Isaac and challenging the claim of Christ to have completed the action of the Aqedah. All three figures stood in the minds of believers for the true inheritance of God's covenant with his people, for the single sacrifice that made ritual pleasing to God, and for the devotion of martyrs who offered their own lives on the altar of sacrificial conflict. The close of the eleventh century saw bloodshed, both self-sacrifice and the extermination of infidels in the name of God, blossom in flowers of evil that have haunted the West ever since, and that have all but obscured Muhammad's vision, and Ibrahim's, that violence is never God's requirement, but only an obvious trial.

VII

Blood Harvest

Each Abrahamic religion can arm itself, if it chooses, with the conviction that its innocent victim, Isaac or Christ or Ismaʿil, models God's desire for how his people should sacrifice themselves for him. Each can find nobility, not only in self-sacrifice, but also in adults' encouragement of children and young people to give their lives. Each can perceive mystical significance in blood that is shed on a scaffold of execution or in a field of battle, blood whose power God revealed on Moriah, Golgotha, or Mina.

After the events of September 11, 2001, and subsequent wars in Afghanistan and Iraq, books and articles on violence and religion have appeared nonstop. The relationship between Islam and militancy against Western societies is so commonly discussed that it has turned into a cliché. By way of compensation, to avoid portraying Christianity as innocent in its confrontation with Islam, publishers and filmmakers have recently revived the Crusades as another favorite subject, this time reversing the portrayal of dashing soldiers of Christ that once was fashionable. Violence and religion can easily seem synonymous to many readers and viewers.

Detailed histories of the Crusades analyze events that are complicated, appalling, and fascinating. Their fascination has also spawned less critical works that are anecdotal, episodic, and sometimes prurient. Yet beneath the surface of events, the Crusades provide an excellent example of what happens when the three Abrahamic religions meet in combat, armed with their paradigms of martyrdom. By attending to how those paradigms have been deployed, and how in their deployment each religion has made the next more dedicated in its violence, we can better understand why modern cultures, no less than their ancient and medieval predecessors, slip easily into Abraham's curse.

Many Muslims—and not only those described as militants—refer to American soldiers stationed in the Middle East as Crusaders. When President Bush asked other nations to join a "crusade" against terrorism after September 11, he was using a common enough figure of speech, but he trapped himself in a stereotype that has plagued American policy in Muslim nations and in much of Europe. Negative responses to his language from abroad reflected more than linguistic neuralgia or anti-Americanism. The underlying logic of the Crusades, which has featured for a thousand years in Western language, sensibility, history, and entertainment, as well as in Muslim analysis of the West, tells us about the position many nations feel they are in now, and it is a frightening position.

The Crusades, and responses to the Crusades, have long influenced relations among three religions that have permeated their cultures, each holding up martyrdom as a central virtue, and sometimes as the absolute requirement of faith. The Crusades offer likely entertainment because the violence, adventure, intrigue, and romance all took place, it seems, a long time ago and far, far away. But the Crusades also illuminate events of our time, in lands that technology has brought as close as our doorstep. They show what once drove, and continues to drive, the willingness of hundreds of thousands of people to give and take lives for religious reasons, as well as out of the loyalty to ideology, country, or community that often takes the place of religion. Wherever people draw together to defend a common way of life, their emotional attachments to one another, and their shared values, they become a social organism, which can call for individual lives to be spent for the good of all.

Religious or quasi-religious motivations obviously do not account for all the twists and turns in the repeated and almost wholly unsuccessful campaigns we call the Crusades. Personal, political, and commercial interests naturally drove the elites that led both sides in violent encounters from which their leaders profited, or attempted to profit. Nevertheless, the evidence regarding public support during the Crusades is unambiguous: even obviously corrupt leaders could count on substantial followings when they went to religious war with the infidel—as Christians and Muslims called one another.

By getting behind the sequence and causal connections of events, and appreciating the underlying power that the image of the martyr has exercised in all three Abrahamic religions, we can understand a motivation for the Crusades, a motivation that has reemerged repeatedly in different forms since the Crusades themselves ended in the temporary exhaustion of the West. With the recent reemergence of conflicts defined in religious terms by the antagonists themselves, coming to terms with the motivation of martyrdom has become imperative.

The demise of the Soviet Union at the end of the twentieth century saw the logic of Cold War replaced by the logic of conflict between Christianity and Islam, with the Jewish state of Israel a principal issue of contention between increasingly antagonistic sides. Nuclear, chemical, and biological weaponry, configurations of national and corporate interests, and instruments of propaganda unprecedented in their power could make the twenty-first century the most destructive since Abraham originally offered to slaughter his son. The Crusading mentality is not merely an artifact of the Roman Catholic Church during the Middle Ages, but offers vivid evidence of what can happen when cultures afflicted with Abraham's curse go to war, unless their sacrificial reflex is somehow contained.

Pope Urban II toured his native France between 1095 and his death in 1099 in order to preach the Crusade, appealing to the common conviction that bloodshed purifies the faithful and pleases God. He called for warriors who would literally bear the sign of the cross on their chests during their journey to Jerusalem, as pilgrim cross-bearers (*croisés* in French, crusaders in English) who could celebrate their release from sin as they went to battle. If they died in their struggle against the heathen, Urban guaranteed with his authority as pope, their sins would be forgiven.

Urban grounded his argument for why Crusaders should go forth to battle with an assessment of their present, sinful condition at home, which could be cured, he promised, by battling abroad. He added a practical edge to his appeal, which amounted to an attempt at social engineering. He predicted that a good war fought against a common foe would at last resolve the problem of internecine squabbles among the bellicose knights of medieval Europe.

Urban gave voice to a sound political instinct, which Ronald Reagan later echoed. After meeting with Soviet leader Mikhail Gorbachev, he once remarked that he thought to himself, "How easy his task and mine might be in these meetings that we held if suddenly there was a threat to this world from some other species from another planet outside in the universe." Debate surrounds the question of whether President Reagan actually thought that an alien invasion was likely, but there is no disputing his insight that engagement with a foreign threat brings domestic unity by displacing the human penchant toward violence outward, from parochial opponents to external enemies.

Yet Urban was thinking, not only politically, but also in terms of the supernatural virtue of giving one's life for the Catholic faith. He believed that fractious knights at home could be transformed into heroic martyrs in the crucible of holy war. By means of both the blood they offered and the lives they took on the way to Jerusalem, he explicitly stated that each Crusader became "a living, holy and pleasing sacrifice" to God.

Urban also made the connection between the Crusaders and the Maccabees before them, comparing Maccabean combat "for rituals and the Temple" to the new and nobler struggle for the *patria*, the "fatherland." His incentive to compete with the memory of the zealots of ancient history sowed seeds in the minds of many Crusaders that quickly blossomed into some of their most despicable atrocities. The speed, vehemence, and scale of their actions defy explanation with routine reference to self-interest.

Historians have often remarked that the Crusades successfully combined Medieval hunger for pilgrimage, penitence, and spoil with assertions of national and papal power. Those observations are valid, but the extraordinary popular energy unleashed by the Crusades has nonetheless puzzled historians, chiefly because they have not adequately factored in the sacrificial dimension of Urban's appeal. Self-*sacrifice*, more than self-interest, is the hidden hand guiding this strange and relentless history.

Popular response to Urban's call exceeded all expectations, in numbers and in zeal. Crusaders became notoriously difficult to control, because they included not only knights, but hosts of untrained enthusiasts, especially from the peasantry. They took the papal grant of forgiveness very much to heart, because Urban promised a reward for the present as well as the future: "he absolved all the penitent from all their sins from the hour they took the Lord's cross and he lovingly released them from all hardships, whether fasting or other mortification of the flesh." Crusading was a license, not only to kill, but also to eat one's fill and indulge other appetites, absolved in advance from the sins of greed, theft, and lust. Battle took the place of the penance, payment, and stringent disciplines usually required for forgiveness.

Pope Urban sought to persuade "men of all ranks, knights as well as foot soldiers, rich as well as poor, to carry aid promptly to those Christians [in Muslim lands] and to destroy that vile race from the lands of your brethren." The response gave him more than he had appealed for. In the First Crusade alone, between 60,000 and 100,000 people—men, women, and children—answered Urban's call. Thousands of them, especially the badly trained, amateurs, and the young, were served up to their Muslim enemies for slaughter in modern-day Turkey, far short of the goal of their "pilgrimage."

But what did death matter? After all, immediate remission of sins and joy for eternity remained heady rewards. The adrenaline of revenge laced these sweet prospects, because Urban had dramatized the depravity of the infidels during his celebrated speaking tour, citing atrocities against Christians such as forced circumcision, disembowelment, and rape.

Retribution and pilgrimage were combined in the Crusades, as has often been remarked, but the aim was salvation. A monk of the time, Guibert of Nogent, appreciated and repeated Urban's aim, saying, "God has instituted in our time holy wars, so that the order of knights and the crowd running in their wake, who, following the example of ancient pagans, have been engaged in slaughtering one another, might find a new way of gaining salvation." Violence had been baptized as the route to heaven for men and women and children who wished to find a way to be free of the corruption of this world despite their own worldly, violent proclivities, and to win their place in heaven with Christ.

Sinners could not make up for their sins personally according to Catholic theology, of course, but recourse to penitential discipline, or the violent shortcut of joining the Crusades, demonstrated sorrow and faith in Christ's atoning gift. Middle English poetry is filled with examples of lyrics recited at the time one paid a recompense for sin, such as the "Invocation to the Cross":

O blissful Crosse, teche us al vertu
   Plesyng to god for oure salvacion,
Quenchyng alle vices in the name of Ihesu
   Raunson payng for oure dampnacion.

That cross, portrayed as the fulfillment of the sacrifice of Isaac and the supernatural altar of God's eternal offering of his Son to himself, was now literally taken up in the Crusades by ordinary sinners, so they would be cleansed of sin for eternity. They grasped the opportunity in their tens of thousands.

The Crusaders' zeal targeted *all* those who rejected faith in Christ. Many militants took out the full vigor of their initial fervor against Jews in their own communities before they even left for the Holy Land, as well as against Jews who lay along their path to Jerusalem. Although their pogroms might seem a grotesque perversion of Urban's aim, the Crusaders were convinced of the family resemblance among all infidels, and it seemed madness to leave the enemy undisturbed at home while fighting them abroad.

In addition to their shared rejection of Christ, circumcision represented a common bond between Muslims and Jews, designed according to the Crusade's propagandists to give "free rein for every kind of shameful behavior." Peter the Venerable, a learned monastic abbot who had the Qur'an translated into Latin in order to refute it, came to the conclusion in 1146 (or 1147) that God rejects "the Jews like the hateful Cain, the Muslims like the worshipers of Baal."

Pogroms became international Christian practice during the centuries of the Crusades. Describing the crowning of Richard the Lionhearted in 1189, Richard of Devizes offers an account that is as chilling in its rhetoric as the atrocities against Jews in England that it depicts were inhuman. Richard first refers to the Eucharist that solemnized the coronation as the sacrifice of Christ. He then links that sacrifice to another, the slaughter by Christian mobs of Jews described as "vermin": "On the very day of the coronation, about that solemn hour, in which the Son was immolated to the Father, a sacrifice of the Jews to their father the devil was commenced in the city of London, and so long was the duration of this famous mystery, that the holocaust could scarcely be accomplished the ensuing day."

Pogroms by Crusaders began as early as 1095 in Rouen and continued into the Rhineland. Campaigns against defenseless Jews punctuated the violent progress of the Crusades, finally far exceeding the Crusades themselves in duration, virulence, and body count. During the twelfth century the primordial logic of the *cherem* and the vocation of self-sacrifice in imitation of Christ fused to produce a genocidal campaign, consigning its Jewish victims to hell on earth and to the devil in death. The plague of sacrificial violence against Jews, unleashed by Cyril of Alexandria during the fifth century (see chapter V) and perfected during the Crusades, continued in Europe until the twentieth-century Holocaust, and its future remains uncertain.

The Crusaders' taste for the torture and decapitation of their victims emerged during a pogrom against the Jews in Worms, according to

written records. The holy warriors took to their method with eager-
ness, and they used it against their enemies generally; later in their
campaign they went to the extreme of unearthing Muslim dead so
as to decapitate them, too. In the case of armed opponents in the
field, however, the Crusaders had to face the inevitable outcome that
when the fortunes of war shifted, their grisly tactics could be turned
around and used against them. Nonetheless, the decapitation of enemies remained a standby Crusader practice, especially useful when
heads could be catapulted into besieged cities, in order to demoralize
their inhabitants.

By the time the First Crusade ended, Crusaders had engaged in
cannibalism at Marrat in 1098, and beheading seemed merciful compared to other means of killing at their hands. Raymond of Aguilers
wrote of the taking of Jerusalem on July 15, 1099: "Some of the pagans were mercifully beheaded, others, pierced by arrows, plunged
from towers, and yet others, tortured for a long time, were burned
to death in searing flames. Piles of heads, hands and feet lay in the
houses and streets, and men and knights were running to and fro
over corpses."

Raymond portrayed this pornographic bloodshed in terms of
sacrifice, specifying that "in the Temple our men were wading up to
their ankles in enemy blood," that some 320 corpses were set ablaze
as a burnt offering, and that the slaughter began on Friday at the ninth
hour, when Jesus was crucified. The Crusaders gathered for Mass in
the alleged place of Jesus' burial, the Church of the Holy Sepulchre,
while the blood of their victims was still on them, so that their devotion was enhanced by the blood that had been shed: their victims',
their comrades', their own—and Christ's.

While Muslim armies could turn the Crusaders' tactics against them,
and Muslim theologians articulated teachings of jihad to address the
new situation, Jewish families and communities had no recourse to
military defense. A Christian chronicler, Albert of Aachen, recorded
that in Mainz in 1096, "The Jews, seeing that their Christian enemies
were attacking them and their children, and that they were sparing

no age, likewise fell upon one another, brothers, children, wives, and sisters, and thus they perished at each other's hands. Horrible to say, mothers cut the throats of nursing children with knives and stabbed others, preferring them to perish thus by their own hands than to be killed by the weapons of the uncircumcised."

A Jewish chronicler, drawing on the example of Abraham, made both the actions and the motivations involved even more explicit in his description of collective suicide: "Each one in turn sacrificed and was sacrificed, until the blood of one touched the blood of another. The blood of husbands mixed with that of the wives, the blood of fathers and their children, and the blood of brothers and their sisters, and blood of rabbis and their disciples, the blood of bridegrooms and their brides . . . the blood of children and nursing infants and their mothers. They were killed and slaughtered for the unity of God's glorious and awesome name."

From the perspective of the biblical and Judaic tradition, the question had to be asked, and it was asked: "Were there ever 1,100 Aqedahs on one day—all of them like the Aqedah of Isaac, son of Abraham?" In the face of this carnage, "Why did the heavens not grow dark and the stars not hold back their splendor?" Isaac ben David, warden of the Jewish community in Mainz, put into brutal action the theology, current since the time of the Maccabees, that explained innocent sacrifice. He killed his children in front of the ark of the Torah in the synagogue, and said, "May this blood be atonement for all my sins."

The horror of the images makes them difficult to believe, and the force of legend and oral retelling is palpable in many stories of the Crusades' Jewish victims. In one famous story, a young mother named Rachel killed her children, one of them named Isaac:

She took her young son Isaac—he was most pleasant—and slaughtered him. . . . As for the lad Aaron, upon seeing that his brother had been slain he shouted, "My mother, my mother, do not slay me"; and he went and hid under a box. Rachel then took her two daughters Bella and Madrona and sacrificed them to the Lord, God of hosts, who commanded us not to compromise our untainted fear of him and to be totally wholehearted with him. When the righteous woman finished sacrificing her three children to our Creator, she raised her voice and called out to her son, "Aaron, Aaron, where are you? I shall not have mercy to spare you either." She pulled him by his leg out from under the box where he had hidden and sacrificed him to God the powerful and the exalted.

Crusaders, enraged that they had been cheated of young lives to kill, beat the sacrificial mother to death.

In perhaps the most disturbing, darkly described tale of preemptive slaughter within a Jewish congregation, a community head (*parnas*) and prospective father-in-law took the lives of both his son, named Abraham, and his son's bride to be, tragically named Sarit (a diminutive form of the name Sarah). When she tried to escape her Aqedah by running away, the *parnas* intervened:

> He called to her, "My daughter, since you did not have the privilege of wedding my son Abraham, you will not marry any Gentile either." He caught hold of her . . . kissed her on the mouth, and raised his voice, wailing together with the maiden. He cried out in a loud voice, bitterly, to all those present, "Behold, all of you, this is the wedding of my daughter, my bride, that I am performing today." They all cried, sobbing and wailing, mourning and moaning. The pious Master Judah said to her, "Come and lie in the bosom of Abraham our father, for in an instant you will acquire your place in the next world and enter into the company of the righteous and pious." He took her and laid her upon the bosom of his son Abraham her betrothed and, with his sharpened sword, he cut her up the middle into two parts; then he also slaughtered his son.

The resonance of these stories with the Aqedah is as manifest as their unremitting violence, inspired by biblical descriptions of cutting sacrificial victims in half. The narratives' total dedication to the ideal of sacrifice pushes aside moral objection to taking the lives not only of one's children, but also of young people who wanted no part of self-sacrifice.

The acts described, of course, were not voluntary or spontaneous oblations of human life; they were reactions either to certain, painful death or to torture that would lead to apostasy or to death. In the face of virulent Christian persecution, self-sacrifice seemed the noblest course. As a Jewish priest said, when he and his friends were surrounded by Crusaders: "Let not the wicked hands of the impure defile us with their abominable rites, but let us offer ourselves as a sacrifice to God brought on the altar of God, total burnt offerings to the most high."

One purpose of these stories is to challenge the underlying sacrificial ideology of the Crusades, by putting the self-sacrifice of Jews above that of the Crusaders. Some details are no doubt exaggerated, and at times surreal, but the narratives serve a serious and specific purpose—to convince Christian authorities to call off and prohibit pogroms while encouraging Jews to remain loyal to their faith. As in the time of the Maccabees and of the revolutionaries against Rome who committed suicide at Masada rather than surrender, the Aqedah motivated the practice of literal self-sacrifice and child-sacrifice among the martyrs of France and the Rhineland at the dawn of the Crusades and later, in order to sanctify the name of God and to ward off assaults by Christian mobs.

In the case of Muslim theology, the teaching of jihad—"struggle" in the way of Allah—has put Ibrahim's and Isma'il's obedience to Allah into practice by means of military confrontations with those who are unfaithful to Allah. Contemporary apologists for Islam often say that jihad principally refers to one's own personal struggle to submit to God, the "interior" jihad, and that only the onslaught of the Crusaders produced the concept of an "exterior" jihad of military conquest. Good, strong evidence partially validates this argument, but it fails as a satisfactory account of jihad, to begin with because the distinction between interior (or "greater") and exterior (or "lesser") jihad predates the Crusades.

Furthermore, the Muslim Aqedah, and its association with Isma'il as faithful son and warrior against idolatry, emerged long before the Crusades. That image has time and again proven an effective motivation for military action, both directly and in stories of martyrs whose virtues mirror Isma'il's.

Muhammad himself led the victorious military campaign from Medina back to Mecca, in addition to other battles. He dedicated himself to cleansing the sanctuary of Mecca, centered on the huge square stone called the Ka'bah. The idols around that stone needed to be removed and destroyed, according to Muhammad's revelation, because that precise place was the earthly counterpart of Allah's heavenly sanctuary directly above Mecca. Pilgrimage there, which involves prayer and sacrifice, is one of the five "pillars" of Islam required of every believer, together with acknowledging Allah as the only God with Muhammad as his prophet, daily prayer five times a day, giving alms, and keeping the fast of Ramadan. When believers—thousands in Muhammad's day, hundreds of thousands in ours—circulate counterclockwise around the Ka'bah seven times, they take part in the dance of the angels in heaven around the Throne of God directly above. Islam, no less than Judaism and Christianity, offers its followers participation in actions connected with the divine world, not merely teachings about God.

War to liberate the Ka'bah therefore involved more than strategic interest, and required no additional moral justification, such as self-defense. Military action is sometimes intrinsic to the practice of Islam, and the Qur'an enjoins jihad in this sense (Qur'an, *Al Baqarah* 2:216). When Muhammad cleared the idols from the Ka'bah, he reproduced the faithfulness of Ibrahim and Isma'il, who had also established the worship of Allah there. The act of clearing the Ka'bah is so intimately connected with the sacrifice of Isma'il that an influential jurist and scholar taught that Muhammad hid the horns of the ram used to redeem Isma'il near the Ka'bah.

Very early *hadith* (that is, stories of sayings and deeds of the Prophet not included in the Qur'an, but preserved among his companions and their followers) portray Ibrahim as a militant warrior for this cause. Ibrahim was so zealous, he used an iron bar to smash heads and limbs off of idols, hanging the instrument of this destruction on the biggest statue he could find. Ibn Ishaq, an eighth-century scholar named after Isaac, told of how Ibrahim's persecutor, Nimrod, ordered the patriarch killed by fire for destroying the idols of the same Kaʻbah, and of how Allah himself extinguished the flames.

Ibrahim, in other words, was a *ghazi*, a warrior—and because he confronted the real prospect of death, he might have been a *shahid*, with the same sense of witness and the same intimation of suffering that the terms *martus* in Greek and *shahad* in Aramaic convey. Muhammad expected to be numbered as a *shahid*, although—like Ibrahim—he was more a model of the warrior. Snatched from the flames designed to kill him, Ibrahim went on to clear the Kaʻbah with the help of his son Ismaʻil. When Ibrahim asked his son for a stone to restore the Kaʻbah, it is said the angel Gabriel fetched the black stone from India that Muslims kiss to this day.

Jihad with its connection to martyrdom proved effective within a context of tribal warfare, and brought Islam international conquests long before the Crusades. In December of 627, the Byzantine emperor Heraclius put an end to what he thought was the greatest threat to his empire, the Persian superpower that Greece and Rome had elevated to mythic proportions, when he defeated the Sassanid dynasty's army at Nineveh. Heraclius took back Jerusalem and restored sacred relics to the Holy City that the Sassanids had plundered. But he overlooked the quarter from which his greatest defeat was impending.

In 630, Heraclius triumphantly returned the "Holy Cross" (the wood on which Jesus had allegedly been crucified) to the Holy City, but he then saw his army, tens of thousands strong, defeated by the new Muslim forces at Yarmuk during August of 636. Jerusalem fell two years later, and the Holy Cross had to be shipped to Constantinople, while the "Holy Lance" that allegedly killed Jesus was removed to Antioch.

The Muslim doctrine of the "four swords" emerged during the early centuries of spectacular triumph:

Allah gave the Prophet Muhammad four swords: the first against the polytheists, which Muhammad himself fought with; the second against apostates, which Caliph Abu Bakr fought with; the third against the People of the Book [Christians and Jews], which Caliph 'Umar fought with; and the fourth against dissenters, which Caliph 'Ali fought with.

This teaching by Al-Shaybani, who died in 804 C.E., helps explain what motivated the enormous success of Muslim raiders, especially during a time when the two superpowers of the era, the Byzantine empire and the Sassanid empire, had largely exhausted themselves in confrontation with one another. Centuries prior to Urban II, Islam had found a way to turn lethal squabbles among clans outward into productive conquests for the *umma*, the community.

Jihad by no means precluded peaceful relations with Christianity. In 800, eastern monks presented Charlemagne with keys to the Church of the Holy Sepulchre and the standard of the city of Jerusalem, along with sacred relics, after long negotiations with the Muslim Abbasids in Baghdad conducted by Isaac, a Jew whom Charlemagne had sent as part of a contact group. But once the Crusades became the norm, resort to anything but violence to gain access to Jerusalem seemed a betrayal to many Christians. Frederick II, the Holy Roman Emperor, led his Crusade more by diplomacy and his own knowledge of Arabic than by force of arms, and arranged for Jerusalem, Bethlehem, and Nazareth to be placed under Christian control in 1229, but Frederick, called "the Infidel Emperor," saw his settlement rejected by the papacy.

The resilience of the Qur'anic teaching is such that it proved adaptable to the cessation of conquest as well as to extension into new territories. The jurist Al-Shafi'i (who died in 820 C.E.) taught that jihad was a *collective* responsibility, not required of Muslims individually, during the period that Islam settled into relatively stable borders with Christian lands. The Crusades, of course, as well as attendant actions such as the Christian "reconquest" of Spain, meant the end of relative stability and signaled the need for a militant definition of jihad.

No single figure better represents the Muslim response to the threat of the Crusades than Saladin, the general born in Tikrit who welded disparate Muslim kingdoms in the eastern Mediterranean basin into a single force, dedicated to Sunni Islam. The triumph of Saladin over the Crusaders was triggered by the ill-advised attempt of the Crusading knight Renaud de Châtillon, beginning in 1182, to destroy Mecca and Medina. This brought to the land of the Ka'bah a threat that neither Muhammad nor the Qur'an had foreseen, but one that clearly justified jihad, serving to help Saladin forge a united opposition.

Renaud at first succeeded to the fateful extent that he nearly kidnapped Saladin's sister in 1187. Saladin vowed he would decapitate Renaud with his own scimitar. After the Battle of Hittin later the same year, he did just that, ordering the execution of two hundred Templars and Hospitallers at the same time.

During his campaign, which included the liberation of Jerusalem, Saladin learned of the death of his little son, named Isma'il. On the Feast of Sacrifice, which commemorates Ibrahim's offering of his son, Saladin made a vow in Jerusalem that would influence the understanding of jihad ever after: "I think that when God grants me victory over the rest of Palestine I shall divide my territories, make a will stating my wishes, then set sail on the sea for their far-off lands and pursue the Franks there so as to free the earth of anyone who does not believe in God, or die in the attempt." One of his biographers, when describing Saladin's victory at Tiberias, relates both the grisly consequences of jihad and the deep conviction that the land needed to be purified of Christianity: "The field of battle became a sea of blood; the dust was stained red, rivers of blood ran freely, and the face of the true Faith was revealed free from those shadowy abominations." In a chilling throwback to the Crusaders' pogroms against the Jews, 'Imad ad-Din observes that "the humiliation proper to the men of Saturday was inflicted on the men of Sunday." Jihad had been unleashed for defensive reasons, but with an intensity and an extension in its reach which, in theory, no one could escape.

The following century the jurist Ibn Taymiyah (1268–1328 C.E.), responding partially to confrontation with Crusaders but chiefly to Mongol invasions from the east, articulated a definition of jihad that made it the literal pinnacle of Muslim faith, based on the Prophet's analogy of dedication to Allah to a camel, "the head of the affair is Islam, its central pillar is the *salat* [prayer], and the tip of the hump is the jihad." This made Ibn Taymiyah say, as he is still quoted on militant Web sites today: "Now, it is in jihad that one can live and die in ultimate happiness, both in this world and in the hereafter."

The bloodied Crusader, the Jewish child literally called an Aqedah, the *shahid* who dies in the midst of the jihad, have confronted one another in battle and met one another in sacrifice—not continuously, but with sporadic intensity—since the eleventh century of the Common Era. Woven into texts and traditions that combine metaphor, archetype, and direct identification with martyrs of the faith, they reach into the symbolic depths of culture, where people can be moved to act for reasons they are often in no position to understand.

Each of these models of martyrdom reflects the most central medieval paradigms of the Abrahamic religions. The Crusader sheds his blood, and the blood of others, to celebrate the redemptive power of Christ's blood at the Church of the Holy Sepulchre. The Jewish children of the Rhineland are new sacrifices of Isaac that exceed the devotion Genesis attributes to Abraham. In the case of Islam, the paradigm of Isma'il at the time of Ibrahim's offering equates death in the context of struggle to the deepest obedience to Allah.

The Feast of Sacrifice (*Id al-Adha*) takes place as part of the *hajj*. Punctuating his procession toward the act of sacrifice, in a way that echoes the response of Ibrahim to Allah, the pilgrim cries, "What is thy command? I am here!" In addition to the animal sacrifice itself, which is set near Mina, where Isma'il was offered, pilgrims take part in a specific imitation of Ibrahim and Isma'il. At Mina there are monuments where, according to tradition, Satan appeared to Isma'il, to lure him into disobedience. Isma'il replies by throwing stones at Satan, and that is what the worshipers do today. They not only stand in Isma'il's place; they do what he did, and embrace the intention to carry that impulse within them when they return from the *hajj*. No less than in the Christian Eucharist and in the Jewish *shofar* at Rosh Hashanah, the Aqedah resonates in the practice as well as in the theology of Islam in a way that makes it inextricable from Muslim faith.

Europe's culture of self-sacrifice has proven no less influential.

When new European slaughters with religious dimensions break out—as they have persistently and catastrophically in Northern Ireland and the Balkans, for example—they are typically dismissed as atavistic throwbacks that prove the rule that Europe as a whole has outgrown wars of religion. Dismissals of that kind mistake the depth of Europe's constitutional dedication to holy war, and require an effort of amnesia.

Northern Ireland and the Balkans may appear to be unusual tragedies, but the Jewish population of Europe was subject to repeated pogroms throughout the Middle Ages and the Renaissance, explosions of Christian *cherem* that erupted when England and France, for example, emerged under Christian monarchies. Just as England saw its Jews expelled in 1290 under Edward I, the Spanish Reconquista forced both Jews in 1492 and Muslims in 1502 to convert or face banishment. Violence in the name of purity, national and religious, was delayed in Germany, partially as a result of the late birth of nationalism there, but it broke out under the Third Reich in a uniquely deadly form because technologies existed during the twentieth century that had not been available before, and because theories of race gave the appearance of scientific truth to the old Crusading attack on Jews.

The monk and chronicler Richard of Devizes had called Jews "vermin" when he described the pogrom of 1189 in cities in England, which became a tradition for centuries in Europe, decimating ghettos. For Nazi theorists, the extermination needed to be "final," because even small traces of "Jewish blood," as they called it, would contaminate Aryan purity. Just as Adolf Hitler magnified Crusader rhetoric in regard to Jews, so he took up Pope Urban's pleas for the defense of the "fatherland," as if a refusal to attack one's enemies preemptively, by self-sacrifice if necessary, were a betrayal of one's native soil and kin. Hitler was brilliant as a propagandist but utterly unoriginal in his message, and the masses who listened to him in Germany were no more culpable than the masses of Christians in France and England and Spain and Hungary centuries earlier who decided to put their swords to nearby enemies while preparing to combat foreign foes.

The theme of the enemy within emerged as a vital factor within the drive to holy war in the West, with results as violent as the Crusades themselves. In France, Crusading zeal targeted the Cathars, a group devoted to a version of Christianity that saw spirit as separate and distinct from the world of flesh. Pope Innocent III was outraged by the Cathar teaching that Mary Magdalene was Jesus' concubine, although his vehemence may have had more to do with the Cathars' denial of papal authority and of the requirement to pay tithes to the Church than with their peculiar teaching about Jesus and Mary. Innocent declared a Crusade against the Cathars in 1209, and the result has been called the first European genocide.

On July 22, 1209, the Feast of Saint Mary Magdalene, Crusaders dispatched by the pope torched the town of Béziers, killing both the Cathars who had fled there and the Roman Catholic population that had refused to give them up. Some fifteen thousand people died that day, including the heretics and those who protected them. One pious chronicler rejoiced "that these disgusting dogs were taken and massacred during the feast of the one that they had insulted."

But what of those in Béziers who were not Cathars and did not approve of Cathar teaching? As the papal legate, Arnaud Amaury, ordered the execution, he was asked how the Crusaders would know Cathars from Catholics. He replied, "Kill them all! The Lord will know his own." That initiated a tradition of killing Cathars that successfully made the transition to killing Protestants after the Reformation, and all but eradicated both groups in France.

The persecution of the Cathars from the thirteenth century on was in several ways a prelude to religious wars during the sixteenth and seventeenth centuries, which resulted in the death of one-fifth of the population of Germany, it has been estimated, prior to the Peace of Westphalia in 1648. Some recent writings on Islam claim that the Muslim world needs the kind of Reformation from which the Christian West has benefited. But the Reformation produced willing martyrs of its own, and spawned a culture of violence in the confrontation between the papacy and the reformers. The Peace of Westphalia came only after millions of deaths, the bankruptcy of the Spanish empire, and the cruel humiliation of German nationalism. The costs of the Wars of Religion have been paid well into the twentieth century, and it is not at all clear that Europe is even today entirely free of that debt. Wishing the Reformation on Islam—whatever that may mean, since the Reformation was grounded in Christian theology—would hold out the prospect of centuries of continuing violence.

By the time of the Peace of Westphalia, Europe—now involving relatively new imperial powers such as Catholic Spain and the Protestant Netherlands—had fought internecine colonial wars as well as wars with indigenous peoples in the lands they conquered. In 1492, the same year as the expulsion of Jews from Spain, Christopher Columbus had made his appeal for funds to Ferdinand and Isabella in terms of freeing eastern lands from the benighted rule of the infidels. Although, given Columbus's self-serving conduct in the New World, it would be ludicrous to characterize him simply as a Crusader, it is equally egregious to deny that one force behind colonialism was the Crusading impulse in a mercantile form.

Each Crusading wave drew power from stories of martyrdom. Catholic and Protestant saints died by burning at the stake, the overwhelming majority at the hands of fellow Christians, and are remembered to this day in the calendars of their churches. Thomas à Becket, hacked to death at the order of his own king, nonetheless shone as "a bright candle on God's candlestick," in the words of William Fitz Stephen. The intrepid conquistador or British settler spurred himself on to a deadly opposition to all "Indians," as well as a taste for slavery, by recounting stories of how they and all the darker races eviscerated male captives, raped women, and maimed children. These tales of horror demanded a single, noble response: the willingness of soldiers to risk their lives, to give the ultimate sacrifice if need be, to kill for the good of civilized people.

Jews were charged with celebrating demonic masses in which they drank the blood of children and ate their flesh as well as with the profiteering and moral degeneracy that are repeated to this day in the *Protocols of the Elders of Zion*. To do battle with this insidious, manipulative foe put every participant in a pogrom at deadly risk—and, of course, justified all manner of violence.

Traveling in Germany forty years ago, I took a photograph of a statue of a soldier dressed as an infantryman. Below this anonymous hero the epitaph read, "Deutschland muss leben, und wenn wir sterben muss": "Germany must live, even if we must die." Without using the names of Isaac and Christ or consciously involving Genesis 22, this statue embodies an attitude toward war as self-sacrificial and noble. In fact, it is the last line of several stanzas written for the First World War, and recycled for the Second World War. One stanza reads:

> God calls us, my wife, God calls us!
> He who made our home, bread, and Fatherland,
> Justice, courage and love his weapons,
> God calls us, my wife, God calls us!
> If we atone for our happiness with mourning:
> Germany must live, even if we must die!

Without a formal Crusade, but with skillful incentives to martyrdom—and threats of ostracism and imprisonment for those who refused military service—Europeans sacrificed millions of their young and countless civilians in wars portrayed on all sides as noble, and often as divinely sanctioned.

Just as, during prolonged contact with Crusaders, teachings of jihad found new intensity and force, so Muslim scholars have most praised the martyrs' flame during times of oppression and resistance. In haunting similarity to the characterization of Thomas à Becket, the Shi'a scholar Murtaza Mutahhari, himself the victim of assassination in 1979, wrote: "The *shahid* can be compared to a candle whose job it is to burn out and get extinguished in order to shed light for the benefit of others. The *shuhada'* are the candles of society." In a funeral oration, his teacher—the Ayatollah Khomeini of Iran—praised Mutahhari and asserted that "Islam grows through sacrifice and the martyrdom of its cherished ones."

Confidence in the efficacy of martyrdom, deeply resonant with early Christian sources, grew as a result of Mutahhari's writings. He successfully made the connection between the Iranian revolution, martyrdom, and jihad: "Islam came to reform society and to form a nation and government. Its mandate is the reform of the whole world.

Such a religion cannot be indifferent. It cannot be without a law of jihad." The Shi'a focus on martyrdom is achieved most visibly in loyalty to Ali, the Prophet's cousin as well as son-in-law, a fabled warrior willing to put his life in danger for the Prophet, the true successor of Muhammad who fell victim to assassination.

Ali's son, Husayn, grandson of the Prophet through his mother Fatima, represented the continuation of that authority. In the Shi'a view, he had every right to be recognized as the caliph, the successor of the Prophet. But Husayn had to battle for this claim against the Umayyad dynasty, which claimed its succession, not by hereditary right, but through its keeping the traditions of the Prophet, the Sunna that are the basis of Sunni Islam. The story of Husayn's martyrdom, a narrative with a ritual rhythm as compelling in its own way as the Aqedah, is a keystone of Shi'a theology that has recently grown in influence within Islam as a whole.

Husayn was martyred with supporters and members of his family during the Battle of Karbala in 680, after a siege that deprived them of water. Husayn's six-month-old son was near death, and his father took him in his arms to ask his Umayyad opponents for water. One of them shot an arrow that killed the infant; Husayn buried his child and then went back to war. When he paused for prayer, he was attacked by arrows and spears, and beheaded as he lay on the ground. His head was put on a pike and his body abused, that abuse marking his status among Shi'a as "leader of the martyrs."

During the festival of Ashura, which commemorates the death of Husayn and his companions, self-wounding and fasting are practiced, and small children—especially boys—are cut in imitation of the wounds inflicted on the martyrs. Much has been made of the comparison between these practices and the Passion Plays and flagellations of the Middle Ages as well as Roman Catholic theology, but Ashura reflects a deep connection to core elements of Islam beyond its more or less striking similarity to some forms of Christian piety.

Because these martyrs die of wounds on the field of battle, they fulfill the paradigm of the warrior-victim, becoming a model for how violence—both inflicted and suffered—becomes holy. At the same time, the emphasis on the thirst of Husayn and his son is a precise link with Isma'il, the ancestor of the Muslims, because Isma'il and his mother, Hagar, were saved from thirst in the desert at Zamzam when Sarah's jealousy forced them away from Ibrahim.

The power of Ashura resides not only in its peculiar importance among the Shi'a, but also in its intensification of the reflex of self-sacrifice that is embedded in the Muslim portrait of Isma'il, crossing sectarian boundaries. The depth of that reflex helps account for how, from the time of Saladin until this day, Muslims can unite in order to defend "the land of the two holy places" (Mecca and Medina), a phrase frequently used, for example, by Osama bin Laden. Husayn and his infant son as remembered during the feast of Ashura subsume key elements associated with Isma'il. Their wounds and death realize in history what Isma'il offered to suffer in vision, completing the sacrifice that remains visionary in the case of Ibrahim and his son.

Just as the logic of the Crusades turned inward within Europe to hunt down Jews, Cathars, Templars, Protestants, and the like, so Saladin's conquests were not limited to Crusaders. Occupying Egypt prior to any contact with the Crusaders, he conquered the Muslim dynasty of the Fatimids and extended the dominance of Sunni Islam. Yet despite his undoubted successes and subsequent fame among Muslims and Christians alike, neither his empire nor his jihad long survived his death. His motivating paradigm of the self-sacrificial warrior nonetheless remains a permanent legacy.

After the time of Saladin, a sense of retrenchment, an inevitable outcome of Europe's episodic expeditions and constant Crusading rhetoric, was exacerbated by the fall of Baghdad to Hulagu Khan in 1258, which shifted the center of gravity of Islam toward the west. Islam's greater proximity to Europe proved perilous during the period of aggressive European colonialism, as when Napoleon invaded and seized Egypt in 1798, only to be supplanted by the British. The perceived need for loyal unity in the midst of a sea of hostility brought about Ottoman attempts to move into central Europe, and campaigns came as far as Vienna in 1683, as well as a succession of wars of internal conquest, climaxing with the Armenian tragedy in 1915 through 1917.

Since the First World War, two reflexes of violent self-sacrifice for the sake of permanent glory—embodied in the Crusader's and the jihadi's willingness to submit to death—have played themselves out in chess moves of point and counterpoint. The alliance of the Ottoman Empire with the Central Powers during World War I came as a reply to memories of constant French and British incursions into the Middle East, and that decision encouraged the victors to carve up Muslim territory into approximately its present quilt of national boundaries at the end of the war.

The British proved to be the major, moving force in a military and economic occupation that required, for example, 135,000 soldiers to deal with insurgency in Iraq in 1920. But Afghanistan showed the way to successful resistance to the British and subsequent invaders: local warlords with intensely loyal *mujahideen* (that is warriors of jihad) proved flexible, invisible, and effective. Since the First World War, three empires—British, Soviet, and American (with European support)—have attempted to occupy Afghanistan. In all three cases, national, industrialized armies with a predominantly Christian cultural identity have confronted local, lightly armed forces with a predominantly Muslim cultural identity.

From both sides of the conflict in each case, detailed accounts of atrocity have made the confrontation into a modern-day Aqedah for one civilization or both, the necessary ordeal of a divinely sanctioned conflict. That is the inadvertent outcome of Pope Urban's logic: the outward-directed violence that seems harmless because it is directed to a faraway enemy in fact only intensifies Abraham's curse, by galvanizing the praise of violence at home and provoking its mirror image abroad, until the violence returns to the doorstep, better armed and raging for blood.

A common response to the connection between the logic of sacrifice and people's tendency to harm themselves and one another is to accept the inevitability of human violence. Indeed, one possible reading of the analysis of this book would support that response. If sacrifice is endemic within human culture since the time of the Neolithic invention of the city, and if offering human victims is a predictable event in sacrificial cultures when they confront crises so severe as to threaten their destruction, then at least sporadic examples of human sacrifice and its equivalents are only to be expected.

Since the Abrahamic monotheisms have inscribed the model of the willing sacrificial victim—be it Isaac, Christ, or Isma'il—within the moral conscience of three millennia of believers, what kind of children would they produce except those prepared to sacrifice their lives for the faith, or—in the secular version of the same Abrahamic reflex—for an ideology, a country, or a cause?

Many people I have spoken with over the years concerning humanity's propensity toward sacrificial violence, particularly in the West, have said that they are resigned to its inevitable repetition. Thomas Carlyle came up with the name "the dismal science" to describe the field of economics, but some of my readers might think of economics as optimistic when compared to the results of considering the theology of sacrifice and violence.

Although I think it is evident that Abraham's curse has taken more lives in its sacrificial violence since the end of Antiquity than it did between the Stone Age until that time, an indisputably dismal conclusion, I see no inevitability in that regression. Rather, the *conviction* that violence is inevitable as well as endemic plays into the worst excesses of our primordial, sacrificial reflex. Historical experience over the long term warns us away from any easy resignation to tragic inevitability.

On the view that Abraham's curse is inevitable, there is a seemingly realistic option in the face of our constitutional proclivity to destroy one another: unleash the violence that always subsists within the logic of sacrifice and direct it toward a good, or at least a relatively nondestructive, end. That apparently sensible program, couched in a deliberate and realistic assessment of human nature, was applied a thousand years ago, and it plunged the West into a series of retributive wars. The Crusades set its own whirl of violence in motion, and many other forces have been sucked into its vortex.

A shattered community at the end of the eleventh century could ask, "Were there ever eleven hundred Aqedahs on one day—all of them like the Aqedah of Isaac, son of Abraham?" Judged by the standards of the twentieth century, that body count of innocent suffering seems small, dwarfed by millions lost to war, extermination, and deliberate deprivation. On any reasonable reading of Western history, war has been given too much of a chance. The fires of martyrdom, once they have consumed people zealous or desperate enough to risk all for the sake of those they love and their beliefs, risk burning everyone and everything else, until there is nothing left to burn.

Waiting for martyrdom to go away, or hoping to direct violence toward acceptable ends, have proven ineffective strategies. Further pursuit of either strategy will likely produce catastrophic results. Abraham's curse is not inevitable, in my view, but continuing reliance on the failed responses of the past will inevitably bring failure, at an ever-escalating cost.

Judaism, Christianity, and Islam, mutually devoted to Abraham and to the Scriptures that reveal the truth about him, share a common responsibility: to mine their spiritual and scriptural resources for the blessing that God promises the patriarch in all three traditions. The time is now for the same Abrahamic religions that have brought their followers to the precipice and beyond the precipice on many, many occasions, to find a safe way down from Mount Moriah.

VIII

The Long Descent

When is martyrdom heroic? When is it evil? Only partisans in war and their propaganda machines make those questions seem easy to answer. Yet some extraordinary actions, whether deliberate or spontaneous, offer profound insights, and suggest where we might find more complete responses to those complex issues.

There is no evidence that, on September 11, 2001, either the passengers on United Flight 93 or their captors had recently read of Abraham's offering in the Bible or of Ibrahim's in the Qur'an. It is doubtful that the image of the patriarch and his child was anywhere conscious in their minds. Nevertheless, the reflex of self-sacrifice, and of sacrificing others, can motivate human beings whether or not the Aqedah is a conscious influence.

The ethic of martyrdom makes self-sacrifice the only real guarantee that believers are truly faithful, and that they will win victory over the forces of unbelief. Historical experience shows that the concomitant insistence on no retreat, no quarter, no accommodation, especially when concentrated on a single enemy, frequently brings defeat—either immediately or at the hands of an unanticipated enemy. Still, once implanted, belief in martyrdom paradoxically thrives when humiliation increases; because defeat appears to be the outcome of weak faith, redoubled zeal seems the only way forward. Attitudes that support martyrdom are widely reported today among young Muslims in occupied lands, precisely because the ethos of self-sacrifice feeds on the experience of dishonor.

At the release of his film *Apocalypto*, which deals with Mayan practices of ritual human slaughter, Mel Gibson commented, "The precursors to a civilization that's going under are the same, time and time again. What's human sacrifice, if not sending guys off to Iraq for no reason?" In differing words, a sense of fatality has also been typical of many people I have consulted while writing this book. They can see what the Aqedah points to, but have no hope that human beings can free themselves from the sacrificial reflex. Inadvertently, they become as stoical as Abraham, trudging up Moriah for the inevitable immolation of those we love most, our progeny.

Mel Gibson's recent career illustrates the double bind many people experience when they confront sacrifice. While *Apocalypto* presents a culture Gibson believes was inevitably "going under," his previous film, *The Passion of the Christ,* glorified sacrifice. The screenplay of *The Passion* might as well have been crafted during the Middle Ages, with its flights of fancy and superstition: perfidious Jews, assorted demons, a pouty Magdalene, gargoyle-faced demons, and even a Temple priest with a buccaneer eye-patch. Whether rejected in *Apocalypto* or embraced in *The Passion of the Christ*, sacrifice remains Gibson's pivotal preoccupation; the ritual offering of human beings is an inevitable outcome, on this increasingly popular view, to be either praised and emulated, or lamented, as it is repeated time and again.

The Scriptures of Israel, the New Testament, and the Qur'an have much in common, but they do *not* share a conviction in the inevitability of sacrificial violence. The wisdom and power of these texts, read with attention, is that they contradict Abraham's curse. The Abrahamic Aqedahs, together with their interpretive traditions, indeed articulate the impulse toward human sacrifice encoded within the myths and reflexes of many civilizations, but they also provide means by which that impulse can be, and has been, turned aside from what seems an inevitable holocaust.

In the end, the Abrahamic Aqedahs show us that what appears to be an unmanageable, self-destructive instinct is no instinct at all in the true sense of that word. Abraham's curse is encoded, not in our genetic makeup, but in our *cultural* constitution. The capacity to shape human behavior in different directions lies within the resources of all three Abrahamic traditions, because culture is not a predetermined reality.

The self-sacrificial reflex is an artifact of the rise of cities, unquestionably deep-seated, but also reversible, or at least malleable. That is why the outcome of the Aqedah in the grounding sources of Judaism, Christianity, and Islam—the Torah, the Gospels, and the Qur'an respectively—is not ineluctable slaughter, but the descent from the mount of sacrifice of both parent and child. That departure from Moriah is the sign of the blessing of Abraham. The clarity and power of Abraham's blessing is designed to reverse his curse.

Abraham's near sacrifice of Isaac produces a sense of horror that all too often obscures how, at the end of the ancient Israelite story as preserved in the Torah, God intervenes definitively to *prevent* Abraham from offering Isaac (Genesis 22:11–14):

> Yahweh's angel called to him from heaven and said, "Abraham, Abraham." He said, "Look—me." He said, "Do not send your hand upon the youth and do not do anything to him, because now I know that you fear God and have not withheld your son, your cherished one, from me." Abraham lifted up his eyes and saw, and looked—a ram behind caught in a thicket by his horns. Abraham went and took the ram and offered it for a sacrifice by fire instead of his son. Abraham called the name of that place "Yahweh Saw," as is said today, "On the mount Yahweh was seen."

Because Abraham saw the ram, the whole course of action changed.

As the events are presented in Genesis, the underlying insight that prevents the slaughter is God's first; Yahweh "Saw" before Abraham did, prevented the sacrifice of Isaac by means of an angel, and showed the ram to the patriarch. The momentum of the story pivots on the act of seeing by God and by Abraham, and then moves in a direction completely different from how it set out at the start.

God reaches that turning point before Abraham can see the importance of the ram. Because "Yahweh Saw" both a better victim, the ram, and the dedication of Abraham, he tells Abraham without ambiguity that he is definitively to cease *all sacrificial action* in relation to Isaac. The test is categorically over, never again to be repeated: "do not do anything to him." Yahweh's insight is so clearly conveyed to Abraham that it can be said—as the Hebrew wording explicitly states—Yahweh "was seen" on Moriah.

The disclosure of Yahweh on the mount, his being "seen" there after he himself "saw," is stated unequivocally in the Hebrew text. The verb in the phrase "Yahweh was seen" is the straightforward word for "see" (*ra'ah*) in a passive form, meaning "was seen" (or possibly "made himself seen," another way of rendering a *niphal* verbal form in Hebrew), and the subject is Yahweh. This is exactly how the Septuagint's Greek renders the Hebrew text, with Yahweh as the subject of the verb.

English translators, both Jewish and Christian, have balked at this natural rendering. They prefer to say—as in the King James Version—"it will be seen," presumably with the ram in mind. But that contradicts the plain sense of the action. The ram did not intervene in the offering, or see any alternative to slaughtering Isaac, while Yahweh unequivocally did just those things. Contextually as well as grammatically, God is the subject: Yahweh "was seen" on Moriah, liberating Isaac by means of his divine intervention.

What has caused the strained tradition of translation into English, which evades the plain sense of the Hebrew text? This is a case of translators caring more about doctrine than wording, and attempting to legislate what the Bible can say. Where seeing God is concerned, the most famous passage in the Hebrew Bible is where Moses asks to see God's face, and is rebuffed with the warning, "You cannot see my face, because man will not see me and live" (Exodus 33:20).

In its immediate context, that proves to be a carefully calibrated statement, because God *does* allow Moses a glimpse of himself in an oblique vision of the divine, at an angle from behind (Exodus 33:23). In other words, what a mortal can't do is see God's *face*, as if God were a human being; God's form nonetheless can and does repeatedly become visible to prophets within the biblical tradition.

The Book of Exodus in particular celebrates prophetic vision of the divine well *before* issuing its famous caution about seeing the face of God. Immediately prior to the giving of the Torah, Moses ascends the mountain of revelation with Aaron, Nadab, and Abihu, together with seventy Israelite elders. According to the explicit statement in Exodus, they all "saw the God of Israel" (Exodus 24:9–11). The verb used here is just as emphatic as what we have in Genesis 22, when Genesis says that God "was seen." Moreover, Exodus 24:11 stipulates that God "did not *send* his hand" against the Israelites who saw him, exactly as Abraham is told not to *"send* his hand" upon his son.

These Scriptures, from Genesis and Exodus both, want it understood that Abraham perceived what Moses and his companions later did—the divine form of God, and that both Abraham and Moses learned how that vision could be safely mediated to others, without the fear of death. A basic theme of the Torah, which only emerges fully when the promise as well as the threat of the Aqedah is appreciated, conveys the prophetic wisdom that human beings can become companions of God, can see him all but face-to-face, without the sacrifice of their lives or their humanity.

Abraham came to that breakthrough of perception into the divine precisely when he was prevented from slaughtering Isaac. The unequivocal divine mandate means that Abraham and his progeny are *never* to consider sacrificing their children again, and that imperative comes with the authority of a vision of God himself.

Why, then, was there a test in the first place?

Developing his celebrated answer to that question, Søren Kierkegaard in *Fear and Trembling* portrayed Abraham as heroic, a true knight of faith whose belief suspended ethical judgment, "transforming a murder into a holy act well pleasing to God." This reading gives classic expression to a view common to existentialist philosophy and modern Christian thought alike, conveyed with Kierkegaard's sweeping phrase, much quoted in philosophical discussion, "the teleological suspension of the ethical." For some reason, perhaps having to do with the existential anxiety with which Kierkegaard imbued Abraham, this principle has escaped identification as another version of saying that the ends justify the means.

In addition to torturing ethical logic, Kierkegaard's interpretation perpetuates a cultural misapprehension common throughout the West. After the biblical period, especially from the fourth century C.E. on (as we have seen), hagiography had its way with Abraham. As the founder of ideals that Judaism, Christianity, and Islam all strive to realize within their societies, Abraham's image is typically burnished and airbrushed to make him into a model of what every believer should be.

But Abraham, the stereotypical hero, is not at all the character the Bible presents. By the time of his test in Genesis 22, Abraham's complex character in fact looks distinctly dubious. The test, after all, comes in a specific sequence, "after these things," as Genesis 22:1 says in Hebrew. What were "these things"? In chapter 20, Abraham had attempted to pass Sarah off as his sister to Abimelech, king of Gerar, to give the impression she was sexually available. Earlier, a similar story about the patriarch and his wife—this time involving Pharaoh in Genesis 12—also reflects this bizarre form of nomadic hospitality, long abandoned by the time the biblical narratives passed from oral tradition into writing.

Even so, the custom was once common enough that Isaac, too, tries to pass *his* wife off as his sister (Genesis 26)—and to the same Abimelech! Each time a patriarch offered to trade his wife away, the storytellers found a way to preserve the lady's honor by a twist in the plot that precluded her having sexual relations with the foreign ruler. But specifically in the case of Genesis 20—soon after the promise of Isaac's birth in Genesis 17 and 18—Abraham's offer of his wife to Abimelech is deeply disturbing. It calls into question, not only whether Sarah will be involved in adultery, but also whether a child born after her encounter with Abimelech will truly be, and will unequivocally be known as, Abraham's.

Abraham is barely saved from an outright lie in Genesis 20:12, because he explains to an understandably annoyed Abimelech—who confronts the patriarch after realizing the true situation—that Sarah is his half sister. But more important in Genesis than Abraham's half truth (or half lie) about Sarah, or even Sarah's reputation, is the issue of Abraham's paternity of Isaac.

Isaac's birth *as Abraham's son* is the sole guarantee of the covenantal future of Israel in the Book of Genesis, and *only Abimelech's virtue preserves both Sarah's sexual fidelity with Abraham and the assurance that her child will in fact be acknowledged as Abraham's.* Abimelech takes the prophetic guidance of God that came to him in a dream and abstains from sex with Sarah. That restraint alone, and certainly not any intervention from Abraham, assures recognition of Isaac as the son of the covenantal promise with Yahweh.

After Isaac's birth, Abraham's character continues to show all the staying power of a weathervane. Sarah tells him to drive away Hagar and Ishmael from the common dwelling with Abraham, Sarah, and Isaac, and Abraham accommodates her desire with either such carelessness or such cruelty that Hagar and Ishmael would have died of thirst except for angelic intervention, when God opened Hagar's eyes to see a well (Genesis 21:8–21). Genesis follows the theme of water, also describing at this time Abraham as making a covenant with Abimelech (Genesis 21:22–33)—rather than with God—concerning water rights in Beersheba. The patriarch even planted a sacred grove there, a practice associated with idolatrous worship in the Hebrew Bible.

The issues of Abraham's bizarre offer of his own wife to Abimelech when she was pregnant with Isaac, his callous attitude toward the life of his older son (Ishmael) as well as that son's mother (Hagar), and his willingness to make covenant with a human sovereign all converge as a strong undercurrent of doubt about his character by the time Genesis 22 laconically begins, "After these things God tested Abraham." Taking the chapter out of its context makes what happens seem unmotivated, an arbitrary test of loyalty arising from God's nature alone rather than from Abraham's character. But that is very far from the case in the presentation of Genesis.

God has good reason to doubt the man he is trying. Within the Book of Genesis by this stage, Abraham is not the noble figure of later tradition, but the subject of testing because his actions and their motivations have become suspect. They are dubious within the presentation of Genesis itself, not merely from a modern perspective. Men by the time Genesis was written were not supposed to pimp their pregnant wives, desert their children and their children's mothers, or enter into covenantal relationship with human rulers and their divinities rather than with God.

Within chapter 22, taken in its own terms, Abraham plods along on automatic pilot from beginning to end, neither complaining when told to carve up his child and burn him, nor celebrating when he gets to keep his son. He had bargained with God for the lives of the people of Sodom (Genesis 18:22–33), but says nothing at all to preserve the life of his child. He is not a Kierkegaardian "knight of faith" at all. He is a brute, and everything about his brutish behavior toward his family—by this point an evident theme in Genesis—emphasizes by contrast God's compassionate intervention. It is God who "saw" in the ram a way out of the dilemma posed by Abraham's character, and God who "was seen" by Abraham, so that the patriarch in the end spares his son's life.

The climax of the story, which delivers its message, insists both that Abraham and his progeny will enjoy the covenantal promise of Yahweh (Genesis 22:16–18) and that Abraham is not to do anything whatever again to threaten harm to Isaac (vv. 12–14). When Abraham returns to Beersheba at the close of chapter 22 (v. 19), he does so on the basis of his covenant with Yahweh rather than with Abimelech, and with a complete and enduring dedication to Isaac as his son and Sarah's. Just as he never came close to threatening the lives of his children again, so he never again offered his wife to Abimelech or anyone like him, and desisted from making covenants that competed with the divine covenant. Abraham came down from Moriah a changed man.

The test of the Aqedah put Abraham back on the track of the covenant. Only a reading of Genesis 22 out of context, with the assumption of Abraham as a stereotypical hero of faith, makes his character and his behavior noble. Traditional midrashim of Judaism fell under the sway of the hagiographic portrait of Abraham, and yet they also found ways, implicit and explicit, to explore their awareness that Abraham's character was more complex and flawed than that of a conventional hero. Ancient interpreters on the whole proved themselves more sensitive than their modern counterparts, Kierkegaard included, to the remorseless logic of this biblical text.

Implicit criticism of Abraham is embedded in the elevation of

Isaac's participation and importance, *the son's* emergence as the principal human actor in the story rather than the father. This comes out
vividly in the interpretation that at the moment Abraham raised his
knife to slay his son, Isaac saw directly into heaven, and perceived the
angels there. Abraham saw them only indirectly, reflected in his son's
eyes. At the heart of the story, the disclosure of divine compassion
that makes human life and Israel's survival possible, Isaac's vision is
clearer than Abraham's.

Some midrashim factor Sarah into the Aqedah of traditional
Judaism—although she is excluded from the bibilical text of Genesis 22—in order to criticize Abraham explicitly. After speaking of
the events on Moriah, Genesis 23:1–2 reports with only incidental
details that Sarah died. A classic midrash, Leviticus Rabbah, makes
what Abraham did responsible for her death. At the same time, this
interpretation embeds the story in the commemoration of the New
Year, when the ram's horn, the *shofar*, is to be blown as the Aqedah is
remembered.

In the midrash contained in Leviticus Rabbah, Isaac returns home
after the Aqedah and tells his mother what happened on Moriah. De-
spairing and bewildered, she asks, "Had it not been for the angel you
would have been slain?" When Isaac confirms that, the scene becomes
searing: "Then she uttered six cries, corresponding to the six blasts
of the *shofar*. It is said, She had barely finished speaking when she
died." Absent from Mount Moriah, Sarah is the only parent emotionally present to her son, and the ram's horn that is blown every New
Year conveys her grief. Every time the *shofar* sounds, those who are
aware of this midrash remember both Sarah's love and Abraham's
hardness of heart.

Not content with this overt preference of Sarah to Abraham in
terms of moral integrity and basic humanity, this midrash goes on
to caricature Abraham as a compulsive sacrificer. Posing the question
of where Abraham had been prior to the burial of Sarah, Leviticus
Rabbah goes on:

Where did he come from? Rabbi Judah son of Rabbi Shimon
said, He came from Mount Moriah. Abraham harbored doubts

in his heart and thought, Perhaps some disqualifying blemish was found in him and his offering was not accepted.

So while his wife has just died of grief at the realization of his heart-lessness, Abraham is still caught up with the impulse to kill Isaac *after God has told him to stop threatening his son's life.*

In this midrash Abraham is stuck in his understanding before the angelic intervention, fretting that his child wasn't pure enough to be sacrificed instead of rejoicing that the son of the covenant had been spared by divine compassion. Sarah wasn't there, but she understands what Abraham cannot grasp, even after a divine vision and voice had shown him the truth. The insight that the impulse to sacrifice his son came from the patriarch himself, rather than from God, links the interpreter who composed this midrash in Leviticus Rabbah directly with Muslim interpreters (discussed in chapter VI), who knew that the impetus for the sacrifice came from Ibraham's atavism, not from Allah's will.

These midrashim take up in their own ways the clear imperative of Genesis 22 itself: to tame the impulse to offer one's children in sacrifice with the awareness that it comes from a false, prideful, and self-interested understanding of divine will. If you want to know what God wants, it is reflected more directly in Isaac's eyes than in Abraham's, in the perspective of the victim rather than the slayer. And the wisdom to act on what is disclosed on Mount Moriah, to blow a *shofar* of grief that will drive away the compulsion to sacrifice in-nocent human life, comes from the parent who cares, not from the parent who commands.

Christianity makes Jesus the ideal sacrifice that Isaac did not quite embody, the perfect model of obedient martyrdom. This suffering Christ inevitably became, both overtly and implicitly, an incentive for his followers to become martyrs. No period of Christian history has been exempt from the attractions of Abraham's curse, or from the conviction that offering young life in a holy cause is noble.

Yet in a scene of haunting power, the Gospels give the lie to any claim that discipleship of Jesus involves giving in wholesale to the ethic of self-sacrifice or child sacrifice. At the decisive moment prior to his arrest and crucifixion, the Gospels insistently portray Jesus, not as heroic, determined, or even stoical, but as doubtful and uncertain, beset by human weakness.

Mark, the earliest of the Gospels, sets out the scene most vividly of them all (Mark 14:32–43):

And they come to a tract whose name was Gethsemane, and he says to his students, "Sit here while I pray." And he takes along Peter and James and John with him, and he began to be completely bewildered and distressed, and he says to them, "My soul is mournful unto death: remain here and be alert." He went before a little and fell upon the ground and was praying so that, if it were possible, the hour might pass on from him. And he was saying, "*Abba*, Father: all things are possible for you. Carry this cup on, away from me! Yet not what I want, but what you!" And he comes and finds them sleeping, and says to Peter, "Simon, are you sleeping? You were not capable of being alert one hour? Be alert and pray, so that you do not come into a test. The Spirit is willing, but the flesh is weak." He again went away and prayed. Having said the same thing, he again came and found them sleeping, because their eyes were weighed down; and they did not know what to reply to him. And he comes the third time and says to them, "Sleep for what remains and repose: it suffices. The hour has come, Look: the son of man is delivered up into the hands of sinners. Be raised, we go. Look: the one who delivers me over has approached." And at once while he is still speaking Judas, one of the Twelve, comes along, and with him a crowd with swords and clubs from the high priests and the scribes and the elders.

This scene, first written in Mark's crabbed, inelegant Greek (which I have put into the closest correspondence to English possible) achieves its power by what it says about Jesus, and by how it weaves his experience of human weakness into the experience of his followers.

Jesus openly admits his weakness, his "soul is mournful unto death," and he wants his disciples near to comfort him. His words are not just a general admission of grief; rather, he speaks in the words of Jonah at Nineveh (Jonah 4:9), another case of a prophet who sorrowed at the vocation given him by God. That is what makes Jesus' anguish at this moment arresting from the outset. Although depicted from the beginning of Mark's Gospel as God's Son, here he is not even sure he can complete his work as a prophet.

Jesus asks for the "hour" to pass him by—and to leave him alive. The term "hour" refers both to his personal fate (the time of his death), and to the moment when everything he has done will reach its climax in the disclosure of God's kingdom. How can God's Son be praying to elude that climactic realization of what he has done and of who he has always been? An ancient critic of Christianity, the second-century classicist Celsus, picked up on the scene in Gethsemane, asking how Jesus could possibly "mourn and lament and pray to escape the fear of death." The contrast in Celsus's mind was between Jesus and philosophical heroes such as Socrates, who faced their deaths with a noble calm.

Had Celsus known the Gospels better, he could have sharpened his criticism—and he no doubt would have. When Jesus asks for "this cup" to be taken from him, that reflects the Aramaic idiom, the "cup of death": yet in Mark he has been predicting his death, and speaking of its necessity, with greater and greater specificity, and explaining to his followers that they had to be prepared to take this same path (Mark 8:31–38; 9:30–37; 10:32–45). He has already said that they would drink the cup that he drinks (10:39) and that his purpose was to give his life for redemption (10:45). His hesitation now, unless it has some deeper purpose, seems not only a matter of cringing in the face of pain and death, but also of denying his divine mission and misleading his disciples. This passage represents a searching challenge to the belief that suffering is necessary, and the way this challenge is posed is key to the whole Gospel's meaning.

The Gethsemane scene in Mark belongs to one of the earliest oral sources in all the Gospels—the account of Jesus' Passion and death crafted by Peter and his companions. Prayer featured vitally in this proto-Gospel, and Peter stressed the importance of intense repetition in prayer. In Gethsemane, Jesus brings his anguish to his *Abba* three times. Peter's source spoke of Jesus' prayer in order to model for believers how they themselves should pray when in distress, not merely to give information about Jesus.

That is the reason for which liturgical rhythms and antiphonal dialogue ripple through the story of Gethsemane. It is designed as a part of Peter's Passion narrative, the story of Jesus' suffering up to and including the moment of his death. Those events were particularly commemorated and recited by Christians every year prior to Easter, the Sunday of the resurrection, the Sunday when converts were baptized after extensive preparation by means of study, vigils of prayer during the night, and fasting. Those converts joined Jesus liturgically in Gethsemane, and searched themselves to see whether they were ready for the "hour"—the decisive moment of potential danger and revelation—that their baptism represented.

In Peter's narrative, the principal human failing to be avoided prior to this decisive moment was not an agonized plea for one's life like Jesus', but the languor that came to disciples during their vigils and preparations (Mark 14:37–38). By contrast, Peter's story *commends and endorses* Jesus' open expression of fear and doubt. This is prayer as it should be—directed to God as one's *Abba*, which in Aramaic means both "father" and "source," and completely open in its acknowledgment of human weakness.

Peter's understanding, although shaped to suit the needs of liturgy, corresponds well to the historical circumstances that Jesus faced. His campaign against the high priestly administration in the Temple—climaxing in his violent expulsion of animals and their vendors—had put him in danger of retaliation. But the complexities of power politics eluded him. He could not have known that the execution of Pilate's protector in Rome (Sejanus) would dispose Pilate to put his military resources and might at the disposal of the high priest, Caiaphas.

Even a few weeks prior to Jesus' action in the Temple, an alliance between Pilate and Caiaphas seemed unimaginable. In Gethsemane, the unthinkable became real. The imminent danger of crucifixion—deliberately the most painful and shameful of deaths, which Roman authority alone could command—only became fully apparent to Jesus when Roman soldiers as well as police from the Temple joined in the attempt to capture him.

In the Gethsemane scene, Peter conveys the moment when Jesus in his mind's eye confronted the might of Rome, not only the anger of the high priest, and asked his God whether such a fate was truly necessary. Peter's portrayal of Jesus' agony of doubt contradicts the conventional view of Jesus as the all-knowing Messiah who is in complete control of his passions. That portrayal of Jesus' omniscience gained traction within the development of the New Testament over time, as one can see by comparing how later Gospels handle the same scene in Mark. Comparing all the accounts, it is obvious that, as time went on, Christians became less and less comfortable with Jesus being indecisive or fearful in the face of death.

Yet as the Gospels progressively insulated Jesus against his own humanity, a process that continued for centuries after the Gospels were written, each still insisted in its own way that Jesus had a choice, whether to remain in Jerusalem and risk death, or to flee with the hope of survival. Even John's Gospel, the latest, and the most stylized of them all in the New Testament where Jesus' humanity is concerned, emphasizes this crucial element of informed decision.

When, in John's Gospel, Jesus speaks of himself as the "good shepherd" who "lays down his life on behalf of the sheep" (John 10:11), that is with a specific understanding (John 10:18): "No one takes it from me, but I lay it down of myself." In principle, according to John's presentation, Jesus might have learned, as Ibrahim did in the Qur'an, that intention alone sufficed for his sacrifice.

Automatic martyrdom, or acquiescence to an abstract command despite one's fear and indecision, is not the portrait of Jesus that the Gospels as a whole convey. Instead, they insist that Jesus, fully aware of the emotions and doubts that were running though him, great and small, made a choice to offer his life for his sheep or, as he goes on to call his followers in John, his "friends" (John 15:12–17). Insight, commitment, and an assessment of circumstance all contribute to his strategic choice. It is *his* choice, and it is unquestionably noble: there is no doubt whatever but that the Christian tradition endorses the model of martyrdom that it inherited from Maccabean Judaism, and further develops that model.

But a crucial aspect of that development—too often overlooked, with grievous consequences—is that the martyr fully deals with his own emotional state as well as with the external conditions he or she confronts. Martyrdom must always be a matter of one's insight into oneself and into the world at one and the same time. Attempting to mimic a single, heroic gesture—despite one's feelings and whatever the circumstances—amounts to playacting, because it does not represent the self-giving on behalf of others that is the purpose Jesus clearly states, by word and by deed.

That is why, from the second century C.E. onward, the Fathers of the Church taught vociferously *against* martyrdom for display. In their argument against overly enthusiastic would-be victims in the Church, they developed an analogy, detailed in chapter IV, between being a martyr and being a soldier. Their purpose was certainly not to recruit Christians into the Roman army. During their time, baptized persons had to forswear professions such as soldiering and even teaching, because they involved making oaths to the emperor that Christians believed were idolatrous, and soldiers were in any case notorious for their lawless behavior.

Rather, early Christian teachers used the comparison of martyrdom with a soldier's motivation to insist that those who witnessed to Christ with their lives had to do so from personal choice as well as with strategic purpose and tactical clarity. Using that carefully designed comparison, as it has been repeatedly used during the history of the Church, to justify sending young people in the name of Christ to wars whose purposes remain unclear to them, represents an abuse of their trust, and of Jesus' memory.

By removing the mask of conventional righteousness from Abraham, and the mask of stoic resignation from Jesus, we encounter underlying and unexpected meanings in the Aqedah. Rather than being the metaphor of sacrifice that every Jew should bear in his flesh to the point of martyrdom, or the archetype of Christ's suffering that each Christian must honor on command, the Aqedah instead contradicts the reflex of self-sacrifice and child sacrifice.

Abraham learns, as other prophets in Israel learned, that the first instinct to honor God is not necessarily the best instinct, and that God might well reject hasty obedience. Jesus discerns, during his final night in Gethsemane, that truly taking up his cross is not an automatic duty, but is only accomplished by means of his conscious appraisal that his death will benefit others, even as it fulfills his own purpose and personality, in revealing God's kingdom.

What happens if we also remove Muhammad's mask? Will the equivalent of the Aqedah in the Qur'an then also take us in a new direction of meaning, and help counteract Abraham's curse?

Of the three masks, Muhammad's is the thickest with parody. From the earliest encounter with Christianity, his revelations in the Qur'an have been dismissed as symptoms of epilepsy, his teaching on marriage as a license for pedophilia and perversion, and his conflicts with his opponents as a pretext for bloodlust. Those calumnies, well established by the time of the Crusades, have been widely repeated since September 11, 2001, especially those linking jihad with an indiscriminate taste for violence.

Muhammad's mask has been elaborated by intellectual fashions as well as by superstitious legends. In a recent book, Minou Reeves has documented how "Christians have claimed that Muhammad deliberately spread a false religion of his own invention, atheists that he pretended to have the support of God in order to manipulate people, liberals that he was an autocrat, authoritarians that he was a libertarian, feminists that he was an exploiter of women, male chauvinists that he was ruled by women. . . . " Muhammad has suffered more contradictory calumnies than even the apostle Paul, and the charge leveled against him and against Muslims as a whole, of promoting gratuitous violence and suicide attacks, has featured prominently in popular culture during the age of "the War on Terror."

A distinguished group of Muslim scholars wrote an open letter to Pope Benedict XVI when he quoted a Byzantine emperor who defamed Islam as a religion that preached only violence. They cited a famous passage from one of the most carefully crafted surahs of the Qur'an, which clearly states that there should be "no compulsion in religion" (2:256 in *Al Baqarah,* "the Cow," a title referring to Moses' commands for sacrifice). Because this surah was composed over an extensive period of time, until shortly before the Prophet's death, there is no question but that its intention is to provide an overall context for other revelations on the resort to force in the Qur'an.

Yet as often happens when apologists defend their faith, the Muslim scholars so emphasized the constraint that the teaching about "no compulsion in religion" exerts on jihad, they did not speak of jihad itself, the perception of which is, after all, the major irritant in Christianity's and the West's attitude toward Islam today. Some surahs instruct Muhammad's followers that, if they encounter those who reject Allah in war, they are to strike to kill (for example, *Al Tawbah* 9:5; *Muhammad* 47:4). The relationship between *Al Baqarah* and the passages that appear elsewhere in the Qur'an shows that unbelievers are not to be subjected to deadly force without reason, and yet *are to be resisted* to the end when war is involved.

Pope Benedict, in the tradition of Peter the Venerable during the Crusades (see chapter VII), clearly promoted a distorted and self-serving view of Islam. Yet the fact remains that, during the course of his life, Muhammad urged believers to military combat against unbelievers and took an active part in leading battles. He did so without apology, as a noble warrior, or *ghazi*, and with all the resources of moral argument and divine revelation at his disposal. The alternative to armed conflict, at the end of the day, was to see the cause of submission to Allah drown in a sea of inhuman behavior and false worship, the two evils that Muhammad resisted to the end.

The Qur'an makes it plain that combat for the cause of Allah is a virtue, and sometimes a duty. Any other teaching in the context of the time would clearly have led Muhammad and his followers to their deaths at the sword of their enemies. The alternative to jihad was the definitive repression of what Muhammad taught was the sole, true revelation of God for the Arabic peoples, and the basis of justice in their society. The social setting of Muhammad, in which the land of Ibrahim was engulfed by violent forces that threatened to submerge the cause of Allah, shaped the Prophet's actions as much as Abraham's identity as a nomad and Jesus' identity as a peasant rabbi.

Calls to accept the burdens of warfare and suffering, whether collectively or individually, became part of the natural idiom for promoting physical jihad within the Qur'an. Soon after the Prophet started to receive revelations in 610 C.E., persecution in Mecca broke out against Muhammad and his fellow adherents to recognition of the one true God. He disputed with his own clan, the Quraysh, and only protection from powerful members of Muhammad's family—especially his prominent wife Khadijah and his uncle Abu Talib—saved him from violence at the hands of powerful defenders of traditional polytheism.

After all, Muhammad said the traditional gods of Mecca were false—human constructions rather than divine reality. This zeal involved him in the lifelong project of removing idols from the Ka'bah, the local pilgrimage site, which he said had been dedicated to the worship of the one God by Ibrahim long before him. Muhammad believed it was his purpose to cleanse the Ka'bah of idolatrous pollution, and to establish the worship of, and submission to, Allah alone, as Ibrahim had done.

More than a hundred of Muhammad's followers abandoned Mecca in 615. Many of them were women, slaves, and poor people who were attracted to his teaching of social justice, but did not benefit from the family protection that Muhammad and more prominent members of his following enjoyed. These defenseless believers fled for their own safety and journeyed to Abyssinia, then under Christian rule. Clearly, traditional polytheists had the upper hand in Mecca and were willing to use force to insist upon their customs of sacrifice to and worship of the Meccan gods.

The Quraysh became ever more dangerous to Muhammad personally. After the deaths of both Khadijah and Abu Talib in 619 C.E., assassination attempts prompted the Prophet to abandon Mecca and his clan connections in order to travel to Medina. Muhammad's self-imposed departure (*hijrah*) from his native city and clan in 622 C.E., in order to preserve his loyalty to Allah and his revelation, involved palpable risks. Emigrating with only about seventy followers, Muhammad, until that time still a working, if no longer prosperous, merchant, forsook the usual defenses offered by clan and city against the frequent raids and battles that characterized caravan culture in Arabia during the seventh century.

In Medina, Muhammad quickly found many more followers than he had in Mecca, perhaps because the prosperous Jewish communities there had prepared the ground for his monotheist faith. One Rabbi, Ka'b Al Akhbar, converted to Islam and became an influential figure in the movement (as we have seen in chapter VI). Muslim numbers grew into thousands, and they entered into a series of raids, skirmishes, and heated battles—common during the period—with other clans in Medina, including Jewish clans after a few years, as well as with the Quraysh who raided from Mecca. Muhammad's teaching from the Medinan period emphasizes the crucial importance of loyalty to Allah in the context of these clan battles (3:157, *Al 'Imran*, the name of the father of Mary, according to the Qur'an): "If you are slain in the way of Allah or die, forgiveness and mercy from Allah are far better than all they amass."

The unequivocal demand for commitment that Muhammad issued repeatedly during his decade in Medina specifically included encouragement, if necessary, to put family and children at risk (*Al Anfal* 8:28, a surah that deals with spoils of war): "Know that your possessions and your children are a trial; and that it is Allah with whom lies immense reward."

That thought is pursued to a more extreme conclusion in the surah called *Al Tawbah* ("Repentance"). Here there is no doubt of the priorities Muhammad sets out on the authority of his divine revelation. Family members are unmistakably relegated in importance as compared to Allah (*Al Tawbah* 9:24): "If your fathers, your sons, your brothers, your wives, your kindred, the wealth you have gained, the commerce you fear to lose, or the homes you love, are dearer to you than Allah, his messenger, or striving in his way—then wait until Allah brings about his verdict!"

Rigorous insistence upon loyalty to God above all other concerns, even those of family, has been a trait of prophecy since at least the biblical Book of Hosea, from the eighth century B.C.E., where the prophet is instructed by God to divorce his wife in order to illustrate that Israel has alienated God in the same way that a promiscuous wife disgusts her husband. In the case of Jesus, the refusal to put any value before God leads to a teaching that is an evident precedent for Muhammad's (Mark 10:29–30): "Amen I say to you, there is no one who has left home or brothers or sisters or mother or father or children or lands for my sake and the triumphant message's, except that shall receive a hundred times over—now in this time—homes and brothers and sisters and mothers and children and fields—with persecutions—and in the age that is coming perpetual life." For good or ill, the prophetic insistence that no value can compare to loyalty to God has perennially put even children in a position subsidiary to faith, and therefore in at least potentially vulnerable positions. Prophets such as Jesus and Muhammad knew that all God had given would ultimately return to him.

Although a great deal makes them comparable in their prophetic personae, Muhammad and Jesus differed profoundly in their relative situations within their societies. Their social differences went hand in hand with their radically divergent views of the uses of power, although each of them spoke as a prophet.

Jesus was a Galilean teacher whose regional background, lack of education, and suspect birth (because he was conceived before his parents resided together) permanently marginalized him from influence and status. When Jesus *did* attempt to use force on behalf of his teaching, by invading the Temple in Jerusalem with his followers in order to eject animals for sale and the people who sold them, he fell victim to the greater authority and brute power of those in charge of the Temple and Pontius Pilate, the Roman prefect.

Muhammad, in sharp contrast, was a prosperous merchant at the time the Qur'an started to be revealed to him, surah after surah. His considerable means, together with his resourcefulness and his willingness to use physical force, assured his survival and prosperity, and that of his movement, against considerable odds.

The fact that the Medinan surah that spells out the religious obligation to fight when occasion demands is entitled "Repentance" indicates how vital combat was to loyalty to Allah in Muhammad's circumstances. In effect and in fact, war became an article of faith (*Al Tawbah* 9:19, 20): "Do you make the giving of drink to pilgrims or the maintenance of the sacred mosque equal to him who believes in Allah and the last day and struggles for Allah's way? They are not equal in the sight of Allah. . . . Those who believe and leave home and strive with property and life in Allah's cause have the higher rank in the sight of Allah."

Because the striving of jihad had become a paramount religious virtue, Muhammad's concern over the years to specify that there should be "no compulsion in religion" becomes understandable. He needed to insist, and he did insist in *Al Baqarah* 2:256, that jihad was a requirement to preserve the freedom to make Islam possible, but emphatically *not* a form of authorization to compel Islam, a compulsion that he taught amounted to a contradiction in terms. True submission to Allah was between Allah and the believer, not a matter of public policy.

Later interpreters for the most part correctly understood Muhammad's stance and systematized his disparate teachings into a doctrine of just war that, in turn, influenced Christian thinkers such as Thomas Aquinas during the Middle Ages. Yet the everlasting rewards promised to those who "struggle" in physical combat link up together into a tantalizing thread within the Qur'an, comparable to the heavenly benefits promised at a later period to Christian Crusaders. That comparison is not coincidental, since Muslim portrayals of the joys of heaven and the pains of hell deeply influenced Christian thought, and inspired poets such as Dante.

Those who are slain in the way of Allah will enjoy the heavenly garden prepared for them according to another Medinan surah (*Muhammad* 47:4–6). That revelation, written at a time of threat of invasion from Mecca, also reveals Muhammad's frustration when the call to jihad was not heard: the faithful say they are awaiting a word of revelation, and when Muhammad gives them one (*Muhammad* 47:20), they look as if they are about to faint dead away.

The example of Ibrahim became sharper in surahs composed in Medina, although the patriarch had featured centrally in Muhammad's thought long before that. But in Medina, Muhammad interacted with interpretive traditions of Jewish communities, including traditions involving the Rabbinic Aqedah. In the midst of his forceful call to physical engagement with enemies, warranted by the threat of annihilation and pursued even at the risk of life, the temptation must have been strong for Muhammad to associate Ibrahim's offering of his son with the dispatch of young men to war.

The Qur'an instead portrays the patriarch's deep attachment to his sons (*Ibrahim* 14:39). In view of the deaths of Muhammad's small sons and the strong identification he felt with Ibrahim, these words are especially touching. It would have been a very small step for Muhammad to see the loss of his own children reflected in the Aqedah, and to use Ibrahim's sacrifice as the basis to demand that believers should sacrifice their children in the cause of Allah. But that is just the step Muhammad did not take.

The Qur'anic Aqedah (*Al Saffat* 37:84–111) instead insists that, as a prophet, Ibrahim followed Allah's lead away from the conventions of idolatry, but also *against* the impulse to assume that Allah required human sacrifice. Muhammad saw Ibrahim and his sons as models of resistance against idolatry (*Ibrahim* 14:35) more than as paradigmatic martyrs. Ibrahim with his son Isma'il is the hero of the cleansing of the Ka'bah in particular, and its establishment for the pure worship of Allah (*Al Hajj* 22:26, the surah on pilgrimage, written both before and after the *hijrah*). This is the task that Muhammad himself completed, when—having taken control of Mecca in 630 C.E.—he dedicated the Ka'bah to the exclusive worship of Allah, removing and destroying the idols that he believed polluted it.

The purpose of cleansing the Ka'bah was not only to permit pilgrimage there to be free of idolatry, but also to assure that sacrifice was offered to Allah alone. Muhammad explicitly associated the duty of pilgrimage with *animal* sacrifice (*Al Hajj* 22:27–28). The location of this sacrifice is crucial (*Al Hajj* 22:33): it is Mina, a place of sacrifice to this day, where Ibrahim's vision took place, and showed what should be offered, and what should never be offered, to Allah.

The association between the Qur'anic Aqedah and the sacrifice at Mina links Ibrahim to every believer. All the action and experience focuses on the single recognition (*Al Saffat* 37:106) that "this was an obvious trial." For that reason, it is crucial for any and all Muslims that Ibrahim and his son's submission to Allah came out of their vision according to the Qur'an, not any literal attempt to go through with human sacrifice.

God intervened with an "immense sacrifice" of an animal (37:107), so that *only* animals are ever to be considered for sacrifice again. Allah wants only these animals, and their physical offering does not please him, "Their flesh and blood does not reach Allah; your devotion reaches him" (*Al Hajj* 22:37). Only evil people could mistake the giving of a child as a duty; Muhammad described (*Al Ma'arij* 70:11–14) sinners willing to sacrifice children, wives, brothers, and kin to save themselves from divine punishment, like Mesha in the Hebrew Bible.

The Qur'an makes the demand for sacrifice categorical: "Therefore to your Lord turn in prayer and sacrifice," says one of the last surahs (*Al Kawthar* 108:2). But in making that requirement, Muhammad could not have been clearer that the means of sacrifice could never be a human offering and that Allah enjoys, not any particular victim that is offered, but the devoted intention that motivates offering.

Islam, the most recent of the monotheisms, is also the most rooted in the primordial impulse of sacrifice, because literal animal offerings are a regular part of its continuing practice. In light of the Muslim Aqedah, believers should know, however, that Allah has never desired, and that they should never offer, any human victim.

Fear of the consequences of self-sacrifice—and of evident abuses of the impulse toward self-sacrifice—has fed a sequence of best-selling books advocating the virtues of atheism. Recent events make their popularity more than understandable; it is impossible not to sympathize with the apprehension that religious conflicts threaten the lives and the well-being as well as the psychic balance of millions of people.

In reaction, Sam Harris blames religion for its implication in wars that threaten to destroy humanity. Christopher Hitchens makes a case for what he calls "anti-theism" on moral grounds: "it is those who calmly recognize that we are alone who may have the better chance of investing human life with such meaning as it might be made to possess." Richard Dawkins has referred to religion as a "delusion" in the titles of two of his recent books.

Criticism of religion as the principal cause of irrational violence among people and nations has been mounted since the Enlightenment. The most recent attempts at theological demolition contribute to that genre and have several traits in common. While they cite examples of religious violence, they either ignore or attempt to explain away the violence of atheist regimes: the French *Directoire*, the

Bolshevik revolution, the Third Reich, Maoist Communism, Pol Pot's movement, and the Rwanda Hutu government, to select a few examples. The many millions of dead that secularist atrocities have left behind eclipse, both in absolute numbers and in the proportion of the populations involved, the victims cited as modern authors' favorite examples of religious violence: the Crusades, the Inquisition, and the perennially hyped Salem witch trials.

The fashion to oppose "religion" and foster "atheism" (or "antitheism," Hitchens's preference) distracts attention from a basic observation regarding human behavior in the modern period. If the root cause of violence were the practice of religion, and particularly religious dogmatism—as was plausibly argued during the seventeenth and eighteenth centuries—then long ago we should have seen a flowering of pacifism in Europe. The reverse has been the case.

The Thirty Years' War was indeed a brutalizing conflict that bled out Europe, broke the Spanish empire, and distorted German nationalism for centuries, but it did end in 1648, bringing the disastrous epoch of pan-European religious war to a close. Yet what followed was not peace, but commercial and political and nationalistic wars during the seventeenth, eighteenth, nineteenth, and twentieth centuries—several of them involving the rest of the world, and not only countries claimed as "colonies"—that made the post-Enlightenment period the bloodiest in the history of the world.

Attempting to blame all the violence that has consumed the West on its religions alone will only work if you make the case quickly, eloquently, and with as little historical perspective as you can possibly get away with. Harris, Hitchens, and Dawkins, none of them historians, share that strategy. Another family resemblance among them is that they cite egregious examples of religious practices and thinkers in order to reduce religion to its most ridiculous expressions, making those examples their stalking horses for religion as a whole.

To Dawkins, religion is "bad poetry," because it is "based upon an obsession with things *representing* other things they slightly resemble, or resemble in one respect." Harris has observed that, if we agree that talking to God through a hair dryer is crazy, then the removal of the appliance does not make the activity sane.

Hitchens's definition of religion is more detailed but equally reductionist, and it illustrates how freely he uses the word "religion" to stand for a whole series of bad behaviors that might afflict any human group: "It is the elevation and collectivization of credulity and solipsism, and the arrangement of these into institutional dogma and creed. It is the attempt to decide what shall be taught, what shall be allowed by way of sexual conduct and speech and even thought, and what shall be legislated. And it is the attempt to make such decisions beyond challenge, through the invocation of a supernatural authority." This pointed and poignant description objects to what reasonable people as a whole find objectionable. But they would object to these oppressions, and I hope resist them, whether the tyrannies involved came in the form of religion, or politics, or economic compulsion.

Hitchens here describes, not only religious totalitarianisms, but totalitarianisms of all kinds, which attempt to put their power and authority above the natural rights of the communities and nations they rule. If the tyrant of such a regime is called the pope (as in the case of Innocent III during the Crusade against the Cathars), that makes him neither better nor worse than the political tyrant called *der Führer* or il Duce, or the commercial tyranny of firms that have knowingly oppressed workers and poisoned the geographical regions from which they profit.

The inadvertent but inevitable consequence of attempts to scapegoat religion for all the ills of civilization is that they turn a blind eye to secular tyrannies, which since the Enlightenment have proved themselves by far the most lethal, oppressive, and dehumanizing forces on earth. Even the worst of recent campaigns of religiously motivated terrorism, whether perpetrated by Al Qaeda against the West or by the Tamil Tigers against the government of Sri Lanka, pale in comparison to the predations of secular institutions such as Hitler's, Stalin's, and Mao's in their quest for political domination and economic gain.

The challenge for secular orientations of thought is not, in the first instance, to add to the Enlightenment's genre of villainizing religion, but to develop ethical standards and arguments that will compete in their effectiveness with religious teachings against violence. Shouldn't firms not only make good on commercial and environmental disasters such as occurred at Bhopal in India, but also assure that nothing

like those iniquities—whether in human or environmental terms—
ever happen again? How can egregious attempts at ethnic cleansing,
in Rwanda and the former Yugoslavia for example, be analyzed and
understood so that they are not repeated?

Judaism, Christianity, and Islam have developed answers to such
questions. They are all shamelessly transcendent in their orientations,
refusing to be limited to the conditions of this world (the *saeculum*,
from which the word "secular" derives). All three Abrahamic faiths in
their differing ways express their common conviction that human beings are the crown of creation, and in their foundational documents
and their rich histories of interpretation they insist that human parents have no right to take the lives of their children, much less other
people's children.

For Genesis, Abraham is a brutal father, whose reckless disregard
for the life of his family had to be tamed by God so that he could
learn compassion. Mark portrays the choice of Jesus to follow the example of Isaac to its ultimate conclusion as beset by ordinary human
weakness, and conditional on his own discernment of how he could
best fulfill his life's purpose. *Al Saffat* remains faithful to the classic,
Qur'anic distinction between the human sacrifice that people in their
misguided zeal, tyranny, or fear consider offering, and the sacrifice of
obedient devotion that is Allah's only delight.

Yet these rich, corrective traditions are largely ignored, and not only
by religion's self-appointed detractors. Osama bin Laden, Pat Robertson, and Meir Kahane are routinely covered in commercial media as
examples of religious authorities who promote violence, directly or
indirectly. They all unquestionably do incite hatred with their aber-
rant theologies, but it is difficult to see who qualified them as authorities in their respective traditions, apart from the same journalists who
claim to lament their influence. Osama bin Laden has no standing in
the interpretation of Islam; Pat Robertson, whose church is a television station, is a publicist rather than a theologian; the Supreme
Rabbinic Court in Israel repudiated Meir Kahane's teachings, and his
political party has been banned.

By giving the impression that bin Laden, Robertson, and Kahane
are what Islam, Christianity, and Judaism truly represent, once their
veneer of civility is removed, journalism plays into the hands of the

equation between religion and violence. Still, when the public at large is given the stark, unnecessary choice between strident Fundamentalism and militant atheism, although both options are bad, twentieth-century experience in the United States shows that the likely victor will be Fundamentalism. For that reason, I have called attention to the distortions that Harris, Hitchens, and Dawkins represent. They are not searching thinkers, but their views are widely cited, and—as the secular equivalent of Fundamentalists—their logic-chopping distortions have spawned a large number of imitators.

Adding secular Fundamentalism to the other kinds on offer will not alleviate violence. Very marginally, trenchant atheists exacerbate an atmosphere of violence by portraying *any* religious expression as threatening. But their influence is all but negligible, because the fact is that only a slim sector of the population accepts their views. When politicians are ridiculed because they believe they talk with God, for example, that assures them more support among people who believe in God than it loses them among those who make atheism into an article of faith. My concern about secularist criticism of religion is not that it is influential, but that it has proven superficial and counterproductive.

Secularists, those who believe that there is no ultimate value beyond this world, have every reason to take up the interests of children, and yet they spend much more energy attacking religion than advocating for children's rights. Because—as Harris, Hitchens, and Dawkins are fond of repeating—the existence of God can be neither proven nor disproven, why should secularists ignore or deny religious teachings and efforts on behalf of children? If religions agree that children, whose lives have autonomous value, represent the best future for humanity, why should secular thought—for whom children represent the *only* possible human future—be more disposed to despise people who believe in God than to encourage the best aspects of their faith and thought?

Neither deep faith nor trenchant atheism inoculates any society against violence. Pretending otherwise only permits people to project their brutal proclivities, which have been with us since before the Iron Age, onto others—and so to justify their own resort to the violence they deplore in their victims. That has been our way for millennia.

Abraham's curse is not inevitable, although belief in its inevitability helps make it so. The resources of the alternative, of Abraham's blessing, have been preserved in our religious traditions, and secular thought—productively reoriented—might be able to envision the benefits of recognizing the autonomy of children in this-worldly terms. The test of human civilizations—our equivalent of the Aqedah—has come, now that our irreducible differences have become apparent and technology and politics have put us in constant, unavoidable contact with one another. Can we move beyond the initial temptation—to destroy or demean those who disagree with us, metaphorically or literally—and descend from Moriah with our children and our heritage intact? If so, we might at last inherit the promise that has been articulated in countless covenants and visions and dreams ever since human beings became capable of speech and put their hopes into words.

The crisis of escalating religious violence that we currently confront is *not* at its most profound level, as has frequently been claimed, between "radicals" and "moderates." That formula invokes the model of what happened to Protestantism in the United States during the nineteenth and twentieth centuries, when mainline denominations embraced the liberal values of democracy, human rights, and critical thought. Desirable though that development might have been, it was not inevitable, and it has been significantly reversed in the United States with the rise of various forms of Fundamentalism.

In any case, religious critiques of made-to-order martyrdom in Judaism, Christianity, and Islam are by no means merely part of an attempt to promote liberal civility. The correction of martyrdom away from brutality, conventional mimicry, and compulsion lies at the root of each of the Abrahamic faiths, and has been articulated in the rich and distinctive interpretive traditions we have encountered in this book. Those genuinely authoritative expressions of religious truth for the faithful point to the key for unlocking the blessing within Abraham's curse.

The more closely the three faiths relate to one another in their mutual challenge to realize the blessing of Abraham, the more quickly that interpretive and ethical key will turn in the lock of Abraham's curse. The rise of mass-market Fundamentalisms in each of the

Abrahamic faiths, complete with religious "authorities" who have no standing beyond their market appeal and the unwise tendency of the secular media to give them undue attention, represents the strongest obstacle to realizing this promise. As long as the obstacle remains, Abraham's curse will persist and grow, with its call for allegedly necessary, mass-market martyrdoms and its lure of utopias just the other side of Armageddon.

Resisting that prospect has featured as part of the purpose of theological reflection within the Abrahamic traditions for millennia, and is now the common vocation of all those who see that we have no human future if we insist on remaining on Mount Moriah. The distinctive voices of the Torah, Jesus Christ, and the Prophet Muhammad agree that Moriah is behind us, never to be visited again. Any voice that calls us back to the mount of human sacrifice, in whatever form it takes in its myriad disguises, is not God's. It is time for us, whether believers or not, to come down to the place of promise, where we can see that no moral value attaches to sacrificing any human life for any cause, with the possible exception of one's own.

Acknowledgments

The Aqedah invites us to understand complex texts and their interpretations as well as forces in human society that no other source in myth or literature lays bare as clearly. If I have uncovered something of the Aqedah's mysterious power and promise, that comes as a result of the counsel and collaboration of many colleagues.

Philip Davies engaged me in academic consideration of the Aqedah at the University of Sheffield, while we were both Lecturers in the Department of Biblical Studies. We collaborated in developing a chronology of the Judaic texts that has become widely accepted, despite initial resistance motivated by apologetic considerations. Always a keen and searching reader, Philip helped me in this project with the same verve and insight he brought to bear on my thinking thirty years ago.

When I moved from Sheffield to Yale University, Jacob Neusner (then at Brown University) encouraged me to extend my engagement with Judaica. Now that we are collaborators at Bard College, he is an ever-present source of wise guidance and detailed comment. In 2005–2006, Professor Neusner and I led a Faculty Humanities Seminar on the Aqedah, sponsored by the National Endowment for the Humanities and organized by Theresa Vilardi at Bard's Institute for Writing and Thinking.

The late David Pierce, long the mainstay of Bard's Department of Religion, introduced me to the anthropological study of sacrifice. René Girard, from the time we first met at a conference at Stanford University, has proven a formative and continuing influence, most of all when we cordially disagree with one another. More recently, another distinguished scholar from Stanford, Van A. Harvey, commented on the working manuscript of this book and helped shape its final form.

Scholars of Islam have deepened the study of religion at Bard College considerably. Lynda Clarke, Salahuddin Muhammad, Jonathan Brockopp, Nerina Rustomji, and Ismail Açar have been extremely helpful to me, both in discussion and in commenting on the working manuscript. Professors Açar, Clarke, and Rustomji were exceptionally generous in offering detailed comments that influenced my wording, and Sam Chilton initiated me into the study of Arabic with forbearance and acuity.

The transfer of this study from conception to page required editorial midwifery. The incentive to undertake the project came from Kenneth Wapner, who has provided expert advice, and from Gail Ross, my literary agent. Andrew Corbin, my editor at Doubleday and a fellow student of the Aqedah, has from first to last appreciated the power and complexity of the issues involved, helping me to find words for the violent mystery of sacrifice, which silence makes more virulent.

Notes

Foreword

3 **the Afro-Caribbean god Ogun, whose knife is believed to liberate vital forces from the victims he sacrifices** In relation to the history and cult of Ogun, see *Africa's Ogun: Old World and New*, African Systems of Thought, edited by Sandra T. Barnes (Bloomington: Indiana University Press, 1997).

4 **Mohamed Atta's bags, left behind in Boston** Found in the suitcase of Mohamed Atta, the Atta letter (as it is usually called) includes prayers, instructions for the last night of life, and a practical checklist of requirements for the operation. The Federal Bureau of Investigation released an untranslated copy of the letter; the British newspaper *The Observer* (September 30, 2001) published a translation.

5 **"when you kill in war, it is an act that is allowed"** The comments of Timothy McVeigh and Yigal Amir come from widely circulated reports: see respectively the Associated Press for June 11, 2001, and CNN for November 7, 1995.

9 **when I first researched the Aqedah in detail** See P. R. Davies and B. D. Chilton, "The Aqedah: A Revised Tradition History," *Catholic Biblical Quarterly* 40 (1978):514–46. Philip Davies followed up our initial article in "Passover and the Dating of the Aqedah," *Journal of Jewish Studies* 30 (1979):59–67. I have also continued to contribute to this discussion: "Isaac and the Second Night: A Consideration," *Biblica* 61 (1980):78–88, reprinted in *Targumic Approaches to the Gospels: Essays in the Mutual Definition of Judaism and Christianity*, Studies in Judaism (Lanham and London: University Press of America, 1986), pp. 25–37; "Recent Discussion of the Aqedah," *Targumic Approaches to the Gospels*, pp. 39–49. Two comprehensive treatments of the question have confirmed our analysis and made it a matter of scholarly consensus: Lukas Kundert, *Die Opferung/Bindung Isaaks*, Wissenschaft-

liche Monographien zum Alten und Neuen Testament 78.1, 2 (Neukirchen-Vluyn: Neukirchener, 1998); and Edward Kessler, *Bound by the Bible: Jews, Christians and the Sacrifice of Isaac* (Cambridge, England: Cambridge University Press, 2004).

11 **"The Parable of the Old Man and the Young"** Wilfred Owen, *Poems*, Poet to Poet Series, edited by Jon Stallworthy (London: Faber, 2004). Owen died in 1918, one week before the armistice. The "Parable" is featured in the third movement (called the Offertorium) of Benjamin Britten's *War Requiem,* first performed on May 30, 1962, for the reconsecration of Coventry Cathedral.

12 **after Walter Lowrie's translation of his work** Kierkegaard had *Fear and Trembling* published under the pseudonym Johannes de Silentio in 1843; Lowrie's translation of the Danish edition appeared in 1941. See Edmund Perry, "Was Kierkegaard a 'Biblical' Existentialist?" *Journal of Religion* 36.1 (1956):17–23.

Chapter I

17 **Human sacrifice, and child sacrifice at that, contradicts what has been called "the Minoan Myth."** See Joseph Alexander MacGillivray, *Minotaur: Sir Arthur Evans and the Archaeology of the Minoan Myth* (New York: Hill and Wang, 2000), p. 312; *Urbanism in the Aegean Bronze Age,* edited by Keith Branigan (London: Sheffield Academic Press, 2001). In regard to Neanderthal culture, see Paul Mellars, *The Neanderthal Legacy: An Archaeological Perspective from Western Europe* (Princeton, NJ: Princeton University Press, 1996), pp. 305–7, 364, 375–81.

22 **By the time the Elohist source was first crafted** Good arguments have been made for dating elements of the Elohist source, or even the source as a whole, much later. But its characteristic concern with prophecy reflects a setting in the ninth century B.C.E. Even those, particularly in Europe, who express skepticism about an early dating of the Elohist source agree that this prophetic emphasis animates Genesis 22. See Friedhelm Hartenstein, "Die Verborgenheit des rettenden Gottes. Exegetische und theologische Bermerkungen zu Genesis 22," *Isaaks Opferung (Gen 22) in den Konfessionen und Medien der Frühen Neuzeit:* Arbeiten zur Kirchengeschichte, edited by Johann Anselm Steiger and Ulrich Heinen (Berlin: de Gruyter, 2006), pp. 1–22.

24 **Human sacrifice emerged as the price required to assure divine favor in building a city** This is well described in *Understanding Religious Sacrifice: A Reader,* Controversies in the Study of Religion, edited by Jeffrey Carter (New York: Continuum, 2003); *Sacrifice in Religious Experience,* Numen Book Series XCIII, edited by Albert I. Baumgarten (Leiden: Brill, 2002); Jon D. Levenson, *The Death and Resurrection of the Beloved Son: The Transformation of Child Sacrifice in Judaism and Christianity* (New Haven: Yale University Press, 1993); Paul Wheatley, *The Pivot of the Four Quarters: A Preliminary Inquiry into the Origins and Character of the Ancient Chinese City* (Chicago: Aldine, 1971).

28 **A sensitive reader might decide to reject the whole story of the Aqedah** See Carol Delaney, *Abraham on Trial: The Social Legacy of Biblical Myth*

(Prince-ton, NJ: Princeton University Press, 1998). She analyzes the murder of a young girl in California on January 6, 1990 (the Feast of the Epiphany of Christ), tracing the influence of the Aqedah on the crime. Delaney describes the murder by quoting, she says, from a "verbatim transcript," but she renders the events in a style reminiscent of Genesis 22, complete with contrapuntal dialogue. Lest anyone miss the biblical connection, she also gives the murderer the pseudonym "Cristos." Delaney accuses the Bible, and in particular the Christian glorification of Isaac, as anticipating Jesus' death, of producing the pattern of behavior that "Cristos" replicated. She follows other scholars, who have argued that sacrifice represents an overt attempt at male dominance. Riane Eisler has argued that "androcracy" distorted the "partnership" model of the Neolithic period, while Nancy Jay has described the blood-rites of the Temple in Jerusalem as a male attempt to imitate women's capacity in bearing children to bring forth life out of blood. See respectively *The Chalice and the Blade: Our History, Our Future* (Cambridge, Mass.: Harper & Row, 1987); *Throughout Your Generations Forever: Sacrifice, Religion, and Paternity* (Chicago: University of Chicago Press, 1992). Jay, Eisler, and Delaney are gifted critics, but their gender-only solutions to the problem of violence assume not only that men are inherently violent in a way that women are not, but also that there is a constitutional dichotomy between the two. I think the evidence in aggregate shows that distorted gender roles emerge as the *outcome* of the Stone Age culture of war, as I describe later in this chapter.

29 **Mesha himself went on to have a monument inscribed** The inscription has been published many times since its identification in 1868. See R. F. Klein, *The Recovery of Jerusalem: A Narrative of Exploration and Discovery in the City and the Holy Land*, edited by Walter Morrison (New York: Appleton, 1872), pp. 389–402; Klaas A. D. Smelik, "The Literary Structure of King Mesha's Inscription," *Journal for the Study of the Old Testament* 46 (1990):21–30.

30 **Clytemnestra let her jealousy show through** For helpful treatments, see Ken Dowden, *Death and the Maiden: Girls' Initiation Rites in Greek Mythology* (London: Routledge, 1989); Dennis D. Hughes, *Human Sacrifice in Ancient Greece* (London: Routledge, 1991); Jennifer Larson, *Greek Heroine Cults*, Wisconsin Studies in Classics (Madison: University of Wisconsin, 1995); Nannó Marinatos, *The Goddess and the Warrior: The Naked Goddess and Mistress of Animals in Early Greek Religion* (London: Routledge, 2000); Kathleen L. Komar, *Reclaiming Klytemnestra: Revenge or Reconciliation* (Urbana: University of Illinois Press, 2003). See the edited Greek text of Euripides with a serviceable English translation (from which I have departed) by Arthur S. Way, *Euripides with an English Translation*, vol. 2, Loeb Classical Library (London: Heinemann, 1919), lines 1024–27.

31 **When President George W. Bush remembered** The White House released a transcript of the address on its electronic site, which I quote here. The two references appear in the same paragraph.

34 **René Girard, a French literary critic turned social anthropologist** Girard's

most systematic work remains *Violence and the Sacred,* translated by Patrick Gregory (Baltimore: Johns Hopkins University Press, 1977). The quotation below is my translation of the original French edition of *Violence et le Sacré* (Paris: Grasset, 1972), p. 153. I have engaged with Girard in the course of my analysis of sacrifice; see *The Temple of Jesus: His Sacrificial Program within a Cultural History of Sacrifice* (University Park: Pennsylvania State University Press, 1992); "The Hungry Knife: Towards a Sense of Sacrifice," in *The Bible in Human Society: Essays in Honour of John Rogerson,* Journal for the Study of the Old Testament supplement Series 200, edited by M. D. Carroll, D. J. A. Clines, and P. R. Davies (Sheffield, England: Sheffield Academic Press, 1995), pp. 122–38; "Sacrifice," *Encyclopedia of Religious and Spiritual Development,* edited by Elizabeth M. Downing and W. George Scarlett (Thousand Oaks, Calif.: Sage, 2006), pp. 393–95.

39 **Diodorus Siculus reported on the ancient practice at Carthage** Didorus goes on in his *Library of History* 20.14.5–7 to compare Euripides' presentation of the sacrifice of Iphigenia. See also 13.86.3 and the discussion in Joyce E. Salisbury, *Perpetua's Passion: The Death and Memory of a Young Roman Woman* (New York: Routledge, 1997), pp. 51–54, who also cites Plutarch, Tertullian and Minucius Felix to this effect. On the archaeological evidence and attempts to discount it, see Lawrence E. Stager, "Carthage: A View from the Tophet," *Phönizer im Westen,* edited by Hans Georg Niemeyer (Mainz, Germany: Zabern, 1982), pp. 155–66; Lawrence E. Stager and Samuel R. Wolff, "Child Sacrifice at Carthage—Religious Rite or Population Control?" *Biblical Archaeology Review* 10 (1984):30–51.

Chapter II

46 **"Blow with a ram's horn before me that I may remember for you the Aqedah of Isaac"** See Rosh Hashanah 16a in the Babylonian Talmud. The quotation in the next paragraph comes from Daniel Boyarin and Seymour Siegel, "Resurrection, Rabbinic Period, Medieval Jewish Philosophy, Modern Period," *Encyclopedia Judaica:* 240–44, 240; details of the cult that arose around Baruch Goldstein are discussed in Israel Shahak and Norton Mezvinsky, *Jewish Fundamentalism in Israel* (London: Pluto, 1999).

49 **Many Jews responded to what they saw as the direct threat to the existence of their religion with the offer of their own lives** See Tessa Rajak, "Dying for the Law: The Martyr's Portrait in Jewish Greek Literature," *The Jewish Dialogue with Greece and Rome: Studies in Cultural and Social Interaction,* Arbeiten zur Geschichte des antiken Judentums und des Urchristentums XLVIII (Leiden: Brill, 2001), pp. 99–133; Eric S. Gruen, "Hellenism and Persecution: Antiochus IV and the Jews," in *Hellenistic History and Culture,* Hellenistic Culture and Society, vol. 9, edited by Peter Green (Berkeley: University of California Press, 1993), pp. 238–64.

54 **According to *Jubilees'* version of the story, the Aqedah was the seventh, climactic test of faith that Abraham faced** As counted by Joseph A. Fitzmyer, "The Sacrifice of Isaac in Qumran Literature," *Biblica* 83 (2002):211–29, 214. Fitzmyer mounts a sustained critique on the argument of Geza Vermes,

who relied on the work of Israel Lévi and H. J. Schoeps earlier in the twentieth century in an attempt to make later Rabbinic interpretations of the Aqedah appear more ancient than the evidence warrants.

59 **Josephus may allude to Agamemnon and Iphigenia in Euripides** See Edward Kessler, *Bound by the Bible*, 101. Kessler, p. 59, also refers to the classical portrayals of Hector and Priam in Homer.

59 **The later, famous case at Masada** Josephus reports (*War* 7.320–401) that in 73 C.E., after a lengthy siege, when it appeared the Romans would soon break through the final defenses, 960 Jewish men, women, and children determined that suicide was preferable to either slavery or execution.

60 **Belief in a life after death** See Isaiah 25:8; 26:19; Ezekiel 37:1–15, and Claudia Setzer, *Resurrection of the Body in Early Judaism and Early Christianity: Doctrine, Community, and Self-Definition* (Boston and Leiden: Brill Academic, 2004), with the review in *Catholic Biblical Quarterly* 68 (2006):158–60; Shmuel Shepkaru, "From after Death to Afterlife: Martyrdom and Its Recompense," *Association for Jewish Studies Review* 24.1 (1999):1–44.

63 **"Aqedah" came into its own, because it was a reference to the way a sheep or a ram was tied up for slaughter** See Tamid 4:1 in the Mishnah and one of the most useful works ever written on the Aqedah, Shalom Spiegel's *The Last Trial*, translated by Judah Goldin (New York: Random House, 1967), pp. xix–xx. See also Aharon (Ronald E.) Agus, *The Binding of Isaac and Messiah: Law, Martyrdom and Deliverance in Early Rabbinic Religiosity*, SUNY Series in Judaica: *Hermeneutics, Mysticism and Religion* (Albany: State University of New York Press, 1988).

65 **Abraham went so far as to nick Isaac's carotid artery** See J. Mann, *The Bible as Read and Preached in the Old Synagogue* (Cincinnati: Union of American Hebrew Congregations, 1940), p. 67; H. J. Schoeps, "The Sacrifice of Isaac in Paul's Theology," *Journal of Biblical Literature* 65.4 (1946):385–92; Eduard Lohse, *Märtyrer und Gottesknecht* (Göttingen: Vandenhoeck & Ruprecht, 1963).

67 **Isaac studied in a heavenly academy** See Martin McNamara, "Melchizedek: Gen 14, 17–20 in the Targums, in Rabbinic and Early Christian Literature," *Biblica* 81 (2000):1–31. As McNamara shows, the Targumim belong within a more generally Rabbinic pattern.

67 **In a midrash on the Maccabean story** See Jacob Neusner, *Lamentations Rabbah: An Analytical Translation*, Brown Judaic Studies 193 (Atlanta: Scholars Press, 1989), 50.1. The midrash names the woman as Miriam, daughter of Tanhum, and has her also suckle her two-and-a-half-year-old son before his death.

68 **Isaac offered his neck willingly for sacrifice** These Aramaic versions, called Targumim, have played a central role in modern discussion of the Aqedah. For texts and discussion (especially of Genesis 22, Isaiah 33:7, and Exodus 12:42) see: for Genesis 22, "The Aqedah: A Revised Tradition History," *Catholic Biblical Quarterly* 40.4 (1978); for Isaiah 33:7, "Recent Discussion of the Aqedah," *Targumic Approaches to the Gospels: Essays in the Mutual Definition of Judaism and Christianity*, Studies in Judaism (Lanham and

London: University Press of America, 1986), pp. 39–49; for Exodus 12:42, "Isaac and the Second Night: A Consideration," *Biblica* 61 (1980):78–88 and *Targumic Approaches to the Gospels,* pp. 25–37; for Leviticus 22:27, Jon D. Levenson, *The Death and Resurrection of the Beloved Son: The Transformation of Child Sacrifice in Judaism and Christianity* (New Haven: Yale University Press, 1993), pp. 183–84.

Chapter III

74 **"his cross" refers to any eventual trial that a *disciple* will face** In any case, although Jesus anticipated the kind of violent rejection that many prophets before him had suffered in Jerusalem, the decision of the Romans to put him to death by crucifixion was the outcome of totally unexpected events in Rome. I have explained the impact in Jerusalem of the execution of the prefect Sejanus in Rome on October 18, 31 C.E., as well as the chain of events leading to the crucifixion, in *Rabbi Jesus: An Intimate Biography* (New York: Doubleday, 2000), pp. 197–268.

76 **a profound and persistent weakness in the work of the "Jesus Seminar":** *The Five Gospels: The Search for the Authentic Words of Jesus,* edited by Robert W. Funk and Roy W. Hoover (New York: Macmillan, 1993), pp. 78–79. John Dominic Crossan's dissent appears in *The Historical Jesus: The Life of a Mediterranean Jewish Peasant* (San Francisco: HarperSanFrancisco, 1991), p. 353. Epictetus's aphorism is translated from *Epictetus: The Discourses as Reported by Arrian, the Manual, and Fragments with an English Translation,* edited by W. A. Oldfather (Cambridge, Mass.: Harvard University, 1985, 1989). Although Edward Kessler has argued that the image of Isaac carrying his wood as if it were a cross in Genesis Rabbah 56:3 is "clearly influenced by the New Testament description of Christ carrying his cross to the crucifixion," most scholars have found it difficult to imagine why the Rabbis responsible for Midrash Rabbah would have assimilated Christian claims; see Kessler, "Binding of Isaac (Akedah)," *A Dictionary of Jewish-Christian Relations,* edited by Edward Kessler and Neil Wenbon (Cambridge, England: Cambridge University Press, 2006), p. 59.

78 **Jesus imputed a new and revolutionary meaning to the significance of the meals he had long enjoyed with his disciples** See my monograph *A Feast of Meanings: Eucharistic Theologies from Jesus through Johannine Circles,* Supplements to *Novum Testamentum* 72 (Leiden: Brill, 1994), and a semi-popular treatment, *Jesus' Prayer and Jesus' Eucharist: His Personal Practice of Spirituality* (Valley Forge, Pa.: Trinity Press International, 1997), as well as *Rabbi Jesus,* pp. 225–30, 248–68.

82 **The author of the Epistle to the Hebrews wrote in Paul's name, but around thirty-one years after Paul's death** See *Rabbi Paul: An Intellectual Biography* (New York: Doubleday, 2004), pp. 161–62, and the more extensive discussion in *Trading Places: The Intersecting Histories of Judaism and Christianity,* with Jacob Neusner (Cleveland: Pilgrim, 1996; also Eugene, OR: Wipf and Stock, 2004).

86 **Augustine's conception of inherited sin** On this and related topics, see *The*

Cambridge Companion to Augustine, edited by Eleonore Stump and Norman Kretzmann (New York: Cambridge University Press, 2001); *Augustine and His Critics: Essays in Honour of Gerald Bonner,* edited by Robert Dodaro and George Lawless (London: Routledge, 2000); *The Augustinian Tradition,* Philosophical Traditions, edited by Gareth B. Matthews (Berkeley and Los Angeles: University of California Press, 1999). On the context in ancient thought dealt with here, see Mary Boyce, *Zoroastrians: Their Religious Beliefs and Practices,* Library of Religion (London: Routledge, 2001); *The Light and the Darkness: Studies in Manichaeism and Its World,* edited by Paul Mirecki and Jason BeDuhn (Leiden: Brill, 2001).

87 **propaganda often portrayed their enemies as guilty of sacrificing and even eating Christians** This kind of accusation goes back a long way. Pagans accused Christians of such practices, and then Catholics accused Gnostics in the same vein; Stephen Benko, *Pagan Rome and the Early Christians* (Bloomington: Indiana University Press, 1984), pp. 54–78. From there, the attribution has prospered; see Daniel Baraz, *Medieval Cruelty: Changing Perceptions, Antiquity to the Early Modern Period,* Conjunctions of Religion and Power in the Medieval Past (Ithaca, N.Y.: Cornell University Press, 2003); R. Po-Chia Hsia, *The Myth of Ritual Murder: Jews and Magic in Reformation Germany* (New Haven: Yale University Press, 1988); W. Arens, *The Man-Eating Myth: Anthropology & Anthropophagy* (New York: Oxford University Press, 1980); and Priscilla L. Walton, *Our Cannibals, Ourselves* (Urbana: University of Illinois Press, 2004).

91 **Their marginal status, neither Jewish nor non-Jewish, and numbering only a fraction of 1 percent of the population of the Roman Empire** See the estimates of Rodney Stark in *Cities of God: The Real Story of How Christianity Became an Urban Movement and Conquered Rome* (San Francisco: HarperSanFrancisco, 2006), p. 67. In my opinion, Stark relies too much on a standard rate of growth of 3.4 percent a year, which causes him to underestimate Christian numbers in the middle of the first century and overestimate them at the beginning of the fourth century; see my review in the *New York Sun* (December 8, 2006). For a good text of Tacitus, who published his work in 116 C.E., see *Tacitus: The Annals with an English Translation, Books XIII–XVI,* Loeb Classical Library, Tacitus V (Cambridge, Mass.: Harvard University Press, 1994). Domitian's persecution, ended by his assassination in 96 C.E., has been a topic of scholarly debate, but I think the evidence is quite clear; in addition to Eusebius, *History of the Church* 3.17–20, see Donald McFayden, "The Occasion of the Domitianic Persecution," *American Journal of Theology* 24.1 (1920):46–66.

Chapter IV

96 **Isaac personally acted as he did "with confidence, knowing what was coming"** See Kirsopp Lake, *The Apostolic Fathers,* vols. I, II, Loeb Classical Library (London: Heinemann, 1912), and the later edition by Bart D. Ehrman (Cambridge, Mass.: Harvard University Press, 2003). I have attempted in this book to cite from the Loeb series, because it is widely accessible and

fairly standard. But for the sake of comparison among documents, I have had to supply my own translations.

97 **The second-century theologian from Samaria named Justin** See André Wartelle, *Saint Justin: Apologies, Introduction, Texte Critique, Traduction, Commentaire et Index* (Paris: Etudes Augustiniennes, 1987), who places the *First Apology* in 153–54 C.E. (p. 35); Paul P. Parvis in "Justin, Philosopher and Martyr: The Posthumous Creation of the Second Apology," in *Justin Martyr and His Worlds*, edited by Sara Parvis et al. (Minneapolis: Fortress, 2007).

99 **Stéphane Audoin-Rouseau and Annette Becker** *14–18: Understanding the Great War* (New York: Hill and Wang, 2002), a translation by Catherine Temerson of *14–18: Retrouver la Guerre* (Paris: Gallimard, 2000).

99 **Pliny, governor of Bithynia and Pontus in Asia Minor** This Pliny is called "the Younger," to distinguish him from his uncle and adoptive father, a famed historian and naturalist. See A. N. Sherwin-White, *The Letters of Pliny: A Historical and Social Commentary* (New York: Oxford University Press, 1985); *Pliny: Letters*, Loeb Classical Library, translated by William Melmoth and W. M. L. Hutchinson (London: Heinemann, 1923).

111 **"one, named Quintus, a Phrygian recently come from Phrygia, cringed when he saw the beasts"** Smyrna, on the western coast of Asia Minor, was a cosmopolitan harbor; evidently, prejudice against those who came from the Phrygian interior was rife there. The slight might also be an early indication of antagonism to the rigorist teachings of Montanus, who also came from Phrygia, and whose movement came to be called "the Phrygian heresy."

111 **Although the total number of martyrs between Stephen's death in 32 C.E. and Constantine's Edict of Milan (which ordered the toleration of Christianity) in 313 C.E. probably came to only a few thousand** The Roman Empire had to deal with the fact that, by 300 C.E., Christians made up some 10 percent of the population; see Robert M. Grant, *Christianity and Society: Seven Studies* (San Francisco: Harper & Row, 1977); and Rodney Stark, *The Rise of Christianity: A Sociologist Reconsiders History* (Princeton, N.J.: Princeton University Press, 1996), with the corrections offered in Stark's *Cities of God: The Real Story of How Christianity Became an Urban Movement and Conquered Rome* (San Francisco: HarperSanFrancisco, 2006). Both Grant and Stark agree with W. H. C. Frend, *Martyrdom and Persecution in the Early Church* (Oxford: Blackwell, 1965) in putting the number of martyrs in hundreds rather than thousands, but in my opinion that estimate is artificially limited by the number of individuals that happen to have been named in extant sources, and by a failure to include deaths by pogrom as martyrdoms. I should also note that Stark's sociological estimates are global, and when he turns to the populations of cities (and even of the Roman Empire as a whole) at any given time, he states conclusions that are at odds with estimates based on archaeological excavations, which I have set out in *Rabbi Paul: An Intellectual Biography* (New York: Doubleday, 2004).

112 **This was an especially vexing matter for Marcus Aurelius** See Anthony

Birley, *Marcus Aurelius: A Biography* (New Haven: Yale University Press, 1987), pp. 202–4. Marcus resolves his problem by accusing the Christians of "sheer opposition"; cf. *Meditations* 11.3 in A. S. L. Farquharson, *The Meditations of the Emperor Marcus Aurelius: Edited, with Translation and Commentary* (Oxford: Clarendon, 1968). Cf. Stephen Benko, *Pagan Rome and the Early Christians* (Bloomington: Indiana University Press, 1986), pp. 41–42. On the incorporation of Stoic concepts within Christianity, see *Rabbi Paul*; and Daniel Boyarin, *Dying for God: Martyrdom and the Making of Christianity and Judaism* (Stanford, Calif.: Stanford University Press, 1999).

113 **By this time Tertullian could simply allude to the motif of Christ bearing the cross being like Isaac carrying the wood** See *An Answer to the Jews* 10. Earlier, *The Epistle of Barnabas* (7.3) achieved great popularity and exerted wide influence by finding prophecies to Christ in the Scriptures of Israel. This tract from Alexandria, written before 135 C.E., said that Jesus offered "the vessel of the spirit, a sacrifice for our sins, in order that the type instituted in Isaac, who was offered upon the altar, might be completed," a motif also taken up by Tertullian's colleague in Gaul, Irenaeus, *Against Heresies* 4.5.4, and by Clement of Alexandria, *Paidagogos* 1.5.23.

114 **Melito's evocation of the suffering of Christ** See Stuart J. Hall, *Melito of Sardis: Peri Pascha and Fragments*, Oxford Early Christian Texts (Oxford: Clarendon, 1979). Editorial work in this case is particularly important, since the textual evidence is fragmentary.

115 **The noblewoman Perpetua recorded her dream prior to her execution** See Rosemary Rader, "Perpetua," in *A Lost Tradition: Women Writers of the Early Church*, edited by Patricia Wilson-Kastner (Lanham, Md.: University Press of America, 1981), pp. 1–32; Joyce E. Salisbury, *Perpetua's Passion: The Death and Memory of a Young Roman Woman* (New York: Routledge, 1997).

116 **"Eating the sacred bread and drinking the sacred wine, Christians were assimilated with their Lord and thus made ready to follow him even unto death"** Bernhard Lang, *Sacred Games: A History of Christian Worship* (New Haven: Yale University Press, 1997), pp. 254–62, and, for example, Cyprian, *Treatise* 9.10. Lang has pursued his analysis in "Opfer," *Neues Handbuch Theologischer Begriffe* 3, edited by Peter Eicher and Angela Schlenkrich (München: Kösel, 2005), pp. 301–11.

Chapter V

121 **This theory, originating in the second century, found its way into the Qur'an as well as a revisionist scholar's work** Qur'an 4.157, *Al-Nisa*, and Hugh J. Schonfield, *The Passover Plot: New Light on the History of Jesus* (New York: Geis Associates, 1965). Basilides's position is described by Irenaeus in *Against Heresies* 1.24.4. Irenaeus's statement about Cerinthus appears in *Against Heresies* 1.26.1. Guy G. Stroumsa, "Christ's Laughter: Docetic Origins Reconsidered," *Journal of Early Christian Studies* 12.3 (2004):267–88, 269–70, follows Georg Strecker in distinguishing among three views: "(1) the one according to which Simon of Cyrene was the substitute of Jesus on the cross (a claim made by Basilides, at least according to Irenaeus); (2) the

one affirming that Christ left Jesus just before his death on the cross (according to Cerinthus and the *Gospel of Peter*); and (3) the claim that Jesus Christ was indeed crucified but did not suffer, that he remained *impassibilis*, as his nature is pneumatic (the claim of the Docetics fought by Ignatius)." See *The Gospel according to Peter* 4:10, 19; 5.20. A similar presentation is found in *The Apocalypse of Peter* from Nag Hammadi (VII.3.81.3–21). Here the "Savior" assures a follower, "He whom you see above the tree, glad and laughing, is the living Jesus. But he into whose hands and feet they are driving the nails is his physical part, which is the substitute. . . ."

123 **To Origen's mind, there is complete transparency between Christ's suffering and that of the believer** *Exhortation to Martyrdom* 30 (cf. 27, 50), written c. 235 C.E. Origen's sermon on Jesus as the "lamb of God" appears in *Homilies on Genesis* 8.9. For his thought-experiment in regard to Satan, see *On First Principles* 3.6.5. His condemnation appears in Philippe Labbe and Gabriel Cossart, *Sacrosancta concilia ad regiam editionem exacta* (Paris, 1671–72).

125 **The crucifixion began that epochal reconciliation, by literally giving the devil his due** *Commentary on Romans* 2.13. His view on the devil appearing in Genesis 22, which ultimately reaches back to *Jubilees*, appears in *On First Principles* 3.2.1. The link with the scapegoat appears in *On First Principles* 3.2.1 and in *Homily 9 on Leviticus 5*. See Eugene Teselle, "The Cross as Ransom," *Journal of Early Christian Studies* 4.2 (1996): 147–70.

130 **he took the bait of a helpless victim so that the fishhook of Christ's divine nature captured him** Gregory's unforgettable comparison appears in "The Great Catechism" 24. "In Praise of Blessed Theodore, the Great Martyr" represents Gregory of Nyssa's panegyric for a serving soldier as a martyr, delivered on February 7, 386. Extended comparison between Isaac and Christ, in Gregory's *De deitate filii et spiritus sancti et in Abraham*, also appears in a fourth-century hymn by Ephrem the Syrian. The causal relationship between the two versions is disputed. Whatever relationship one supposes, there can be no doubt of the growth of this image during the fourth century. See Marc Bregman, "Aqedah: Midrash as Visualization," *Journal of Textual Reasoning* 2.1 (2003); Franz Nikolasch, "Zur Ikonographie des Widders von Gen 22," *Vigiliae Christianae* 23 (1969):197–223.

132 **When Sejanus, praetorian prefect of Rome, was strangled by imperial order on October 18, 32 C.E.** Sejanus's fate is discussed in the ancient histories of Dio Cassius, Suetonius, and Tacitus, supported by other sources; see David Shotter, *Tiberius Caesar* (London and New York: Routledge, 1992). For the story of forced self-consumption, see Plutarch, *Cicero* 49; Anthony Everitt, *Cicero: The Life and Times of Rome's Greatest Politician* (New York: Random House, 2001), p. 319.

134 **not only Christ, but the Church as a whole, had lived the pattern of Isaac** Eusebius, *Praeparatio Evangelica* 9.19–20 and Claire Lavant and Françoise and Jean-Claude Gaven, *Ambroise de Milan: Abraham* (Les Pères dans la foi 74) (Paris: Migne, 1999), 2.1.1; 1.8.67, 79.

134 **Later in the fourth century, in Callinicum** For the sad events at Callinicum,

see F. Homes Dudden, *The Life and Times of St. Ambrose*, vol. 2 (Oxford: Clarendon, 1935), pp. 371–79.

135 **Stories of virgin-martyrs resisting the sexual assaults of pagan princes and consuls** See Peter Brown, *The Body and Society: Men, Women, and Sexual Renunciation in Early Christianity* (New York: Columbia University Press, 1988). Another good example of fourth-century themes is the anonymous Aqedah in one of the Bodmer papyri; see Pieter W. van der Horst and Martien F. G. Parmentier, "A New Early Christian Poem on the Sacrifice of Isaac," *Le Codex des Visions*, Recherches et Rencontres 18, edited by André Hurst and Jean Rudhardt (Geneva: Droz, 2002), pp. 155–72, a version of the Aqedah that also granted Sarah an enhanced role.

136 **"the child being led to the sacrifice by his father indicates through symbol and outline that neither human strength nor the greed of the conspirators led our Lord Jesus Christ to the cross, but the desire of the Father"** Edward Kessler, *Bound by the Bible: Jews, Christians and the Sacrifice of Isaac* (Cambridge, England: Cambridge University Press, 2004), pp. 125, 132, citing *Pascal homilies* 5 and *Glaphyrorum in Genesim.* Augustine's paraphrase of Genesis 22 appears in *The City of God* 16.32 and his understanding of the millennium in *City of God* 20.9. His statement in regard to "heretics, Jews, and pagans" in a united front against the unity of the Church appears in Sermon 62.18.

138 **literal payment grew as a method of righting wrongs within early medieval Europe** See Peter Brown, *The Rise of Western Christendom: Triumph and Diversity, 200–1000 A.D.* (Cambridge, Mass.: Blackwell, 1996); Thomas Pollock Oakley, *English Penitential Discipline and Anglo-Saxon Law in Their Joint Influence*, Studies in History, Economics and Public Law, edited by the faculty of Political Science of Columbia University, vol. CVII, no. 2; whole no. 242 (New York: Columbia University Press, 1923).

138 **Anselm, the archbishop of Canterbury who died in 1109, converted Cyril of Alexandria's suggestion into a fully renovated ransom theory** *Cur Deus Homo* 1.7; see David Brown, "Anselm on Atonement," *The Cambridge Companion to Anselm*, Cambridge Companions to Philosophy, edited by Brian Davies and Brian Leftow (Cambridge, England: Cambridge University Press, 2004), pp. 279–302.

139 **the blood on the Temple Mount reaching up to the bridles of the Crusaders' horses** See Raymond d'Aguilers, *Historia Francorum qui ceperunt Iherusalem*, translated by John Hugh Hill and Laurita L. Hill (Philadelphia: American Philosophical Society, 1968); Eileen Dugan, "Jerusalem in the Crusades," *Journal of Religion and Society* 2 (in the Supplement Series, 2007). For the medieval exchange between Abraham and Isaac, see Alfred W. Pollard, *En-glish Miracle Plays, Moralities and Interludes* (Oxford: Clarendon, 1927), lines 305–8; 337–40; Peter Braeger in "Typology as Contrast in the Middle English *Abraham and Isaac* Plays," *Essays in Medieval Studies* 2 (1985):131–53.

Chapter VI

144 **In a vivid sermon widely disseminated on the Internet** Published without attribution in a Nigerian newspaper, *Daily Sun* (January 21, 2005), the sermon was picked up by Islam Online and another site, Islaam. As the sermon is repeated, the specific targets of militant concern vary. For example, the Nigerian version speaks of Somalia, rather than Iraq.

148 **The original Aqedah of Islam, as revealed to Muhammad** See the widely used edition 'Abdullah Yûsuf 'Ali, *The Meaning of the Holy Qur'ân: New Edition with Qur'anic Text (Arabic), Revised Translation, Commentary and Newly Compiled Comprehensive Index* (Beltsville, Md.: Amana, 2003), and *The Holy Qur'an with English Translation and Commentary* (Hazrat Mirza Tahir Ahmad; Tilford, England: Islam International Publications, 1988), although renderings here are my own.

149 **Bernard Lewis and Daniel Pipes** Among their many works, see Bernard Lewis, *The Crisis of Islam: Holy War and Unholy Terror* (New York: Modern Library, 2003); Daniel Pipes, *Militant Islam Reaches America* (New York: W. W. Norton, 2002), the quotation coming from p. 135, along with the estimate that "Islamists constitute a small but significant minority of Muslims, perhaps 10 to 15 percent of the total population."

150 **The prophecy of an inevitable "clash of civilizations"** See Lewis, "The Roots of Muslim Rage," *Atlantic Monthly* 266.3 (September 1990):47–60; Huntington, *The Clash of Civilizations and the Remaking of World Order* (New York: Simon & Schuster, 1996). A collection of essays opposed to the characterization of Islam by Lewis and Huntington conveys the theme of its criticism in its title, *The New Crusades: Constructing the Muslim Enemy*, edited by Emran Qureshi and Michael Sells (New York: Columbia University Press, 2003).

153 **the angel Gabriel came to him as a man** See Neal Robinson, *Discovering the Qur'an: A Contemporary Approach to a Veiled Text* (Washington, DC: Georgetown University Press, 2002); Muhammad Husayn Haykal, *The Life of Muhammad,* translated by Isma'îl Râgî A. al Fârûqî (North American Trust Publications, 1976); Yahiya Emerick, *The Life and Work of Muhammad,* Critical Lives (Indianapolis: Alpha, 2002); A. Guillaume, *The Life of Muhammad: A Translation of Ishâq's Sîrat Rasûl Allâh* (New York: Oxford University Press, 2003); *The Biography of Muhammad: The Issue of the Sources,* Islamic History and Civilization, edited by Harald Motzki (Boston: Brill, 2000).

155 **A useful monograph** Reuven Firestone, *Journey in Holy Lands: The Evolution of the Abraham-Ishmael Legends in Islamic Exegesis* (Albany: State University of New York Press, 1990), p. 135. See also "Merit, Mimesis, and Martyrdom: Aspects of Shi'ite Meta-Historical Exegesis on Abraham's Sacrifice in Light of Jewish, Christian, and Sunni Muslim Tradition," *Journal of the American Academy of Religion* 61.1 (1998):93–116. These are critical analyses of Muslim sources, but their treatment of Judaic and Christian sources is jejune and dated. See also *The Binding (Aqedah) and Its Transformations in Judaism and Islam: The Lambs of God,* Mellen Biblical Press Series 32,

edited by Mishael Maswari Caspi and Sascha Benjamin Cohen (Lewiston, N.Y.: Mellen Biblical Press, 1995); and *Opfere Deinen Sohn! Das Isaak-Opfer in Judentum, Christentum und Islam,* edited by Bernhard Greiner, Bernd Janowski, and Hermann Lichtenberger (Tübingen: Francke, 2007).

156 the *Liber Antiquitatum Biblicarum* For an illuminating treatment, see K. van der Toorn and P. W. van der Horst, "Nimrod Before and After the Bible," *Harvard Theological Review* 83.1 (1990):1–29. See *Liber Antiquitatum Biblicarum* 6 and the *Book of Jubilees* 12. The passage from Genesis Rabbah mentioned below appears at 38.13; see H. Freedman, *The Midrash Rabbah: Translated into English with Notes, Glossary and Indices: Genesis* (London: Soncino, 1977).

159 inference of that kind has become a normal part of scholarship Biographies of Muhammad have followed this principle through for better than a hundred years. As a method, it is the soundest approach to the task of biography on the basis of religious scriptures, and for that reason I adopted it in my book, *Rabbi Jesus.* A clear presentation of the method is developed in Rudi Paret, *Mohammed und der Koran: Geschichte und Verkündigung des arabischen Propheten,* Kohlhammer Urban-Taschenbücher 32 (Stuttgart: Kohlhammer, 1980).

164 An interpreter who died in 923 C.E., Al Tabari, See William M. Brinner, Franz Rosenthal, and Moshe Perlmann, *The History of al-Tabari,* Bibliotheca Persica (Albany: State University of New York Press, 1987–91). The relevant passages are II.293–319.

166 "if we blew ourselves up, we would go directly to Paradise" See the report of Constance de Bonnaventure in *Le Figaro* (July 7, 2007), 20 (supplement).

167 a dispute between Ishmael and Isaac See Genesis Rabbah 55:4. The account of Satan's role in the tale is a variant of an earlier Judaic interpretation, which appears in the Babylonian Talmud (tractate Sanhedrin 89b); Lukas Kundert, *Die Opferung, Bindung Isaaks*, Wissenschaftliche Monographien zum Alten und Neuen Testament 78 & 79, vol. 2 (Neukirchen-Vluyn: Neukirchener, 1998), pp. 54–61; and Avivah Gottlieb Zornberg, *Genesis: The Beginning of Desire* (Philadelphia: Jewish Publication Society, 1995), pp. 97–98. The allusion to Job cannot be mistaken. Abraham makes a feast at the time Isaac was weaned (Genesis 21:8), much as Job's family enjoyed feasting (Job 1:25). All this bounty invites Satan to taunt God in regard to Abraham, "This old man—you granted him at a hundred years old fruit of the womb, yet of all the banquet that he made, he did not have one turtledove or one chick to offer to you!" This prompts God to reply, "If I were to say to him, 'Sacrifice your son to me,' immediately he would be sacrificed!"

169 by an angel digging a miraculous well for them See Brannon Wheeler, *Prophets in the Quran: An Introduction to the Quran and Muslim Exegesis* (London: Continuum, 2002), pp. 96–98, 103–4.

Chapter VII

172 **When President Bush asked other nations to join a "crusade"** See Peter Ford, "Europe Cringes at Bush 'Crusade' against Terrorists," *Christian Science Monitor* (September 19, 2001). The quotation of President Reagan comes from a White House transcript of a speech delivered in 1985 at Fallston High School in Maryland.

174 **each Crusader became "a living, holy and pleasing sacrifice"** Thomas Asbridge, *The First Crusade: A New History* (Oxford: Oxford University Press, 2004), p. 66, quoting Robert the Monk, *Historia Iherosolimitana*. Sources are helpfully presented in Edward Peters, *The First Crusade: The Chronicle of Fulcher of Chartres and Other Source Materials* (Philadelphia: University of Pennsylvania Press, 1998); and Robert Levine, *The Deeds of God through the Franks: A Translation of Guibert de Nogent's Gesta Dei per Francos* (Rochester, N.Y.: Boydell, 1997).

175 **Urban promised a reward for the present** As the historian Orderic Vitalis said of Urban in 1135; see Jonathan Riley-Smith, *The First Crusade and the Idea of Crusading*, The Middle Ages Series (Philadelphia: University of Pennsylvania Press, 1986), p. 28. The following quotation is from Aziz S. Atiya, *Crusade, Commerce and Culture* (New York: Wiley, 1966), 21, citing Fulcher of Chartres.

175 **between 60,000 and 100,000 people** See Asbridge, p. 40. Anna Comnena, the Byzantine emperor's daughter, is the source of the most specific estimate, of 10,000 knights, 70,000 infantry, and many camp followers who made it as far as Constantinople. Casualties and desertions were enormous. Asbridge estimates at only 13,300, the Crusader force that finally took Jerusalem (p. 300), even smaller than the tragic 30,000 of the "Children's Crusade" of 1212, who set off for death and slavery (Atiya, p. 85). The quotation of Guibert de Nogent comes from Riley-Smith, p. 149.

176 **"Invocation to the Cross"** Frank Allen Patterson, *The Middle English Penitential Lyric: A Study and Collection of Early Religious Verse*, Columbia University Studies in English (New York: Columbia University Press, 1911), p. 138.

177 **"free rein for every kind of shameful behavior"** See John V. Tolan, *Saracens, Islam in the Medieval European Imagination* (New York: Columbia University Press, 2002), p. 135, citing Guibert de Nogent. On Peter the Venerable, see Jeremy Cohen, *Sanctifying the Name of God: Jewish Martyrs and Jewish Memories of the First Crusade* (Philadelphia: University of Pennsylvania Press, 2004), pp. 3–4.

177 **slaughter by Christian mobs of Jews described as "vermin":** From J. A. Giles, "Chronicle of Richard of Devizes," *Chronicles of the Crusades* (London: Bohn, 1848), section 3.

178 **"Some of the pagans were mercifully beheaded"** Asbridge, pp. 316, cf. 87, 193, 273–74. The following citation is taken from Atiya, pp. 61–62. Among other informative and readable histories, see Jonathan Riley-Smith, *The Crusades: A History* (New Haven: Yale University Press, 2005); Christopher Tyerman, *God's War: A New History of the Crusades* (Cambridge, Mass.: Belknap, 2006).

179 **"mothers cut the throats of nursing children with knives"** These and the following examples come from Jeremy Cohen, *Sanctifying the Name of God*, pp. 5–6, 13, 61–64, 74, 107–8, 143–44; see also Shlomo Eidelberg, *The Jews and the Crusaders: The Hebrew Chronicles of the First and Second Crusades* (Madison: University of Wisconsin Press, 1977); and Robert Chazan, *In the Year 1096: The First Crusade and the Jews* (Philadelphia: Jewish Publication Society, 1996).

181 **the teaching of jihad** See Atiya; Robert Irwin, "Islam and the Crusades, 1096–1699," *The Oxford Illustrated History of the Crusades,* edited by Jonathan Riley-Smith (Oxford: Oxford University Press, 1997), pp. 217–59, 225–27; Rudolph Peters, *Jihad in Classical and Modern Islam: A Reader*, Princeton Series on the Middle East (Princeton, N.J.: Markus Wiener, 1996); Reuven Firestone, *Jihād: The Origin of Holy War in Islam* (New York: Oxford University Press, 1999); Khalid Yahya Blankinship, *The End of the Jihad State: The Reign of Hisham Ibn 'Abd Al-Malik and the Collapse of the Umayyads*, SUNY Series in Medieval Middle East History (Albany: State University of New York Press, 1994).

182 **Muhammad hid the horns of the ram used to redeem Isma'il near the Ka'bahh** Ahmad b. Muhammad b. Hanbal (d. 863 C.E.), cited in Brannon Wheeler, *Prophets in the Quran: An Introduction to the Quran and Muslim Exegesis* (London: Continuum, 2002), p. 104. The following *hadith* is from Ibn Abbas (d. 690 C.E.), as cited in Wheeler, pp. 89–90. The next story, from Ibn Ishaq (d. 772 C.E.), is cited by Wheeler, pp. 91–92.

183 **Muhammad expected to be numbered as a *shahid*** Richard Bonney, *Jihad: From Qur'an to bin Laden* (Basingstoke and New York: Palgrave Macmillan, 2004), p. 36. The story about Gabriel and the black stone comes from Suddi (Abu Muhammad Isma'il b. 'Abd al-Rahman b. Abi Karimah al-Suddi d. 749 C.E.), quoted in Wheeler, p. 100. For discussion of the teaching of Al-Shaybani, see Bonney, p. 53.

185 **Saladin made a vow in Jerusalem** According to Saladin's hagiographer, Baha' ad-Din, quoted in Francesco Gabrieli (translated by E. J. Costello), *Arab Historians of the Crusades*, The Islamic World Series (Berkeley and Los Angeles: University of California Press, 1984), pp. 100–101, cf. p. 104. The next citation is from 'Imad ad-Din, pp. 18–29; see Gabrieli, pp. 134–35.

185 **a definition of jihad that made it the literal pinnacle of Muslim faith** Atiya, p. 133, makes the case that pilgrimage had provided a major dimension of this teaching, as in the case of the Crusades. See also Bonney, p. 116.

186 **"What is thy command? I am here!"** Ahmad Kamal, *The Sacred Journey, the Pilgrimage to Mecca* (San Jose: toExcell, 2000), pp. 35, 85–86, 88, 91. It is notable that after joining in throwing stones at Satan, as Isma'il did, "the pilgrim should cut the hair," a symbolic act of self-sacrifice.

188 **One pious chronicler** Pierre des Vaux-de-Cernay, *The History of the Albigensian Crusade: Peter of les Vaux-de-Cerny's Historia Albigensis*, translated by W. A. and M. D. Sibly (Woodbridge, UK: Boydell, 1998), p. 51 (paragraph 91), 292; and the *Dialogue Concerning Miracles* by Caesar of Heisterbach.

190 **"Germany must live, even if we must die!"** Heinrich Lersch, in a song called

"Soldatenabschied"; *Lersch, Heinrich, 1889–1936: Ausgewählte Werke in zwei Bänden,* edited by Johannes Klein (Düsseldorf: Diederichs, 1965–66).

190 **Mutahhari's writings** Richard Bonney, *Jihad,* pp. 242, 238, 240. On Husayn and Shi'a practice, see Annemarie Schimmel, "Karbala and the Imam Husayn in Persian and Indo-Muslim Literature," *Al-Serat* 12 (1986); James A. Bill and John Alden Williams, *Roman Catholics & Shi'i Muslims: Prayer, Passion, & Politics* (Chapel Hill: University of North Carolina Press, 2002).

193 **insurgency in Iraq in 1920** See Niall Ferguson, *The War of the World: Twentieth Century Conflict and the Descent of the West* (New York: Penguin, 2006); and Bonney, pp. 234–38.

Chapter VIII

196 **Attitudes that support martyrdom** See Joyce M. Davis, *Martyrs: Innocence, Vengeance, and Despair in the Middle East* (New York: Palgrave Macmillan, 2003). The Associated Press, September 25, 2006, reported Mel Gibson's statement. See *Mel Gibson's Bible: Religion, Popular Culture, and The Passion of the Christ,* edited by Timothy K. Beal and Tod Linafelt (Chicago: University of Chicago Press, 2006).

199 **"it will be seen"** Along with the choice of "it" as the subject, rather than "Yahweh" or "he" (if it is preferred to associate "Yahweh" with the mount rather than make it the subject of the verb), the use of the English future tense in the King James Version and its derivatives takes the focus off of God, referring instead to some ritual to be repeated in the future, when rams will be offered. But the imperfect tense in Hebrew can be taken either as the past or the future, and contextually the former is more sensible here.

200 **"transforming a murder into a holy act well pleasing to God"** *Fear and Trembling and The Sickness unto Death,* translated by Walter Lowrie (Princeton, N.J.: Princeton University Press, 1941), p. 64. The same portrayal permeates the analysis of Hugh C. White, *Narration and Discourse in the Book of Genesis* (Cambridge, England: Cambridge University Press, 1991), p. 191, and has become a staple of literary criticism. Jo Milgrom cogently attacks Kierkegaard's position as convenient to "justify almost any atrocity"; *The Binding of Isaac: The Akedah—A Primary Symbol of Jewish Thought and Art* (Berkeley, Calif.: Bibal, 1988), pp. 19–23. Jon D. Levenson rightly attributes Kierkegaard's interpretation to the Pauline tradition of portraying Abraham as a hero of faith; *The Death and Resurrection of the Beloved Son: The Transformation of Child Sacrifice in Judaism and Christianity* (New Haven: Yale University Press, 1993), pp. 125–42. The intimation of Abraham's idolatry at Beersheba is raised by Mishael Maswari Caspi and Sascha Benjamin Cohen, *The Binding [Aqedah] and Its Transformations in Judaism and Islam: The Lambs of God,* Mellen Biblical Press Series 32 (Lewiston, NY: Mellen Biblical, 1995), p. 7.

204 **Isaac saw directly into heaven** This interpretation is found in the Targums Pseudo-Jonathan and Neofiti at Genesis 22:10. For a treatment, see "The Aqedah: A Revised Tradition History," *Catholic Biblical Quarterly* 40 (1978):514–46. For the midrash that follows, see Leviticus Rabbah 20.2 in

The Midrash Rabbah: Leviticus, translated by J. J. Slotki, edited by H. Freedman and Maurice Simon (London: Soncino, 1977). These interpretations anticipate Wilfred Owen's.

207 **the second-century classicist Celsus** Quoted in Origen's work of the third century, *Contra Celsum* 2.24; see Henry Chadwick, *Contra Celsum: Translated with an Introduction and Notes* (Cambridge, England: Cambridge University Press, 1953). On the Aramaic idiom of the "cup," see Roger Le Déaut, "Goûter le calice de la mort," *Biblica* 43 (1962):82–86. For a technical discussion of the Gethsemane scene and its sources, see Raymond E. Brown, *The Death of the Messiah*, vol. 1, The Anchor Bible Reference Library (New York: Doubleday, 1994), pp. 146–234.

208 **directed to God as one's *Abba*** The echo with the Lord's Prayer and its wording is deliberate in Mark; see *Jesus' Prayer and Jesus' Eucharist: His Personal Practice of Spirituality* (Valley Forge, Pa.: Trinity Press International, 1997).

211 **"Christians have claimed that Muhammad deliberately spread a false religion of his own invention"** Minou Reeves with P. J. Stewart, *Muhammad in Europe* (New York: New York University Press, 2003). The letter to Pope Benedict was signed by thirty-eight scholars from around the world, sent on October 12, 2006, and reported in *Islamica Magazine.* Benedict not only cited an inflammatory comment, but also discounted the importance of the surah *Al Baqarah*, which insists that true faith cannot be compelled, suggesting that later passages in the Qur'an superseded it. In making that argument, he showed himself out of touch with critical scholarship and prejudicial in his exegesis. As a convenient resource in addition to those cited in chapter VI, see the online translations and transliteration of the University of Southern California Muslim Students Association, which also includes introductions by Syed Abul 'Ala Maudoodi taken from his book, *The Meaning of the Qurān*, translated by Ch. Muhammad Akbar, edited by A. A. Kamal (Lahore, Pakistan: Islamic Publications, 1980–).

218 **books advocating the virtues of atheism** See Harris, *The End of Faith: Religion, Terror, and the Future of Reason* (New York: Norton, 2004), and *Letter to a Christian Nation* (New York: Knopf, 2006); Hitchens, "The Future of an Illusion," whose title simply echoes Freud's, in *Love, Poverty, and War* (New York: Nation, 2004), pp. 333–38, 334; Dawkins, *Unweaving the Rainbow: Science, Delusion and the Appetite for Wonder* (Boston: Houghton Mifflin, 1998), and *The God Delusion* (Boston: Houghton Mifflin, 2006). Quotations are from Dawkins, *Unweaving the Rainbow,* 180–83, where he is dependent upon Frazer's outdated work on sacrifice; Harris, *Letter to a Christian Nation*; and Hitchens, "Future of an Illusion," p. 338.

Index